The Greening of Economic Policy Reform
Volume II: Case Studies

Edited by
Wilfrido Cruz
Mohan Munasinghe
Jeremy Warford

The World Bank
Washington, D.C.

Environment Papers are published to communicate the latest results of the Bank's environmental work to the development community with the least possible delay. The typescript of this paper therefore has not been prepared in accordance with the procedures appropriate to formal printed texts, and the World Bank accepts no responsibility for errors. Some sources cited in this paper may be informal documents that are not readily available.

The chapter "Economic Policies for Sustainable Resource Use in Morocco" by Ian Goldin and David Roland-Holst first appeared in *The Economics of Sustainable Development* (1995, Ian Goldin and L. Alan Winters, editors), copyrighted and published by Cambridge University Press, and is reprinted with the permission of Cambridge University Press.

Related World Bank publications include *Economywide Policies and the Environment* by Mohan Munasinghe and Wilfrido Cruz (World Bank Environment Paper No. 10) and *Environmental Impacts of Macroeconomic and Sectoral Policies* (forthcoming) edited by Mohan Munasinghe.

Library of Congress Cataloging-in-Publication Data

Warford, Jeremy J.
    The greening of economic policy reform / Jeremy Warford, Mohan
Munasinghe, Wilford Cruz.
        p.   cm.
    Includes bibliographical references.
    Contents: v. 1 Principles—v. 2. Case studies
    ISBN 0-8213-3797-1
    1. Sustainable development—Case studies.   2. Economic policy—
Case studies.   3. World Bank   I. Munasinghe, Mohan, 1945–   .
II. Cruz, Wilfredo.   III. World Bank.   IV. Title.
HC79.E5W36   1997
333.7—dc20   95-39068
                                                                    CIP

CONTENTS

VOLUME II

Tables

Figures

FOREWORD

Recent years have seen a wide range of economywide policy reform programs which have been undertaken in developing countries to address macroeconomic problems, such as those affecting international trade, government budgets, private investment, wages, and income distribution. Reform programs also address broad sectoral issues, such as those relating to agricultural productivity, industrial protection, and energy use. The economywide mechanisms for attaining these goals include altering the rates of exchange or interest, reducing government budgets, promoting market liberalization, fostering international openness, enhancing the role of the private sector, and strengthening government and market institutions—often coupled with pricing and other reforms in key sectors such as industry, agriculture, and energy.

Although these policies are typically not directed explicitly toward influencing the quality of the natural environment, they may, nonetheless have major impacts upon it, either positive or negative. This book is the second of two volumes that address these economic policy and environment interactions. The case studies in this volume (and the synthesis of key principles in Volume I) show that there are significant payoffs in attempting to understand such impacts better and to act upon them. Positive impacts of economywide reforms on the environment can be used to build constituencies for reform. Potential negative impacts need to be analyzed, monitored, and mitigated.

The importance of addressing economywide reforms and environmental management in an integrated manner has received growing recognition. As noted in the Bank's Annual Report on the environment, most country assistance strategies (CAS) now address the environmental challenges facing each country (World Bank, 1995, *Mainstreaming the Environment*). The CAS is the principal statement of the World Bank's overall development strategy in a given country. In some country assistance strategies, the links between environmental problems and their underlying causes are discussed (e.g., natural resource or energy price distortions). In others, the focus is on government efforts to address environment issues at the country level. Recent examples include the CAS for Chile, China, Hungary, Latvia, Niger, Senegal, Swaziland, and Thailand. For example, in Senegal, although the main focus is on stimulating economic growth, the environment is listed as one of five problem areas that need specific attention.

Environmental considerations are also featured in CAS discussions of sectoral policies and lending programs. These include water resource management (e.g., Brazil, India, FYR Macedonia, and Peru), urban sanitation (most countries), energy efficiency (China, and various countries in Eastern and Central Europe), industrial pollution control (Brazil, China, Ghana, and Thailand), mining (Estonia, Ghana, Peru, and Poland, among others), and agriculture (especially countries in Africa and Latin America) (World Bank, 1995, *Mainstreaming the Environment*).

In some instances, the direction of environmental impacts stemming from economywide policy reform is fairly straightforward. The extent of the impact, however, invariably requires empirical analysis. In more complex cases, even the direction of the impact is ambiguous. Although much literature of a theoretical nature on this topic is emerging, there has still recently been little empirical work addressing the links between economywide policies and the environment. In view of their location-specific nature, involving a range of economic, physical, institutional, and cultural variables, there is a clear need for more case study material to enhance our understanding of these relationships.

The case studies presented in this volume, which have been carried out within the World Bank over the last several years, are a contribution to this objective. They have already provided the basis for a comprehensive paper on economywide policies and the environment that was approved by the Bank's Board of Executive Directors, and presented at a special session of the 50th Anniversary Annual Meetings of the World Bank and International Monetary Fund in Madrid, October 1994 (World Bank, 1994, *Economywide Policies and the Environment: Emerging Lessons from Experience*). The case studies reflect a wide range of country situations and environmental problems. Pollution issues are addressed with reference to air quality and energy use in Poland and Sri Lanka, while a variety of natural resource-related issues are covered in the other studies: deforestation and land degradation in Costa Rica, migration and deforestation in the Philippines, degradation of agricultural lands due to overgrazing in Tunisia, fertility losses due to extension of cultivated areas in Ghana, water resource depletion in Morocco, and wildlife management in Zimbabwe.

The case studies also utilize a variety of analytical methods to illustrate the different approaches available for identifying the environmental implications of economywide reforms. These methods range from those tracing the links between economic incentives and resource use through direct observation, to others relying on more complex economic modeling of policies and their environmental effects. In all the studies, however, the analytical approach uniformly requires identifying key environmental concerns and relating these to the agenda of priority sectoral and macroeconomic reforms under consideration. The analysis underscores the formidable difficulties of developing a general methodology to trace all possible environmental impacts of a package of adjustment reforms. At the same time, it offers evidence that careful case-specific empirical work may help identify better ways to deal with potentially serious impacts of specific economywide policies on high-priority environmental problems. We obviously have a long way to go before environmental impact assessment of economic policies can be used systematically in public decisionmaking; nevertheless, this work helps to reinforce the case that imperfect knowledge should not be an excuse for inaction. In many important cases, the potential environmental consequences of economic policies may be discernible, and the direction in which compensatory or defensive measures should go, is quite apparent.

Andrew Steer
Director
Environment Department

Vinod Thomas
Director
Economic Development Institute

The World Bank
Washington, D.C.

ACKNOWLEDGMENTS

We acknowledge the comments and suggestions that were received during the course of many discussions, workshops, and reviews, from colleagues within and outside the World Bank. These include Richard Ackermann, Dennis Anderson, Maria Concepcion J. Cruz, Luis Constantino, Partha Dasgupta, Mohamed El-Ashry, Ved Gandhi, Christopher Gibbs, Gunnar Eskeland, Stein Hansen, T. J. Ho, William Hyde, Emmanuel Jimenez, Ronald MacMorran, Karl-Göran Mäler, Paul Martin, David Pearce, Jorn Rattsoe, Robert Repetto, Iona Sebastian, Robert Schneider, Anand Seth, Hu Tao, Adriaan Ten-Kate, Laura Tuck, Hirofumi Uzawa, and David Wheeler. We have attempted to address all their comments and are solely responsible for any remaining inadequacies.

We are especially grateful to our case study authors: Gregory Amacher, Robin Bates, Jan Bojö, Robert Cunliffe, Boguslaw Fiodor, Herminia Francisco, Ian Goldin, Shreekant Gupta, Ramon Lopez, Paul Martin, Peter Meier, Stephen D. Mink, Kay Muir-Leresche, Zeinab Partow, Annika Persson, David Roland-Host, and Tilak Siyambalapitiya.

Publication of this book was sponsored by the Environment Department and the Economic Development Institute of the World Bank. We thank Mohamed T. El-Ashry, Andrew Steer, Vinod Thomas, and Hatsuya Azumi for their support.

This book has also benefitted greatly from comments received when a condensed version was presented to the Board of Executive Directors of the World Bank, as well as at a special Environment Seminar convened at the Fiftieth Anniversary Annual Meetings of the World Bank and the International Monetary Fund in Madrid.

The complex research program behind this book was made manageable by the excellent Economywide Policies and Environment project team. We especially thank Adelaida Schwab, Noreen Beg, Shreekant Gupta, Annika Persson, and Nalin Kishor. Karen Danczyk assisted with the editorial work; Luz Rivera and Daisy Martinez provided secretarial support. Jay Dougherty and Rebecca Kary of Alpha-Omega Services, Inc., provided editorial and layout services.

The project was supported in part by generous contributions from the governments of Norway and Sweden.

Wilfrido Cruz, Mohan Munasinghe, and Jeremy J. Warford

CONTRIBUTORS AND EDITORS

Gregory Amacher is Associate Professor, Forestry Department, Virginia Polytechnic Institute.

Robin Bates is Principal Economist, Industry and Energy Department, World Bank, Washington, D.C.

Jan Bojö is Senior Environmental Economist in the Environmentally Sustainable Development Division, Technical Department, Africa Region of the World Bank.

Wilfrido Cruz is Environmental Economist at the Environment and Natural Resources Division of the Economic Development Institute of the World Bank. He was formerly Economist at the World Resources Institute, a leading environmental policy research organization.

Robert Cunliffe is an Ecologist at the World Wildlife Fund, Zimbabwe.

Boguslaw Fiodor is Professor, Instytut Ekonomil, Adademia Ekonomiczna, Wroclaw, Poland.

Herminia Francisco is Associate Professor, Economics Department, College of Economics and Management, University of the Philippines at Los Baños.

Ian Goldin is Chief Executive, Development Bank of Southern Africa, South Africa.

Shreekant Gupta is Chief of the Environmental Economics Unit, National Institute of Public Finance and Policy, New Delhi, India.

Ramón López is Professor, Department of Agricultural and Resource Economics, University of Maryland, College Park, Maryland.

Peter Meier is Chief Economist of IDEA, Inc., Washington, D.C.

Stephen D. Mink is Senior Economist, Middle East and North Africa Region, World Bank, Washington, D.C.

Kay Muir-Leresche is Senior Lecturer at the University of Zimbabwe, Department of Agricultural Economics and Extension, Harare, Zimbabwe.

Mohan Munasinghe is Distinguished Visiting Professor of Environmental Management, University of Colombo, Sri Lanka. He is on leave from the World Bank, where he was Chief of the Pollution and Environmental Economics Division, Environment Department.

Zeinab Partow is a Researcher, Banco de la Republica, Bogotá, Colombia.

Annika Persson is a Consultant in the World Bank Policy Research Department, Washington, D.C.

David Roland-Host is Associate Professor of Economics, Mills College, Oakland, California.

Tilak Siyambalapitiya is head of the Generation Planning Branch, Ceylon Electricity Board, Sri Lanka.

Jeremy J. Warford is Visiting Professor of Environmental Economics, Centre for Social and Economic Research on the Global Environment, University College, London. He was formerly Senior Adviser in the Environment Department and Economic Development Institute, the World Bank.

1

Natural Resource Management and Economywide Policies in Costa Rica: A Computable General Equilibrium (CGE) Modeling Approach

Annika Persson and Mohan Munasinghe

CURRENTLY, THE ECONOMIC ANALYSIS of environmental issues relies mainly on project level studies, using cost-benefit analyses and environmental assessments. However, economywide policies (both macroeconomic and sectoral) frequently have much more powerful environmental effects than mere project level investments. Some progress has been made in identifying the environmental consequences of sectoral policies involving, for example, energy, water or agricultural pricing. Nevertheless, the impacts of broad macroeconomic reforms (such as exchange rate devaluation, trade liberalization, privatization, and other fiscal and monetary stabilization policies) on natural resource and pollution management are far more difficult to trace. This hampers efforts to design better sustainable development strategies that meet economic, social, and environmental criteria in a more balanced way (Munasinghe 1993).

This chapter, with minor format and presentation changes, was initially published in the *World Bank Economic Review,* Vol. 9, No. 2 (pp. 259–85). With permission, it is presented here with the other case studies from the Economywide Policy and Environment Project.

In the case of the World Bank, for example, the general lack of knowledge about links between economic policies and the environment has delayed attempts to gradually expand the application of environmental analysis to cover economywide or policy-based lending—the second largest use of Bank resources (about $5.8 billion annually, or 27 percent of total lending in 1993). It has also hampered efforts to develop more effective national environmental action plans (NEAPs) (these are prepared by borrowing countries, with Bank assistance, to help determine priority activities to address national environmental issues).

A recent study argues that many instances of environmental damage are due to market failures and policy distortions, exacerbated by unemployment, landlessness, and poverty (Munasinghe et al. 1993). Therefore, broad policy reforms which usually promote efficiency or reduce poverty, also should be generally beneficial for the environment. However, some of these reforms may have negative environmental effects, depending on pre-existing (and often localized) constraints—such as inadequately defined property or resource rights.

It is important for decisionmakers to be able to trace the complicated paths by which macro-level policy changes ultimately affect incentives for efficient resource use at the micro level of firms or households. The objective is not necessarily to modify the original broader policies (which have conventional economic or poverty related goals), but rather to design more specific or localized complementary measures that remove economic distortions or constraints (Munasinghe and Cruz 1994). These additional measures would help mitigate negative effects or enhance positive impacts of the original policies on the environment. Such complementary actions would include both market-based approaches (like Pigouvian taxes on environmental externalities or allocation of limited pollution rights coupled with marketable permits), as

well as nonmarket methods (such as command-and-control techniques).

The ideal approach is a "general equilibrium" analysis that traces both the economic and environmental effects of economywide policy reforms. When such comprehensive methods are not possible in developing countries where data and skills are scarcer, "partial" approaches that help to identify the most important impacts of economywide policies, are frequently used. Because the full consequences of a policy are not traced, both quantitative and qualitative results of the partial equilibrium model may be wrong. For example, taxes that are not "lump sum" may carry over from the sector for which they were intended into other sectors of the economy and affect consumption and production decisions there as well. In this context, the main purpose of this paper is to investigate the effects of economywide policies in Costa Rica on forest areas and the environment (Persson 1994). We also seek to determine whether new measures involving the allocation of property rights to these forests will yield different results when analyzed using a general equilibrium model than by applying a more conventional partial equilibrium approach.

In the remainder of this section, the main issues, analytical approach and results, are summarized. The next section describes previous work on Costa Rica and the environmental priorities. The applicability of CGE models to such problems is discussed in the section, *The modeling approach*. Further details of the model and data used here are presented in the next two sections. Finally, the last two sections summarize the chief results and conclusions of the study. Annex 1-A provides more information on the model.

Deforestation and soil erosion are major environmental problems in Costa Rica. Some data on forest clearing over time are shown in Table 1-1. To evaluate how sectoral and economywide policies can help control deforestation, the CGE model used here highlights the economic activities and factors that specifically affect deforestation in Costa Rica. The model goes beyond standard approaches in two important respects. First, it can simulate the effect of introducing property rights on forest resources, thus encouraging sustainable management of forests by private individuals who value future returns to forestry. Second, it includes markets for logs and cleared land: loggers deforest to sell timber to the forest industry and for exports, and squatters clear land for agricultural production and for sale to the agriculture sector as the latter expands and requires more land.

The model retains features that are fairly standard in most CGE models. The tradable sectors—forestry, agriculture, and industry—are price takers in the world market, while infrastructure and services produce nontraded output. To focus on the natural resource sectors, the domestically mobile factors include, aside from capital and (skilled and unskilled) labor, cleared land and logs. The supplies of both labor and capital are exogenous. The demand for these factors arise from the producing sectors (agriculture, industry, etc.) and from the deforestation activity of loggers and squatters. The supply of cleared land is initially based on Costa Rica's total land area that has been deforested. However, additional cleared land is made available from increased deforestation. This rate of land clearing depends on the definition of property rights as well as on taxes (or subsidies) that affect the forest and agricultural sectors. In addition, the expansion of squatting activities augments the cleared land factor. Agricultural production provides the demand for cleared land.

Poorly defined property rights in Costa Rican forests play an important role in deforestation. The model indicates that correction of this market failure would reduce deforestation. If property rights are well defined and the interest rate is exogenous, the value that loggers assign to preserving the forests is crucial. In order to stop deforestation, the benefits from preserving the forests must be significantly higher than the value of the logs and the cleared land.

In the model, tax policies may generate unexpected side effects, and substitution effects between inputs in the producing sectors may be important. Therefore, when possible impacts of macroeconomic policies are investigated the general equilibrium approach generates results that are different from those derived from a partial equilibrium analysis.

Status of Forests in Costa Rica

Deforestation in Costa Rica is proceeding at a rapid pace, and there is a growing concern about this both inside the country and from environmental organizations in the rest of the world. Ministerio de Recursos Naturales, Energía y Minas (1990) mentions the following economic and ecological benefits that Costa Rica may lose if deforestation continues: access to construction materials and other wood products, unchecked species of plants and animals that have possible and future uses for consumption and industrial production, recreation and ecotourism, control of erosion and sedimentation, and education and research possibilities. The greenhouse effect and concerns about the rich biological diversity in Costa Rica may be important to other countries and environmental organizations.

Deforestation and erosion are the main environmental problems in the country (Blomström and Lundahl 1989; Foy and Daly 1989). Originally, most of Costa Rica was forested, but in 1977 only 31 percent (16,000 square kilometers) remained covered with forests. Blomström and Lundahl (1989) estimate that in 1983 14 percent of the area was still covered with forests. Solórzano et al. (1991) give the more conservative estimate that about 40 percent of the land is still covered with forests. This difference is probably due to differences in what types of forests were investigated. The lower estimates probably concern only primary forests, whereas the higher estimates include secondary forests and intervened forests (Sader and Joyce 1988).

Most of the deforestation has occurred since 1950. If deforestation continues at the current rate, the commercial forests of Costa Rica will be exhausted within the next five years. The life zones with the highest rates of deforestation are the tropical wet forests; these are also the life zones in which biodiversity levels are highest (Solórzano et al. 1991).

Carriére (1991) describes the process of deforestation as taking place in several stages. First, a logging company involved in high-grading clears a vehicle tract to extract lumber. Thereafter, the road is improved by the government due to pressures from lobbying groups, and this in turn enables local peasant families to clear and use the remaining forest for subsistence agriculture until the decreasing yields force them to sell or abandon the land, depending on whether it is titled or not. However, the land is still suitable for pasture and is therefore assembled by urban-based real estate companies and sold to cattle ranchers. After a few years, the land is almost completely degraded and unsuitable for any kind of economic use. This view is shared by Keogh (1984).

The Costa Rican government is taking steps to preserve the forests. More than 13,000 square kilometers has been designated as national parks, although in the past deforestation had been encouraged to diversify the country's production away from coffee and banana crops (Biesanz et al. 1987).

The following four groups as responsible for deforestation in Costa Rica (Lutz and Daly 1990):

1. The timber industry may be responsible for deforesting as much as 20,000 hectares annually. Logging requires a special permit from the government, but about half the trees are cut illegally.

Domestically cut logs are processed locally and are used typically in construction. Exports of wood and wood products are small, and imports are negligible. The current import tariff on logs is 5 percent (Lutz and Daly 1990). Efficiency in the forestry sector is low,

and only a few species are commercially utilized. About 54 percent of the logs are processed, and of these about half finally reach the market (Ministerio de Recursos Naturales, Energía y Minas 1990). The main part of the logs used in the timber industry is bought from sources other than the industry itself.

2. Banana firms and other companies are expanding their plantations rapidly.

The main products cultivated in Costa Rica are rice, coffee, fruits, sugarcane, beans, maize, and sorghum (Hugo et al. 1983). Lutz and Daly (1990) state that erosion is visible in some areas, but that farmers "do not produce in obviously unsuitable ways to destroy the environment. For example, living fences are widely used, which reduce erosion, and protective forest cover is left intact next to creeks, on contours or steep slopes, etc."

The Costa Rican tax structure for income and property taxes is regressive. Sales taxes and other indirect taxes constituted 70 percent of the total tax revenues in 1970, and there are indications that this figure may still be high. Although property taxes are low (in some cases about 1 percent of the actual market value), property and income tax evasion is a problem that costs the country approximately 100 billion colones a year. A remedy may be to raise the price of land by increasing land taxes, increase tax collection rates, and prosecute tax evaders more effectively.

3. Cattle ranchers have expanded their activities rapidly at the expense of forested areas in recent decades. However, this type of land conversion may be limited now since most of the land that can be sustainably used for pasture has already been cleared.

In the 1950s and 1960s there was a large increase in investment in cattle, encouraged by foreign aid and investment, as well as government aid in the forms of credit and provision of infrastructure. This increase of cattle ranching caused deforestation to increase rapidly. The pasture trend boomed in the 1970s, but since then profits have decreased. More than 70 percent of the farmland is in pasture, while only 2.5 percent is in coffee, and 1.1 percent is in bananas (Biesanz et al. 1987).

4. Squatting is taking place on both privately owned and government land. Some of the squatters produce agricultural outputs, but others sell the cleared land to cattle ranchers or other land owners. Buyers who buy "in good faith" from squatters are not prosecuted. About twice as much is paid for cleared land as is paid for forests.

Squatting is an important cause of deforestation in Costa Rica. By clearing the land, it is possible to get formal ownership to the land (Blomström and Lundahl 1989) or in some cases at least to the "land improvements." Squatting by smallholders nowadays appears to constitute a less significant part of the deforestation in an overall context, although it may be locally important (Lutz and Daly 1990).

If ownership may be obtained with no costs other than the clearing of the land, the forests can be seen as a type of common property while the cleared land is perceived as traditional private property. However, in the case of Costa Rica, it is not the traditional case of undefined property rights where there is an open access resource (cf., for example, Dasgupta 1982). Here we are looking at insecure land tenure. This implies that there is no crowding effect on the stock of the resource, which is what occurs when each agent maximizes his own profit without taking the effect on the stock of the resource into account. Instead of the traditional open access problem, we have a form of short-term property rights when deforestation occurs, but the property rights to the standing forests are not protected. The logger or squatter will continue deforestation only until the marginal cost of deforestation equals the marginal revenue, because of this structure of property rights. The social cost of deforestation will then be higher than the private cost since "the world's" willingness to pay for the preservation of the Costa Rican forests will not be included in the private cost. That the difference in cost functions is a major cause behind deforestation in the developing world is shown in Chichilnisky (1993), where a north-south trade model is developed, and the difference in trade patterns between north and south is explained by a difference in property rights. Thus, deforestation would be driven by the difference in private and social objectives. For example, the loggers' main interest may be the profitability of the logging operation itself without much consideration about future, alternative uses of the land.

Another critical economic factor may be the existence of higher private discount rates, i.e., deforestation may be caused by discounting the future value of the forests. A high discount factor implies that future gains from the forests is of much less value than the gains from deforestation today. The impacts of tropical forests are often more significant in the long term than in the short term. However, the regenerative capacity of tropical forests is low, and the discounting of future environmental benefits may often make it more profitable to harvest forest resources as quickly as possible. Forest investments, like replanting, take a long time to yield returns, and individuals therefore find little attraction in conservation and reforestation activities. In many developing countries, private market rates are very high and often exceed the rate that would be socially justifiable (Barbier, Burgess, and Markandya 1991). Poor people often face even higher discount rates because of credit constraints.

The Modeling Approach

As may be concluded from the above, the main reasons for deforestation and thereby erosion are the following:

- The price of land is too low, since the total social opportunity value of the rain forests is not included.

- Undefined property rights make the private cost of deforestation lower than the social cost of deforestation.

- Discount rates may be too high. This implies that the value of future gains from the forests are lower than the gains from deforestation today.

- In addition, economywide policies such as the tax system may cause deforestation.

Computable general equilibrium (CGE) models have been applied before to environmental problems—mainly issues involving air pollution and pollution taxes. A short discussion of some CGE models relevant to the approach developed here is provided below.

Bergman's (1990a) model is designed to simulate the effects of environmental regulation and energy policy on the Swedish economy. The environmental market failure is in this case corrected by the creation of a market for emission permits. The cost of emission permits for carbon dioxide, sulfur, and nitrogen is incorporated in the cost functions.

Jorgenson and Wilcoxen (1990) analyze the economic impact of environmental regulations on the U.S. economy. This is done by simulating long-term growth with and without environmental regulations. The share of abatement costs in total costs is estimated for each industry, as well as the share of investment in pollution control equipment and the cost of pollution control devices in motor vehicles. The model is run with and without these costs, to estimate the economic impacts.

There are not many examples of CGE models dealing with the impact on the economy of overexploitation of natural resources. Panayotou and Sussangkarn (1992) construct a model against the background of environmental problems in Thailand. The sources of the environmental issues are economic growth, exchange rate problems, and government policies (such as agricultural policies and taxation, and the land tenure system) promoting deforestation. The approach implies that every unit of production in each producing sector produces, for example, a fixed amount of air pollution or deforestation. The environmental impacts are not part of the model per se—the environmental degradation or improvement is not fed back into the model so as to affect future production and consumption decisions. The results include the findings that export taxes on rice and rubber increase investment in soil conservation, increase the use of agrochemicals, and shift land from rubber to rice.

Not much work has previously been done on the modeling of undefined property rights in a general equilibrium context, where the results may differ from those of a partial equilibrium model. Devarajan (1990) suggests that a fruitful approach may be to incorporate a partial equilibrium model in the general equilibrium framework by removing the first order condition that labor must be paid the value of its marginal product in some sectors and replace it with a condition that reflects the suboptimal behavior of the sector. This will enable an analysis of the effects on deforestation of policy interventions in the system. It is emphasized that the model has to be dynamic in order to take account of both the stock and the flow effects of deforestation.

Unemo (1993) models the suboptimal use of land in Botswana, caused by overgrazing of cattle due to undefined property rights of the land. Land is seen as an open access resource, and the effects of overgrazing are incorporated in the cattle owner's production function in the form of crowding effects. The quantity of output is determined not only by the number of cattle the individual owns, but by the whole population of cattle grazing on the land. The results include the finding that a fall in the price of diamonds considerably increases pressure on land, as mining becomes less profitable relative to cattle ranching.

In order to model property rights related behavior in Costa Rican forests, it is assumed that the private cost of deforestation is lower than the social opportunity value of the forests when property rights are undefined. When property rights are defined, the social value of the rain forests will be incorporated in the utility functions of the squatters and therefore in the private cost of deforestation. This approach facilitates the analysis of the role of undefined property rights, and follows the approach used by Chichilnisky (1993).

General Features of the Model

This model is a static CGE model of an open economy, although it has certain implicit dynamic features, since the discount rate is included in the future valuation of forested land. It differs from the standard approach of CGE modeling by the inclusion of undefined property rights and by the modification of the functioning of the markets for logs and cleared land. This is discussed in detail below. Land cleared by squatters is assumed to be sold to the agricultural sector.

The model has two types of sectors. The tradable-producing sectors (T-sectors) FOREST, AGRICULTURE, and INDUSTRY are assumed to be price takers on the world market in the standard Heckscher-Ohlin fashion. The nontradable-producing sectors (N-sectors) are INFRASTRUCTURE and SERVICE.[1] In addition, there are two sectors that clear land.

---

[1]The subsectors of the input-output table are aggregated into the five production sectors as follows: FOREST (forestry and fishing); AGRICULTURE (bananas, unprocessed coffee, sugarcane, cacao, basic grains, cotton, tobacco, livestock, other agricultural, coffee processing, grains milling, sugar refining); INDUSTRIES (meat and milk, fish tinning, edible oils, bakeries, other manufactured goods, drink, tobacco products, textiles and clothing, leather and shoes, timber and furniture, paper and printing, chemical products, oil refining, tire products, plastic and rubber, glass and ceramic, construction materials, metal products, electric products, transport equipment, other manufacturing); INFRASTRUCTURE (construction, transport, electricity, gas and water); SERVICES (banking and finance, commerce, ownership of dwellings, general government).

LOGGERS clear land for the purpose of obtaining LOGS for the FOREST industry and for exports, and SQUATTERS clear land and sell it to the AGRICULTURE sector.

The domestic intersectorally mobile production factors are unskilled labor (ULABOR), skilled labor (SLABOR) and capital (CAPITAL). Logs (LOGS) and cleared land (DLAND) are specific to the sectors FOREST and AGRICULTURE, respectively, although logs can be traded on the world market. No reafforestation is possible in the model.

The key elements of the CGE model are introduced below. A more detailed mathematical description is given in Annex 1-B.

Factor market equilibrium and the stock of forested land

The supplies of both labor and capital are assumed to be exogenously given and, for factor markets to clear, these supplies must equal the demands for labor and capital, respectively. Demands arise from the producing sectors plus the amounts used for deforestation by squatters and loggers. The demand for each production factor (like capital or labor) within both the T and N sectors, as well as the deforestation sectors, is given by the partial derivative of the cost function for the relevant sector with respect to the price of the same production factor. There is demand for unskilled labor for deforestation by both loggers and squatters, but only loggers generate demand for capital.

Costa Rica's total area has been divided into two types of land: cleared land and forested land. Cleared land is produced through deforestation. The production of cleared land will depend on the definition of property rights as well as taxes and subsidies on the factors of production and the profits in the FOREST and AGRICULTURE sectors.

Logs are assumed to be tradable. Therefore, the demand for forest land by the logging sector and the world market price determines the rate of deforestation. This demand is equal to the partial derivative of the logging cost function with respect to the user cost of logs plus the net export of logs.

The supply of cleared land is composed of the stock of cleared land, plus deforestation by squatters (the production of cleared land by squatters is further discussed in the next sub-section, *Technology, costs, and producer behavior*). The demand for cleared land is the demand from the AGRICULTURE sector, which is set equal to the partial derivative of the agriculture sector cost function with respect to the user cost of cleared land.

The combination of production factors can be influenced by taxes and subsidies. Thus, a given user price will be greater (smaller) than the corresponding supply price by a percentage tax (subsidy).

Technology, costs, and producer behavior

The production factors have been aggregated into a composite input, Y. DLAND is combined with CAPITAL to yield an aggregate R, which in turn is combined with LOGS to generate M. The latter is combined with SLABOR to produce V, which is combined with ULABOR to yield the composite factor input, Y. This aggregation is accomplished through the use of constant elasticity of substitution (CES) production functions. The technology is specified to exhibit constant returns to scale. The relation between inputs and output is given by typical Leontief production functions for each sector.

Since the technology exhibits constant returns to scale, the marginal cost and the average cost of production in a given sector can be expressed as a linear function of prices, relevant input/output coefficients, and indirect tax rates.

Producers are assumed to maximize profits. The producer output prices, P_i, in the tradables-producing sectors are given by the world market prices. Assuming perfect competition, this implies that pure profits are nonpositive, output is non-negative and positive only if pure profits are equal to zero.

In the nontradables-producing sectors, the sector-specific capital is endogenously adjusted so that price equals marginal cost.

Prices, domestic demand, foreign trade and market clearing

For a good produced in the tradables-producing sectors, the domestic producer price is equal to the world market price of the identical good, and in the nontradables-producing sectors, the domestic user price is equal to the producer price times the tax rate.

The intermediate demand of a good is given by the technology assumptions. Domestic final demand is given by a linear expenditure system, derived from the consumers' utility maximization.

To equilibrate the market for a good, the net export for that good is defined as the difference between domestic supply and demand.

Deforestation sectors

In this model, there are two sectors that are responsible for deforestation, as discussed below. They interact with the rest of the economy through their demands for capital and labor, by supplying forest products and clear land to the rest of the economy, and through the changes in relative prices of factor inputs and the sectoral outputs.

The logging sector

The logging sector is assumed to have a capital intensive technology (Repetto 1988). Further, the technology is assumed to exhibit decreasing returns to scale in order to reflect the diminishing amount of available forests, as well as the fact that much of the logging is done illegally. The production of LOGS is assumed to depend only on two factors of production: LABOR and CAPITAL. A loglinear production function is used. Since the technology used to model the diminishing yields in deforestation exhibits decreasing returns to scale, this implies that the returns to the production factors fall with increased deforestation. Deforestation for land and deforestation for logs are assumed to be independent of each other, and therefore the increased deforestation for logs does not affect the returns to deforestation for land, and vice versa. However, increased deforestation for logs implies decreasing yields in the logging sector, and increased deforestation for land implies diminishing returns in the squatting sector.

In the case of undefined property rights, loggers take only the private cost of deforestation into account. When property rights are well defined, the opportunity value of saving the forests is included in the loggers' cost function.

Squatters

The forested land cleared by squatters is seen as a common property, although there is no crowding effect since the stock of forested land is not included in the squatters' production function. The base case assumes undefined property rights. This section is inspired mainly by Johansson and Löfgren (1985).

The squatters have a production function for cleared land that increases monotonically with labor inputs. Their total revenue from clearing the land is the price paid for the cleared land. Part of the land cleared by squatters is sold to the AGRICULTURE sector; the rest is used for subsistence agriculture by the squatters themselves. However, since both activities occur, the returns at the margin must be the same in each case. The squatters are assumed not to sell the timber from their deforestation, as discussed in the section, *Status of Forests in Costa Rica*. Other uses of the timber, such as for firewood, are assumed to be negligible.

The squatters' total private cost for the clearing of the land will depend only on the amount of labor needed in order to clear the land when property rights are undefined. This is the private cost, which does not include the future value of the forests and the cost of

environmental damage. Therefore, the total social cost of deforestation is this private cost plus the future benefits from cleared forests that are foregone by clearing the land today. The future value of the forests is assumed to be greater than the value of the forests today.

The analysis of the definition of property rights can then be accomplished through the simulation of two regimes. In the case of undefined property rights, the present-day squatters do not take the future value of the forests into account. When property rights are well defined, the squatters own their land and do take the future value of the forests into account. The owners of forested land (i.e., the "squatters aware of the future"), decide whether to preserve the forests or clear land.

When property rights are undefined, there is no market for the forests available to squatters. A simple partial model of land clearing by squatters (in which each squatter receives an equal share of the private profits) is used to show that land will be cleared until marginal cost equals marginal revenue. This result corresponds to maximization of private profit, given the insecure land tenure.

When property rights are well defined, there is a market for the forests. The squatters take the future value of the forests into account, and they can choose to clear forested land or to preserve the forests. This is consistent with the condition for socially optimal forestry—that a tree should be harvested when the market value is equal to the shadow value (Hellsten 1988). This result corresponds to the optimization of net social benefits.

It can be deduced from the foregoing that more land will be cleared when property rights are undefined rather than when property rights are well defined. This is because the squatters' marginal cost of deforestation is lower when property rights are undefined, rather than when property rights are well defined, and the cost includes the future value of the forests. MR is the marginal revenue curve.

A more detailed analysis of the supply function indicates that when property rights are well defined, deforestation will be increased by (a) a change of technology towards more efficient use of labor in the production of cleared land, (b) an increase of the time preference rate, and (c) an increase in the supply price of cleared land. Conversely, deforestation is reduced by increases in: (a) the future value of the forests; and (b) the price of labor.

When property rights are undefined, the clearing of land is not affected by the future value of forests and the rate of time preference. The effects of other variables are the same as in the earlier case.

The profit maximization condition for the squatters in the general equilibrium model includes a term reflecting the opportunity value of saving the forests for alternative uses or deforestation in a later period. When property rights are undefined, the weight given to this term is zero, since future tenure of the forest is uncertain. When property rights are well defined, this term is included in the profit maximization.

Macroeconomic closure and measures of welfare

The current account is assumed to be constant, and the current account surplus is defined as the sum of net exports. There are three welfare measures in the model: (a) the disposable income (which is implicitly determined from the current account), (b) the green gross national product (which is determined as the sum of factor incomes plus a term that diminishes with increased deforestation to reflect the negative welfare effects of deforestation), and (c) utility (which is determined from the consumer's utility function). Utility maximization results in a linear expenditure system for goods, based on a transformed Cobb-Douglas utility function.

Base Case Data, Assumptions, and Limitations of the Model

The data used in this version of the model originate from Briceño (1986),[2] the University of Costa Rica, and the Costa Rica National Accounts (Central Bank 1990). However, the sectors of production are not consistent between the two studies, and data were therefore adjusted in Raventós (1990). The input-output matrix in Annex 1-B, Table 1B-1 has been calculated from the disaggregated data used in Raventós (1990 and 1991). The remaining differences have been added to the net export column. Land use data are shown in Annex 1-B, Table 1B-2. The economic rent to timber has been calculated from Solórzano et al. (1991). Deforestation in 1986 was assumed to equal average deforestation between 1973 and 1989. The value in 1986 prices was calculated using the increase in the consumer price index between January 1985 and December 1986 (calculated from Solórzano et al. 1991). The rent to the production factor DLAND was subtracted from the rents to CAPITAL in the agricultural sector, and the LABOR used for land clearing by squatters was subtracted from the LABOR used in the same sector.

The LABOR and CAPITAL used for logging were subtracted from the payments to those factors in the forest sector. Logging is assumed to be responsible for half of total deforestation, while land clearing by squatters is assumed to be responsible for the other half.

No estimates of elasticities of substitution between production factors are available. It is reasonable to assume that they are imperfect substitutes, and all substitution elasticities were therefore assumed to be less than one. As a base case, the substitution elasticity between LAND and CAPITAL in the sector AGRICULTURE was set at 0.5. The substitution elasticity between the capital aggregate R and LOGS was assumed to be 0.8 in the FOREST sector, and the substitution elasticity between

---

[2]Calculated from Solórzano et al. (1991).

the aggregate M and LABOR was set at 0.8 in all producing sectors. Compared to other studies, such as Bergman (1990a and 1990b), these values appear reasonable. The remaining elasticities concern aggregates involving land and logs in sectors which cannot use those factors as inputs in production, and therefore the shares of those inputs in production always have to be zero. Those elasticities where set to zero, which is consistent with a fixed coefficient (Leontief) technology.

The parameters in the production functions for squatters and loggers are judgment-based estimates, assuming a labor-intensive technology for the squatters and a capital-intensive technology for loggers.

In concluding this section, we note several limitations in the data and model formulation. First, because of the various data adjustments, the results of the simulations are mainly indicative and not necessarily precise quantitative measures.

Second, since the model developed in this paper is essentially static, the results are comparative snapshots of different policy experiments. A more dynamic version of the model is being developed, which takes the stock and flow effects into account, and derives valid results for a longer-term planning horizon.

Third, the approach developed here does not include some other possible linkages with deforestation. Migration and population growth are two causal factors that may be important (Harrison 1991), but they are not investigated. Furthermore, the model neither allows for reafforestation, nor includes erosion and other external effects of deforestation. The economic valuation of such environmental effects (to incorporate them in the conventional economic analysis) would be a formidable task (see, for example, Munasinghe 1993).

Results

Simulations of different policy experiments and the definition of property rights generated some results that are different from what could be expected from the partial equilibrium

framework discussed earlier. This is due to substitution effects in the producing sectors.

The current situation with undefined property rights was taken as a base case. As a first step, property rights were defined, and the opportunity value of the forests (the H-value) was set 28 percent higher than the value derived from deforestation (Solórzano et al. 1991). The discount rate was set at 10 percent. The results are displayed in Table 1-2. A comparison of the first and second columns shows that the definition of property rights results in a dramatic decrease in deforestation, and an increase in the net import of logs (not shown in the table). Activity in the forest sector declines significantly, since this sector is relatively capital intensive and the price of capital is elevated. Deforestation by squatters ceases, and activity in the agricultural sector declines, but to a smaller extent than the forest sector, since the existing stock of land remains. The welfare measures remain constant, since consumption of different goods is unchanged.

Sensitivity analysis (remaining columns in Table 1-2) shows that even a relatively small opportunity value of forests (e.g., H=0.0792) will decrease deforestation dramatically. However, for deforestation to cease completely, a high value (H=0.4792) is required. Both the opportunity value of forests and the interest rate are exogenous to the model. Varying the interest rate while keeping opportunity value fixed shows that high interest rates promote deforestation, and vice versa.

The results of varying the interest rate may be deduced from Table 1-2, since a decrease in the interest rate is equivalent to an increase in the opportunity value, and vice versa. The equivalent of Table 1-2 in terms of interest rates is shown in Figure 1-3. We can conclude that though deforestation is increasing with interest rate, the relationship is not linear.

Next, the effects of taxes on logs, land, unskilled labor, and capital were investigated, as summarized in Table 1-3. A 10 percent tax increase on logs generated predictable results, with no deforestation from loggers and no production in the forest sector. Resources were shifted to the agricultural sector, with an increase in deforestation for land and an increase in total deforestation. The increase in total deforestation can be explained by lowered prices of capital and unskilled labor, resulting from the discontinued production in the forest sector. The tax increase actually results in a higher level of utility, as well as an increase in "green" gross domestic product (GDP). Smaller tax increases than 10 percent generated the similar results, with the forest sector declining and the agricultural sector expanding as taxes on forest products were increased.

Taxes and subsidies on land generate expected results, with a corresponding change in deforestation by squatters and roughly constant deforestation by loggers. Both the tax and the subsidy are distortionary, and reduce utility as well as income and GDP.

A 10 percent tax increase on unskilled labor adversely affects the forest sector, but logging continues and logs are exported. The price of unskilled labor in the deforestation sectors are actually reduced, since those sectors are considered informal in the sense that their activities are to a large extent illegal, and the sectors remains unaffected by government tax policies. Resources are shifted to the agricultural sector, with a large increase in land clearing by squatters as a result. The agricultural sector gains an advantage relative to the industry sector, and industrial production is reduced. These results also hold for the experiments with capital tax policies.

Substitution effects prove to be important for policy experiments involving tax changes on goods produced in tradables sectors, as summarized in Table 1-4. The effects of tax changes on goods from the forest sector generate small economywide effects, since this sector is small compared with the others. The industrial sector (which uses forest products relatively intensely as an intermediate input) gains from the tax reduction and grows, while the forest sector itself suffers. The effects are reversed for a doubling of the tax on forest products. Deforestation remains largely unaffected in both cases.

When the tax on agricultural products is reduced to half, the agricultural sector actually decreases. The industrial sector benefits because of its extensive use of agricultural products as intermediate inputs, and the forest sector is reduced. Deforestation for logs remains constant, while deforestation for land is somewhat reduced. Utility, income and green GNP measures are reduced. A double tax on agricultural products generate the opposite effects. A tax on products from the industrial sector generate the same effects as a tax on agricultural products, although the magnitude of the changes is larger.

Conclusions

The results of the CGE study support the more conventional partial equilibrium approach that establishing property rights tend to decrease deforestation. The reason is that such rights allow forest users to capture the future benefits of reduced logging damage today. Initially, this potentially avoidable loss is presumed to be 28 percent of the value of the residual stand, based on a recent environmental accounting study (Solórzano et al. 1991). Using an interest rate of 10 percent, the simulation indicates that deforestation is dramatically reduced to 5 percent of the base level as both the logging and squatters sectors internalize the losses associated with deforestation, and reduce corresponding activities. Significant reductions in deforestation occur even when the estimate of logging damage is substantially reduced. The CGE results concerning the effects of discount rate changes parallel the predictions of partial equilibrium models—higher interest rates promote deforestation, while lower interest rates contribute to conservation.

Beyond confirming the direct results of partial equilibrium analyses, the CGE approach also makes an important contribution by clearly identifying the indirect effects arising from intersectoral linkages. This impact must be combined with the direct effects attributable to policies that are specific to the forest sector—to determine the total impact. For example, partial equilibrium analysis predicts that stumpage price increases will act directly to reduce logging. On the other hand, the model shows that while deforestation from logging will indeed decline, total deforestation nevertheless increases. This phenomenon arises from indirect linkages captured by the general equilibrium analysis. The contraction of the logging and forest industry sectors causes a shift of resources toward agriculture and, as agriculture expands, deforestation increases.

The importance of such indirect effects is also demonstrated in the analysis of economywide policy changes, such as an increase in the wage rate. Because of intersectoral resource flows, the general equilibrium model captures effects of changes in wages that are different from partial equilib-

rium results. If the wage of unskilled labor were increased (e.g., due to minimum wage legislation), the model predicts that deforestation could worsen instead of declining. Although logging declines due to increased direct costs of higher wages, this is more than offset by the indirect effect of intersectoral flows since the industrial sector (where minimum wage legislation is more binding) is much more adversely affected by the higher labor costs. Labor and capital thus tend to flow to agriculture, leading to the conversion of even more forest land for farming.

Finally, both these last two examples underline the importance of pursuing sectoral reforms in the context of growth. Without alternative employment opportunities, reducing logging activities will tend to direct labor and capital resources toward agriculture, industry, and other sectors. Expansion of some of these sectors may lead to a second round of effects on forestry, which could ultimately result in more severe deforestation.

Table 1-1: Percent of Total Land Area in Forests and Agriculture

Year	1963	1973	1986
Agriculture	30	40	57
Forest	67	57	40

Source: Solórzano et al. 1991.

Table 1-2: Effects of Different Future H-Values (10 billion colones)

	Undefined	Defined property rights		
H-Value	0.0000	0.4792	0.2792	0.0792
Utility	0.0232	0.0232	0.0232	0.0232
GNP	3.1962	3.1972	3.1971	3.1971
Income	3.7681	3.7679	3.7679	3.7679
Deforestation				
Squatters	0.0020	0.0000	0.0000	0.0000
Loggers	0.0020	0.0000	0.0002	0.0010
TOTAL	0.0040	0.0000	0.0002	0.0011
Production				
Forest	0.0552	0.0713	0.0711	0.0691
AGRI	1.3984	1.3876	1.3876	1.3879
IND	1.8477	1.8416	1.8417	1.8424

Table 1-3: Effects of Taxes on Production Factors (undefined property rights; 10 billion colones)

	Base case	tax logs	subs logs	tax land	subs land	tax ulab	subs ulab	tax cap	subs cap
Utility	0.0232	0.0243	0.0214	0.0231	0.0226	0.0229	0.0232	0.0232	0.0233
GNP	3.1962	3.2017	3.1848	3.1960	3.1757	3.1797	3.1965	3.1943	3.1958
Income	3.7681	3.7748	3.7561	3.7678	3.7592	3.7620	3.7679	3.7680	3.7682
Deforestation									
Squatters	0.0020	0.0044	0.0004	0.0000	0.0255	0.0210	0.0000	0.0020	0.0020
Loggers	0.0020	0.0000	0.0018	0.0020	0.0019	0.0029	0.0013	0.0036	0.0011
TOTAL	0.0040	0.0044	0.0023	0.0020	0.0273	0.0239	0.0013	0.0056	0.0031
Production									
Forest	0.0552	0.0000	0.1562	0.0672	0.0000	0.0000	0.0689	0.0515	0.0574
Agriculture	1.3984	1.4204	1.3748	1.3877	1.5122	1.4922	1.3877	1.3987	1.3983
Industry	1.8477	1.9248	1.7017	1.8430	1.7656	1.7946	1.8424	1.8487	1.8471

Table 1-4: Effects of Taxes on Final Products (undefined property rights)

	Base Case	Halve tax on forest	Double tax on forest	Halve tax on agriculture	Double tax on agriculture	Halve tax on industry	Double tax on industry
Utility	0.0232	0.0229	0.0240	0.0135	0.0459	0.0064	0.0572
GNP	3.1962	3.1941	3.1980	3.1589	3.2815	3.1324	3.3253
Income	3.7681	3.7669	3.7709	3.7317	3.8544	3.7051	3.8984
Deforestation							
Squatters	0.0020	0.0020	0.0020	0.0019	0.0022	0.0018	0.0025
Loggers	0.0020	0.0020	0.0020	0.0020	0.0020	0.0020	0.0020
TOTAL	0.0040	0.0040	0.0040	0.0039	0.0042	0.0038	0.0045
Production							
Forest	0.0552	0.0528	0.0609	0.0405	0.0902	0.0160	0.1363
Agriculture	1.3984	1.3984	1.3985	1.3258	1.5706	1.3964	1.4030
Industry	1.8477	1.8503	1.8418	1.9243	1.6663	1.8268	1.8909

Figure 1-1: Main Linkages of the CGE Model

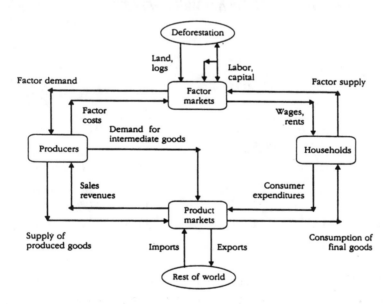

Figure 1-2: Resource Flows and Data Adjustments

	Forest	Agriculture	Industry	Service	Infrastructure	Squatters	Loggers	Net export	Domestic demand	Total demand
Forest										
Agriculture										
Industry		Intermediate demand				Deforestation sectors		Final demand		Total production demand
Service										
Infrastructure										
Squatters		+lsq								Defor. demand
Loggers	+logf									
Labor capital	−lgl −lgk	−lsq −lv				+lsq	+lgl +lgk			Factor demand
Land Indtax		+lv								
		Indirect taxes								Government revenues
Total		Output-producing sectors				Deforestation		Total final demand		

lsq = labor input in squatting; logf = logging; lgl = labor input in logging; lgk = capital input in logging; lv = land value

Figure 1-3: Effects of Interest Rates When Property Rights Are Well Defined

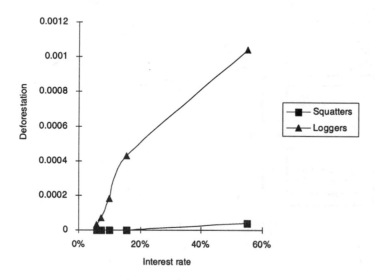

Annex 1-A: Summary of CGE Model Structure

Factor market equilibrium and the stock of forested land

The supplies of labor and capital are assumed to be exogenously given. According to Shephard's lemma the demand for a production factor within a sector is the partial derivative of the cost function with respect to the price of the same production factor. The market equilibrium conditions for capital, unskilled labor, and skilled labor, respectively, can be written

$$U = \sum_{j \in T,N} \frac{\partial C_j}{\partial P_U^U} + l^{sq} + l^{\log} \tag{1}$$

where P_K^U is the user price of CAPITAL and $k^{\log}$ is the CAPITAL used in deforestation by loggers, and

$$L = \sum_{j \in T,N} \frac{\partial C_j}{\partial P_L^U} + l^{sq} + l^{\log}. \tag{2}$$

where P_U^U is the user price of UNSKILLED LABOR, l^{sq} and $l^{\log}$ is the LABOR used in deforestation by squatters and loggers, respectively, and P_L^U is the user price of SKILLED LABOR. Equations (1) and (2) state that the supplies of labor and capital must equal the demand from the producing sectors plus the amount used for deforestation by squatters and loggers.

Costa Rica's total area has been divided into two types of land: cleared land and forested land. Cleared land is produced through deforestation. The production of cleared land will depend on the definition of property rights, and taxes and subsidies will depend on the factors of production and the profits in the FOREST and AGRICULTURE sectors.

It is assumed that there is a world market for LOGS. The market equilibrium condition for LOGS can then be written

$$\alpha d^{FOREST} = \frac{\partial C_{FOREST}}{\partial P_F^U} - f^{nexp} \tag{3}$$

where d^{FOREST} is deforestation from the LOGGING sector, P_F^U is the user price of logs, f^{nexp} is the net export of logs, and α is a fixed coefficient reflecting the amount of timber extracted per unit of deforested land. The production of LOGS is further discussed in the section, *The logging sector*.

The value of the deforestation is calculated here from the loss of standing volume in Solórzano et al. (1991). The coefficient α was assumed equal to one. There is no general agreement among biologists regarding the amount of biodiversity loss resulting from high-grading. If the value of deforestation is defined to represent biodiversity loss as well as loss of standing volume, and high-grading causes large losses of biodiversity, this modified coefficient would still be close to one. An alternative interpretation, consistent with the view that the biodiversity loss is proportional to the number of trees extracted, is that squatters and loggers each remove half the timber following the process described in Carriére (1991a and 1991b). In this case also, the modified coefficient would be nearly equal to one. Thus the model is valid for either of the last two interpretations, but the actual value of the economic loss would have to be adjusted upwards. Due to the lack of data on the value of biodiversity, the first approach of valuing only the timber was selected, since it is a conservative estimate. However, the true value of the loss of forests is higher.

The supply of cleared land is composed of the stock of cleared land, DL^*, plus deforestation by squatters, d^o. The production of cleared land by squatters is further discussed in the section, *Squatters*.

The demand of cleared land is the demand from the AGRICULTURE sector. The market equilibrium condition can then be written:

$$\frac{\partial C_{AGRICULTURE}}{\partial P_{DL}^U} - DL^* - d^o = 0.$$

(4)

The combination of production factors can be influenced by taxes and subsidies. The user price, P_j^U, will exceed the supply price, P_j^S, by a percentage tax, T_j:

$$P_j^U = P_j^S(1+T_j); \quad j = DLAND, \ LABOR, \ CAPITAL$$

$$P_{LOGS}^U = P_{LOGS}^{WM}(1+T_{LOGS})-$$

(5)

In the case of LOGS, the supply price is determined by the world market price.

Technology, costs, and producer behavior

The production factors have been aggregated into a composite input, Y, using CES functions. The technology is specified to exhibit constant returns to scale. The relation between inputs and output is given by sectoral Leontief production functions of the following type:

$$X_j = \min \left[\frac{Y_j}{A_j}, \frac{X_{ij}}{a_{ij}}\right] \quad i, j \in T, N$$

(6)

where X_j is the gross output in sector j, Y_j is a composite input of production factors in sector j, X_{ij} is input of output from sector i in sector j, and A_j and a_{ij} are Leontief input-output **coefficients**. Since the technology exhibits constant returns to scale, the marginal cost and the average cost of production in sector j can be written as

$$C_j = P_{Yj}A_j + \sum_i P_i^D a_{ij} + t_j; \quad i, j \in T, N$$

(7)

where C_j is the marginal and average cost in sector j, P_{Yj} is the producer price of the composite input of production factors, P_i^D is the domestic price of sector i output, A_j is the use of production factors per sector j output, a_{ij} is the use of sector i input per sector j output, and t_j is indirect tax per unit of sector j output.

Producers are assumed to maximize profits. The producer output prices, P_i, in the tradables producing sectors are given by the world market prices. Assuming perfect competition, this implies that pure profits are nonpositive, and that output is non-negative and positive only if pure profits are equal to zero:

$$P_i - C_i \leq 0; \qquad i \in T$$

$$(P_i - C_i)X_i = 0; \quad i \in T$$

$$X_i \geq 0; \qquad i \in T$$

(8)

In the nontradables-producing sectors, the sector-specific capital is endogenously adjusted so that price equals marginal cost:

$$P_i = C_i; \quad i \in N$$

(9)

Prices, domestic demand, foreign trade, and market clearing

For goods produced in the tradables-producing sectors, the domestic producer price is equal to the world market price of identical goods, and in the nontradables-producing sectors, the domestic user price is equal to the producer price times the tax rate:

$$P_i^D = (1+\sigma_i)P_i^W e = (1+\sigma_i)P_i; \quad i \in T, \tag{10}$$

$$P_i^D = (1+\sigma_i)P_i; \quad i \in N \tag{11}$$

where P_i^D is the domestic user price of goods produced in sector i, P_i^W is the world market price of good i, P_i is the producer price of good i, e is the exchange rate, and σ_i is the ad valorem tax rate on good i.

The intermediate demand of good i is given by the technology assumptions. Domestic final demand (D) is given by utility maximization (equation 35). The net export (Z) is determined as the difference between domestic supply and demand. The market equilibrium conditions then become

$$X_i = \sum_{j \in T,N} a_{ij} X_j + D_i + Z_i; \quad i \in T \tag{12}$$

$$X_i = \sum_{j \in T,N} a_{ij} X_j + D_i; \quad i \in N \tag{13}$$

Deforestation sectors

In this model, there are two sectors that are responsible for deforestation. They are discussed below.

The logging sector

The logging sector is assumed to have a capital-intensive technology (Repetto 1988). Further, the technology is assumed to exhibit decreasing returns to scale in order to reflect the diminishing amount of available forests, as well as the fact that much of the logging is done illegally. The production of LOGS is assumed to depend only on two factors of production: UNSKILLED LABOR and CAPITAL. The loglinear production function is

$$d^{FOREST} = (k^{\log})^{\alpha}(l^{\log})^{\beta}, \quad \alpha + \beta < 1 \tag{14}$$

Undefined property rights

From profit maximization, we have that the demands for CAPITAL and UNSKILLED LABOR are

$$(k^{\log}) = \left(\frac{P_K}{\alpha P_{FL}(l^{\log})^{\beta}}\right)^{\frac{1}{\alpha-1}}$$

$$(l^{\log}) = \left(\frac{P_U}{\beta P_{FL}(k^{\log})^{\alpha}}\right)^{\frac{1}{\beta-1}} \tag{15}$$

Hence, the production function for LOGS can be written as

$$(d^{\log}) = \left(\frac{P_K^U}{\alpha P_{LOGS}(l^{\log})^{\beta}}\right)^{\frac{\alpha}{\alpha-1}}\left(\frac{P_U^U}{\beta P_{LOGS}(k^{\log})^{\alpha}}\right)^{\frac{\beta}{\beta-1}} \tag{16}$$

Well-defined property rights

When property rights are well defined, the logging companies take the opportunity value of the forests into account. The opportunity value is represented by a function $H(d)$, and is exogenous to the model. Hence, in the case of well-defined property rights, the logging sectors demand for UNSKILLED LABOR and CAPITAL, respectively, are

$$(l^{\log}) = \left(\frac{P_U^U + \dfrac{\partial H(d)}{\partial(l^{\log})}}{\beta\, P_{LOGS}(k^{\log})^\alpha} \right)^{\frac{1}{\beta-1}}$$

$$(k^{\log}) = \left(\frac{P_U^U + \dfrac{\partial H(d)}{\partial(k^{\log})}}{\alpha\, P_{LOGS}(l^{\log})^\beta} \right)^{\frac{1}{\alpha-1}}$$

$$(17)$$

Squatters

The forested land cleared by squatters is seen as a common property, although there is no crowding effect, since the stock of forested land is not included in the squatters' production function. The base case assumes undefined property rights, although property rights are not undefined in the traditional sense. Instead, it can be seen that a form of short-term property rights is created; because of the short time horizon, the opportunity value of keeping the forests is not taken into account.

The squatters have a monotonically decreasing production function for cleared land with ULABOR as the only factor of production:

$$d^o \ = \ d(l^{sq}) \ = \ l^{sq^\gamma}; \quad \gamma < 1. \tag{18}$$

with
$$d(0) \ = \ 0,$$
$$d_l(l^{sq}) \ > \ 0,$$
$$d_{ll}(l^{sq}) \ < \ 0, \tag{19}$$
and
$$\lim_{n \to \infty} d(l^{sq}) \ = \ B, \tag{20}$$

where n is the number of squatters, l^{sq} is the labor used in the clearing of the land, and B is the total amount of land available for deforestation.

The squatters total revenue from clearing the land is the price paid for the cleared land:
$$I^s(d^o) = P_{DL}^S\, d^o \tag{21}$$
where $P_{DL}{}^S$ is the supply price of cleared land. Part of the land cleared by squatters is sold to the AGRICULTURE sector, and part of the cleared land is used for subsistence agriculture by the squatters themselves. However, since both occur, the revenue must be the same in both cases. The squatters are assumed not to sell the timber from their deforestation. Other uses of the timber, such as for firewood, are assumed to be negligible, and are therefore set to zero.

The squatters' total private cost for the clearing of the land will depend only on the amount of labor needed in order to clear the land when property rights are undefined,

$$C^s(d^o) = P_L^{sq} d^{-1}(d^o) \tag{22}$$

where P_{Lsq} is the price of labor in squatting. This is the private cost, and it does not include the future value of the forests and the cost of environmental damage. The total social cost of deforestation includes the future value of the cleared forests foregone by clearing the land today. The future value of the forests is assumed to be greater than the value of the forests today:

$$\frac{H(F)}{1+i} > 1. \tag{23}$$

Undefined property rights

When property rights are undefined, the land is seen as a common property. There is no market for the forests available to squatters. The production of cleared land by squatter i is

$$d_i^o = \frac{1}{N} d(l^{sq}). \tag{24}$$

where N is the total number of squatters, and the squatters' total production of cleared land is

$$d^o = \sum_{i=1}^{N} d_i^o \tag{25}$$

The total private profit from clearing the land is

$$g^s(d^o) = I^s(d^o) - C^s(d^o) \tag{26}$$

of which each squatter receives an equal share:

$$g_i^s(d^o) = \frac{1}{N} g^s(d^o) \tag{27}$$

However, for the sector as a whole, land will be cleared until marginal cost equals marginal revenue. From the profit function, we have that the squatters' demand for ULABOR is

$$l^{sq}(P_{DL}, P_U) = \left(\frac{P_U}{\gamma P_{DL}}\right)^{\frac{1}{\gamma-1}} \tag{28}$$

and the supply of cleared land is

$$d^o = \left(\frac{P_U}{\gamma P_{DL}}\right)^{\frac{\gamma}{\gamma-1}} \tag{29}$$

Well-defined property rights

When property rights are well defined, there is a market for the forests. The squatters take the future value of the forests into account, and they can choose to clear forested land or to preserve the forests. This is consistent with the condition for socially optimal forestry that a tree should be harvested when the market value is equal to the shadow value (Hellsten 1988). Assuming that all squatters are identical, and that every squatter owns $1/N$ of the land that previously was available for squatting, the total private profits from clearing the forested land is now (Johansson and Löfgren 1985):

$$g^{fs}(d^o) = P_{DL}^s d^o - C^s(d^o) - \frac{H(d^o)}{1+i} \tag{30}$$

Deforestation will occur until marginal cost equals marginal revenue, and from the profit function, we have that

$$l^{sq} = \left(\frac{P_U + \dfrac{\partial(H(l^{sq^\gamma})/(1+i))}{\partial l^{sq}}}{\gamma P_{DL}} \right)^{\frac{1}{\gamma-1}}$$

(31)

$$d^o = \left(\frac{P_U + \dfrac{\partial(H(l^{sq^\gamma})/(1-i))}{\partial l^{sq}}}{\gamma P_{DL}} \right)^{\frac{\gamma}{\gamma-1}}$$

(32)

This result is equal to the result of the social optimization problem.

Macroeconomic closure

The current account is assumed to be constant. This implies that

$$\sum_{i \in T, N} P_i Z_i = S$$

(33)

where S is the current account surplus. Equation (33) indirectly determines the disposable income *(I)*.

The gross national product is determined as the sum of factor incomes, plus a term reflecting the value of diminished deforestation:

$$GNP = P_K^U K + P_L^U L + P_U^U U + P_{DL}^U DL^* + \sum \sum_{j \in T, N} t_i X_j - \Delta(d^o + d^{\log})H(1) + \Pi(d^{sq}) + \Pi(d^{\log}).$$

(34)

The model is solved by maximizing consumer utility subject to a budget constraint:

$$\text{Max} \quad U = \prod_{i} D_i^{b_i} \sum_i b_i = 1, \ i \in N, T$$

$$s.t. \quad I - \sum_i P_i^D D_i = 0$$

(35)

Annex 1-B: Input-Output and Land Use Data, Costa Rica

Table 1B-1: Base Case Data for Costa Rica, 1986 (10 billion colones)

	FOREST	AGRI	IND	INFRA	SERVICE	CONS	NEXP	TOTAL
forest	0.0003	0.0022	0.0391	0.0002	0.0000	0.0124	0.0011	0.0552
agri	0.0004	0.4033	0.2488	0.0000	0.0000	0.3535	0.3924	1.3984
ind	0.0137	0.1405	0.7390	0.3418	0.1343	1.4426	-0.9643	1.8477
infra	0.0004	0.0293	0.0826	0.0647	0.0684	0.8366		1.0821
service	0.0038	0.0602	0.1546	0.1487	0.2160	1.1230		1.7062
land		0.2070						0.2070
logs	0.0022							0.0022
capital	0.0176	0.2052	0.2168	0.1633	0.5256			1.1285
ulab	0.0141	0.2714	0.1525	0.1754	0.1439			0.7573
slab	0.0002	0.0045	0.0999	0.1299	0.4904			0.7250
indtax	0.0025	0.0747	0.1145	0.0580	0.1276			0.3773
total	0.0552	1.3984	1.8477	1.0821	1.7062	3.7681	-0.5708	9.2870
GNP	2.6148							

Note: indtax = indirect tax; nexp = net export; slab = skilled labor; ulab = unskilled labor.
Source: Calculated from a disaggregated input-output table constructed by Edgar Briceño, University of Costa Rica, San Pedro, and Costa Rica National Accounts. The adjustments have been calculated from Solórzano et al. (1991).

Table 1B-2: Land Use Data

	1963		1973		1986	
	Hectares	Percent	Hectares	Percent	Hectares	Percent
Agriculture	1,544,796	30.09	2,048,512	39.90	2,944,616	57.36
Primary forest	3,154,280	61.44	2,666,005	51.93	1,760,622	34.30
Secondary forest	299,011	5.82	283,571	5.52	292,850	5.70
Other	135,593	2.64	135,593	2.64	135,593	2.64
Total	5,133,680	100.00	5,133,681	100.00	5,133,681	100.00

Source: Calculated from Solórzano et al. (1991).

Bibliography

Alsabah, M. S. S. 1985. *General Equilibrium Analysis of Government Expenditures in an Oil Exporting Country: The Case of Kuwait.* Ph.D. dissertation, Harvard University.

Banco Central de Costa Rica. 1990. *Cuentas Nacionales de Costa Rica 1980–1989.* December.

———. 1991a. *Cuentas Agropecuarias 1980–1989.* January.

———. 1991b. *Estadísticas del Sector Industrial Manufacturero 1980–1989.* March.

Barbier, E. 1989. *Economics, Natural Resources and Development. Conventional and Alternative Views.* London: Earthscan Publications Ltd.

Barbier, E., J. Burgess, and A. Markandya. 1991. "The Economics of Tropical Deforestation." *Ambio* 20(2).

Benjamin, N. C. 1990. "Investment, the Real Exchange Rate, and Dutch Disease: A Two-Period General Equilibrium Model of Cameroon." *Journal of Policy Modeling* 12(1):77–92.

Benjamin, N. C., S. Devarajan, and R. J. Weiner. 1989. "The 'Dutch' Disease in a Developing Country: Oil Reserves in Cameroon." *Journal of Development Economics* 30:71–92.

Bergman, L. 1988. "Energy Policy Modeling: A Survey of General Equilibrium Approaches." *Journal of Policy Modeling* 10(3).

———. 1990a. "Energy and Environmental Constraints on Growth: A CGE Modeling Approach." *Journal of Policy Modeling* 12(4):671–91.

———. 1990b. "General Equilibrium Effects of Environmental Policy: A CGE-Modeling Approach." Research Paper 6415. Economic Research Institute, Stockholm.

Biesanz, R., K. Biesanz, and M. Biesanz. 1987. *The Costa Ricans.* Englewood Cliffs, N.J.: Prentice-Hall.

Bishop, R., and S. Andersen (eds.). 1985. *Natural Resource Economics. Selected Papers.* Boulder, Colo., and London: Westview Press.

Blomström, M., and M. Lundahl. 1989. *COSTA RICA en landstudie.* Blickfång Centralamerika, Latinamerika-institutet, Stockholm.

Bojö, J. 1991. "Economics and Land Degradation," *Ambio* 20(2).

Briceño, Edgar. 1986. "Input-Output Tables for Costa Rica." Unpublished data. San Pedro, Costa Rica: University of Costa Rica.

Brook, A., D. Kendrick, and A. Meeraus. 1988. *GAMS—A User's Guide.* Redwood City, Calif.: Scientific Press.

Burns, D. 1986. *Runway and Treadmill Deforestation: Reflections on the Economics of Forest Development in the Tropics.* London: Earthscan.

Carriére, J. 1991a. "The Crisis in Costa Rica: an Ecological Perspective." In D. Goodman and M. Redclift (eds.), *Environment and Development in Latin America. The Politics of Sustainability.* New York: Manchester University Press

Carriére, J. 1991b. "The Political Economy of Land Degradation in Costa Rica." *International Journal of Political Economy* 21(1): 10–31.

Chichilnisky, G. 1993. "North-South Trade and the Dynamics of Renewable Resources." *Structural Change and Economic Dynamics* 4(2).

Cruz, W., and R. Repetto. 1992. *The Environmental Effects of Stabilization and Structural Adjustment Programs: The Philippines Case.* Washington D.C.: World Resources Institute.

Dasgupta, P. 1982. *The Control of Resources.* Oxford: U.K.: Basil Blackwell.

Dasgupta, P., and K.-G. Mäler. 1990. "The Environment and Emerging Development Issues." *Proceedings of the World Bank Annual Conference on Development Economics 1990.* Reprint.

Denevan, W. M. 1988. "Causes of Deforestation and Woodland Degradation in Tropical Latin America." In L. Fortmann and J. W. Bruce (eds.), *Whose Trees? Proprietary Dimensions of Forestry.* Rural Studies Series. Boulder: Westview Press.

Dervis, K., J. de Melo, and S. Robinson. 1982. *General Equilibrium Models for Development Policy.* Press Syndicate of the University of Cambridge, Cambridge.

Devarajan, S. 1990. *Can Computable General Equilibrium Models Shed Light on the Environmental Problems of Developing Countries?* Paper prepared for WIDER conference on "The Environment and Emerging Development Issues," Helsinki, September 3–7, 1990.

Edelman, M. 1985. "Extensive Land Use and the Logic of the Latifundio: A Case Study in Guanacaste Province, Costa Rica." *Human Ecology* 13(2).

Fisher, A. 1981. *Resource and Environmental Economics.* Cambridge, U.K.: Cambridge University Press.

Forsund, F. 1985. "Input-Output Models, National Economic Models, and the Environment." In A. V. Kneese and J. L. Sweeney (eds.), *Handbook of Natural Resource Economics*, Vol. I. New York: North-Holland, Elsevier Science Publishers.

Forsund, F., and S. Strom. 1980. *Miljf og ressurs fkonomi.* Oslo: Universitetsforlaget.

Foy, G., and H. Daly. 1989. "Allocation, Distribution and Scale as Determinants of Environmental Degradation: Case Studies of Haiti, El Salvador and Costa Rica." Environment Working Paper No. 19. Washington, D.C.: World Bank.

Harrison, S. 1991. "Population Growth, Land Use and Deforestation in Costa Rica, 1950–1984." *Interciencia* 16(2).

Hartshorn, G., L. Hartshorn, A. Atmella, L. Diego Gómez, A. Mata, L. Mata, R. Morales, R. Ocampo, D. Pool, C. Quesada, C. Solera, R. Solórzano, G. Stiles, J. Tosi, A. Umaña, C. Villalobos, and R. Wells.

1982. *COSTA RICA Country Environmental Profile. A Field Study.* San José: Tropical Science Center.

Hellsten, M. 1988. "Socially Optimal Forestry." *Journal of Environmental Economics and Management* 15:387–94.

Hugo, V., V. Gonzalez, R. Jimenez, and T. Vargas. 1983. *Problemas Económicos en la Decada de los 80.* San José: Agencia para el Desarrollo International.

Johansson, P. O., and K. G. Löfgren. 1985. *The Economics of Forestry and Natural Resources.* Oxford, U.K., and New York: Basil Blackwell.

Jorgenson, D. W., and P. J. Wilcoxen. 1990. "Intertemporal General Equilibrium Modeling of U.S. Environmental Regulation." *Journal of Policy Modeling* 12(4): 715–44.

Keogh, R. M. 1984. "Changes in the Forest Cover in Costa Rica through History." *Turrialba* 34(3):325–31.

Larson, B. 1991. "The Causes of Land Degradation along 'Spontaneously' Expanding Agricultural Frontiers in the Third World: Comment." *Land Economics* 62(2): 260–66.

Lutz, E., and H. Daly. 1990. "Incentives, Regulations, and Sustainable Land Use in Costa Rica." Environment Working Paper No. 34. Washington, D.C.: World Bank.

Mäler, K.-G. 1985. "Welfare Economics and the Environment." In A. V. Kneese and J. L. Sweeney (eds.), *Handbook of Natural Resource Economics,* Vol. I. New York: North-Holland, Elsevier Science Publishers.

Ministerio de Recursos Naturales, Energía y Minas. 1990. *Estrategia de Conservación para el Desarrollo Sostenible de Costa Rica.* San José: ECODES.

Moltke, K. von. 1990. "International Economic Issues in Tropical Deforestation." *World Outlook,* summer.

Munasinghe, M. 1993. *Environmental Economics and Sustainable Development.* Washington D.C.: World Bank.

Munasinghe, M., and W. Cruz. 1994. *Economywide Policies and the Environment*. Washington D.C.: World Bank.

Munasinghe, M., W. Cruz, and J. Warford. 1993. "Are Economywide Policies Good for the Environment?" *Finance and Development* 30(3):40–44.

Panayotou, T., and C. Sussangkarn. 1992. "Case Study for Thailand." In D. Reed (ed.), *Structural Adjustment and the Environment*. Boulder, Colo., and Oxford, U.K.: Westview Press.

Persson, A. 1994. "Deforestation in Costa Rica: Investigating the Impact of Market Failures and Unwanted Side Effects of Macro Policies Using Three Different Modeling Approaches." Beijer Discussion Paper Series No. 48, Stockholm.

Raventós, P. 1990. *Commercial and Tax Reform in Costa Rica in the Mid 1980's* (preliminary version). Alajuela, Costa Rica: INCAE.

Raventós, P. 1991. Personal communication. INCAE, Costa Rica, July.

Repetto, R. 1988. "Economic Policy Reform for Natural Resource Conservation." Environment Department Working Paper No. 4. Washington, D.C.: World Bank.

Sader, S., and A. Joyce. 1988. "Deforestation Rates and Trends in Costa Rica, 1940 to 1983." *Biotropica* 20(1):11–19.

Schelhas, J. 1991. "A Methodology for Assessment of External Issues Facing National Parks with an Application in Costa Rica." *Environmental Conservation* 18(4).

Shephard, R. W. 1981. *Cost and Production Functions*. New York: Springer-Verlag.

Solórzano, R., R. de Camino, R. Woodward, J. Tosi, V. Watson, A. Vásquez, C. Villalobos, J. Jiménez, R. Repetto, and W. Cruz. 1991. *Accounts Overdue. Natural Resource Depreciation in Costa Rica*. San José and Washington, D.C.: Tropical Science Center and World Resources Institute.

Southgate, D. 1990. "The Causes of 'Spontaneously' Expanding Agricultural Frontiers in the Third World." *Land Economics* 66(1):93–101.

Thrupp, A. 1981. "The Peasant View of Conservation." *Ceres*, July-August.

Unemo, L. 1993. "Environmental Impact of Government Policies and External Shocks in Botswana—A CGE-Model Approach," Beijer Discussion Paper Series No. 26.

Varian, H. 1984. *Microeconomic Analysis*. New York: W. W. Norton & Company.

Wilen, J. E. 1985. "Bioeconomics of Renewable Resource Use." In A. V. Kneese and J. L. Sweeney (eds.), *Handbook of Natural Resource Economics,* Vol. I. New York: North-Holland, Elsevier Science Publishers.

2

Evaluating Economywide Policies
in the Presence of Agricultural Environmental
Externalities: The Case of Ghana

Ramón López

THE CLOSE DEPENDENCE OF RURAL INCOME on environmental factors in poor areas of the world is by now widely accepted. Excessive deforestation, significant declines in natural biomass, and reduction in soil quality, in many cases induced by rapid population growth, have been identified as key factors explaining an apparent fall or stagnation of rural income in Africa and in certain areas of Latin America and Asia (ADB, ECA, and OAU 1984; FAO 1986). The fact that a significant part of the land used in farming and most forested areas in developing countries are controlled through various forms of common property and, sometimes, public property, has been emphasized as a source of resource overexploitation (Perrings 1989; Sinn 1988; Glantz 1977; Allen 1985; López and Niklitschek 1991).[1]

The author is grateful to Erik Lichtenberg for useful comments.

1. Feder et al. (1988) have empirically documented the negative effects of insecure land tenure property rights on agricultural productivity.

Whether indigenous common property resource controls do cause overexploitation (i.e., whether the "tragedy of the commons" applies) has been the subject of much controversy. Various authors have argued that traditional communities develop controls on the use of the resources inducing socially efficient exploitation (Dasgupta and Mäler 1990; Larson and Bromley 1990). That is, traditional systems would internalize the potential externalities arising from lack of individual resource ownership. Whether or not this is true can only be elucidated through empirical work. To our knowledge, the only empirical test of the commons' efficient resource exploitation hypothesis has been developed by López (1993) for western Côte d'Ivoire. López rejects this hypothesis, documenting socially excessive deforestation and biomass depletion which causes large income losses for the rural communities.

The large number of studies focusing on the implications of rural environmental degradation have permitted a qualitative understanding of how the income of rural communities is affected by policies that directly or indirectly impinge on resource utilization patterns. However, these qualitative analyses have not yet been followed by empirical work that would allow us to obtain a clearer idea of the *quantitative* importance of the environment as a factor of production.[2] The absence of such estimates has, of course, made it impossible to measure the effects of government policies on agricultural income although suitable theoretical models on this subject do exist (e.g., López and Niklitscheck 1991; Deacon 1992).

The principal purpose of this study is to estimate the value of environmental resources as factors of agricultural production and to measure the potential effects of various economywide policies on agricultural income by explicitly accounting for such environmental effects.

In doing this, we estimate a production function that, in addition to the conventional inputs, accounts for the effects of environmental factors. The main environmental factor included in the analysis is the role of land degradation. Based on these estimates, we are able to obtain an idea of the extent of overexploitation of the environmental resource (i.e., the extent by which fallow periods are too short). In doing this analysis, we use a unique data set for an area in western Ghana. These data match household survey information from twelve villages covering the period 1988 through 1989 with remote sensing data on (a) area under closed forest, (b) area under natural bush (fallow area), and (c) density of biomass in the fallow areas. The detailed survey includes data on production, land use, employment, use of conventional inputs, and demographic characteristics for a large number of farm-households in the twelve villages. Field visits to the area provided important qualitative information to complement the survey and remote sensing data.

A secondary goal of the study is to relate the agricultural implications of overexploitation to the wider economy. A simple general equilibrium model is used to measure how agricultural price policies, trade policies, and wage and public sector employment policies are likely to affect the contribution of agriculture to national income. Because of data limitations, this second part of the exercise is necessarily provisional and less detailed than the first. Thus, the results have to be interpreted in this light. Our motivation is mainly to illustrate how unintended environmental impacts of economywide policies in agriculture could also have possible consequences on national income. For example, it is not clear that complete elimination of tariffs and export taxes will necessarily cause an increase in national income (or better welfare)

---

[2]An exception is the above-mentioned study by López (1993) who obtained estimates for the contribution of biomass to agricultural production and for the effects of output prices or biomass and agricultural productivity.

in the presence of other distortions. Based on empirical estimates of the magnitude of the various distortions, environmental and conventional, we try to measure the impact of reducing import protection and export taxation on national income. Additionally, we discuss the consequences of using primarily wage cuts or public employment reductions to limit the fiscal deficit in the presence of multiple distortions.

Evaluating economywide policy reform in the context of environmental externalities constitutes a major challenge. First-best instruments to remove existing externalities are not always available, and the transaction costs associated with them can be extremely high. Setting first-best taxes is in many cases politically difficult and, moreover, many governments, particularly in poor developing countries, do not have the administrative and legal capabilities to enforce first-best regulations. This may leave second best approaches as the only options to mitigating the negative effects of externalities. The environmental impact of economywide policy reforms may, in this context, considerably affect the quantitative and even qualitative effect of these reforms on production and eventually on national income and welfare.

The chapter is organized as follows: in the section, *Policy Issues in Ghana*, we provide a brief review of the evolution of the Ghanaian economy as well as a discussion of the major current policy issues. The empirical estimation of the production function and of land cultivation decisions is presented in the section, *Estimating Production Functions and Land Allocation Decisions*. The general equilibrium model is presented in the section, *General Equilibrium Simulations*, where we also discuss the results of simulating various policy reform scenarios. The final section presents our conclusions.

Policy Issues in Ghana

Since 1983 the government of Ghana has introduced structural reforms to stabilize and liberalize the economy. The real exchange rate has been adjusted to levels that are consistent with external equilibrium; the public sector has been downsized; protection to the industrial sector has been substantially decreased; and prices of agricultural goods, particularly exportables (cocoa), have been brought to levels much closer to international prices. The above reforms have had a positive impact on economic performance.

Despite the impressive depth of the reforms, there are still several remaining policy issues:

(a)　Although quantitative import restrictions have been completely eliminated, the industrial sector is still protected via tariffs. The average import tariff rate including special taxes is about 20 percent ad valorem with considerable variations across goods.

(b)　Although the industrial sector is the most important import substitution sector, a few agricultural goods, mostly cereals, are also protected via import duties that reach about 18 percent.

(c)　The implicit export tax on cocoa is still substantial, about 24 percent ad valorem (this implicit tax has been reduced from almost 50 percent in 1985).

(d)　The public sector deficit is still large, and efforts are now under way to reduce it. This requires both large further reductions in employment in the public sector and, possibly, additional cuts in real wages paid by the public sector.

Each one of the above policy issues implies a potential need for further policy reforms. These additional reforms include further decreases in protection to the import substitution sector, further cut on the implicit export tax to agriculture and wage and public employment reductions to control the public deficit.

Estimating Production Functions and Land Allocation Decisions

In the context of traditional agricultural systems prevailing in western Ghana, the predominant cultivation practice is shifting cultivation. This involves long cycles over which land is cultivated for one or two years and left idle for four to ten years to restore its productive capacity. The fallow or rest period allows the natural vegetation to re-emerge and generate biomass that is used as natural fertilizer in the next cultivation period. Also, the root system of the natural vegetation provides physical support to the inherently unstable tropical soils. At the same time, the patches of bush spread out over the land help protect the cultivated areas from erosion, flooding, and other detrimental factors. This provides the rationale for postulating that biomass constitutes an important factor of agricultural production, and that its depletion, via more extensive cultivation and the shortening of fallow periods, is likely to have a negative effect on productivity. In this section, we estimate an extended production function that allows us to empirically measure the importance of natural biomass as a factor of production vis-à-vis the more conventional factors of production.

Another important feature of traditional systems is that land property rights are not in general well defined. A large proportion of the land available in a village is reserved exclusively for use by the villagers. The land is generally owned by the community (based on lineage) rather by individuals, but its use by outsiders is normally restricted. That is, this is a classic case of common property with closed or highly restricted access for external potential users. The community control of the resources is consistent with and facilitates the shifting cultivation practices. The individual has exclusive rights on the land that he or she actually cultivates, but, once the land is left idle in fallow, the land can be reallocated by consensus and consent of the village chief.

Common property in these conditions does not necessarily imply overcultivation of the resource. It is possible that the community exerts certain controls on the allocation of the land to allow for its optimal exploitation. The controls may be inadequate or insufficient; in which case the community as a whole may experience income losses, associated with excessive loss of biomass, erosion, and flooding. Based on estimates of the production function and land allocation decisions, we provide here some clear indication that indeed such controls are not sufficient and that too much land is cultivated. Fallows are too short and the village communities could significantly increase their total income by reducing the cultivated area.

Since individual farmers can move around within the village land areas in search of land to cultivate, the relevant biomass variable needs to be defined at the village level as well. Thus biomass is defined as the total village area under fallow times the average vegetation density per acre of fallow. These data are obtained from remote sensing based on satellite observations for each village area in 1988 and 1989 (see Annex 2-C). We have data on ten villages in western Ghana. These data were matched with Living Standards Survey (LSS) data (World Bank 1993), which provide information on sixteen farm-households sampled in each village and each year. The household data that we use are output value, family and hired labor used by the farm-household, land cultivated by each farmer, farm tools and labor used, use of fertilizers or other purchased inputs, and some demographic variables, such as education, age, family size, and ethnic background. In estimating the land allocation decisions we also use data on wages deflated by output prices per village.

Production function estimation

Table 2-1 provides various estimates of a double-log production function for the ten villages in Ghana. Not all household data turned out to be consistent, and some household data were simply nonexistent. For this reason, we could use data for 139 households from the ten villages and over a period of two years. For the environmental variable, we used two variables, one that accounts only for the proportion of fallow land in the village area and another one that considers biomass volume properly defined as area under fallow times the average biomass density per acre of fallow. The use of fallow land as a factor of production is appropriate, since fertility of the land actually cultivated is determined by the proportion of land under fallow.[3] Besides the fertility effect, the level of biomass in the areas surrounding the cultivated land patches help protecting against flooding and other physical damages.

The estimates of the production function appear highly plausible. Moreover, the goodness-of-fit statistic is large, and the degree of stability of the coefficients is quite remarkable. The estimates of the effect of the biomass variable are statistically significant and are comparable in magnitude with those associated with conventional factors. We also used other variables, such as fertilizers used and family education, but these variables turned out extremely insignificant. The fact that only a small proportion of all farmers use fertilizer and usually in small amounts may explain the lack of significance of this variable. Also, education is quite homogeneously low among most farmers, and thus the lack of explanatory power of this variable. The estimates suggest that farmers who produce cocoa tend to be more productive than those who do not, and that productivity declined in 1989 vis-à-vis 1988. A possible reason for the positive correlation between productivity and cocoa production could be that cocoa producers are usually more integrated into the agricultural extension systems and other government support services than farmers that do not produce cocoa.[4]

The high and significant value of the ordinary least squares (OLS) coefficients of the environmental variable (Table 2-1, Column 1) indicates that the environmental factor is a very important determinant of agricultural productivity. Another possible interpretation, however, is that a village may have more biomass than another because it has better soil quality and climate, which allow the natural vegetation to grow faster. This better climatic and soil characteristics would also lead to more productive agriculture in this village, and thus the positive correlation found between output and biomass would be spurious. Two approaches were followed to check the relevance of this interpretation: (a) we used area under fallow per village as an instrument for biomass volume, and (b) we control for village specific characteristics such as climate and soil quality using village dummy variables.[5]

The area under fallow variable need not suffer from the shortcomings discussed above. Fallow area is not likely to be positively correlated with soil quality and good climatic conditions. Nonetheless, it is positively correlated with biomass density. In a sense, fallow area is an almost ideal instrument for

---

[3]This is clearly appropriate under the assumption of steady state, i.e., when the stock of biomass is constant. Outside the steady state the relationship between cultivated land fertility and the proportion of fallow land is less direct and is also affected by the rate of biomass accumulation or depletion. However, even outside the steady state, cultivated land fertility is still affected by the proportion of fallow land.

[4]Additionally, we used two dummy variables (Dummy size A and B) to control for the possibility of technological differences associated with either extremely small or extremely large farm sizes (i.e., for farm sizes outside the mean ± 3 standard deviations range). Further, we also use a dummy variable (Dummy 89) to control for possible changes in productivity due to weather or other reasons between 1988 and 1989.

[5]Procedure (a) is consistent with a long-run interpretation because biomass density depends on the proportion of the land under fallow in steady state (see López 1993).

biomass.[6] The fact that using the village fallow area variable as an instrument yields highly significant and positive estimates for the effect of biomass (see Table 2-1, Columns 2 and 3) suggests that the causality interpretation—that more biomass causes greater agricultural productivity—is correct.

Using village specific dummies should control for unobserved variables, such as climate and soil quality, and thus eliminate the influence of such variables from the coefficients associated with the other explanatory variables.[7] The use of village-specific dummies (rather than household dummies) is an adequate procedure because the biomass variable used is also defined at the village level. Column 3 provides the estimates obtained using village-specific dummy variables and the instrumental variables estimators. The estimators of the biomass coefficients remained large and significant. Thus, both procedures suggest that there is a meaningful causal relationship going from the level of the environmental factors to agricultural output.

Apart from the statistical significance of the coefficients associated with biomass, it is important to emphasize their quantitative levels. The biomass coefficient estimated using instrumental variables and controlling for village dummies was 0.17 (Table 2-1, Column 3). This means that the contribution of biomass to agricultural production is about 17 percent, or equivalently, that the share of biomass in total agricultural production once this factor is measured at its shadow value is 17 percent. This compares with a contribution of 26 percent for land cultivated, 25 percent

for labor and 26 percent for capital. Since the share of agricultural output in national gross domestic product (GDP) is about 50 percent, this means that the contribution of biomass to national income is about 7.5 percent. Thus, the stock of biomass is an important determinant of not only agricultural production but also of total GDP. A 10 percent reduction of the biomass stock, for example, could lead, ceteris paribus, to a fall in agricultural output of the order of 1.7 percent and to a reduction of aggregate GDP of 0.75 percent.

Land cultivation decisions

Table 2-2 provides estimates of the land cultivation decisions by the individual farmers.[8] Column 1 provides estimates conditional on a given level of family size, while the estimators in Column 2 are obtained by assuming that family size is endogenous. In this sense, the estimates in Column 2 can be interpreted as more long-run than those in Column 1. The key variable here is the agricultural wage deflated by the output price. This variable is defined per village for each year. Its coefficient suggests that the wage rate exerts a negative effect and that the agricultural output price has a positive effect on land cultivated. The elasticity for the wage rate is about -1 for the short-run estimates (Column 1) and about -1.26 for the long-run estimates (Column 2).

Thus, increasing agricultural prices or wage reductions cause an expansion in the cultivated area and, therefore, a reduction in the fallow area and a fall in biomass, which in turn reduces agricultural productivity. According to the estimates in Table 2-2, the elasticity of land cultivated with respect to agricultural output price is in the 1 to 1.26 range. The other explanatory variables have all the expected signs and are significant. Family size has a large positive effect on the amount of land cultivated. This finding is very consistent

---

[6]If anything, fallow area should be negatively correlated with soil quality and good climatic conditions. One could reasonably argue that villages that have good soils and climate would tend to cultivate more land (and hence have less fallow) because land is more valuable.

[7]The village dummies also account for other village specific variables such as distance to markets, transportation facilities, etc.

---

[8]The conceptual basis for the derivation of the land use specification is provided in Annex 2-A.

with the idea that population pressure is an important factor behind environmental degradation. Capital equipment represented by the number of tools and implements owned by a household also exerts a positive effect on the area that families cultivate. Similarly, it appears that, other conditions being equal, established local residents (Ashanti and Bron tribes) tend to cultivate less land than relatively new immigrants (the rest of the population).

Tradeoffs between expansion of cultivated land, biomass, and agricultural productivity

The estimates of the production function expose the tradeoffs associated with expanding the cultivated land. The direct positive effect of expanding cultivation on production has to be weighted against the negative effect of such an expansion on the level of biomass and, therefore, on output. To evaluate this tradeoff, it is necessary to quantify the effect of cultivated land on the level of biomass. Total biomass can be expressed as total fallow area times the average biomass density per acre of fallow land,

$$\theta = \eta \cdot (\bar{x} - x) \tag{1}$$

where η is average biomass density per acre of fallow land, $\bar{x}$ is total land area in a village, and x is the total land cultivated. Thus, $\bar{x} - x$ is the area under fallow. The average density η is not independent of the area cultivated either. Following López (1993), we can postulate a simple specification for the dynamics of η,

$$\ddot{\eta}_t = \tilde{\alpha} - \left(\frac{x}{\bar{x}}\right)\eta_t \tag{2}$$

where $\bar{\alpha} > 0$ represents the natural growth of vegetation, and $x/\bar{x}$ is really the rate of depreciation of biomass in the context of a rotational system. In the long run when the level of biomass becomes stable, we have that

$\dot{\eta}_t = 0$. In this case,

$$\eta = \tilde{\alpha}\left(\frac{\bar{x}}{x}\right) \tag{3}$$

That is, the level of biomass density in the long run is inversely related to the proportion of the total land area that is cultivated. Using (3) in (1), we obtain

$$\theta = \tilde{\alpha}\bar{x}\left(\frac{\bar{x}}{x} - 1\right) \tag{1'}$$

That is, the total biomass volume is decreasing with the proportion of cultivated land $(x/\bar{x})$ and increasing with the rate of growth of natural vegetation, $\tilde{\alpha}$. From (1') it is clear that the elasticity of total biomass with respect to area under cultivation can be defined by

$$\frac{d \ln \theta}{d \ln x} = -\left(\frac{1}{1 - x/\bar{x}}\right) \tag{4}$$

If, for example, 25 percent of the village land is cultivated $(x/\bar{x} = 0.25)$, increasing cultivated land by 1 percent will decrease total biomass by 1.33 percent, or equivalently, the elasticity is -1.33.

Using (4) and the estimated coefficients for the land cultivated and biomass variables, one can calculate the full effect of increasing cultivated land on agricultural output.[9] If, for example, we use the estimates in Column 3 of Table 2-1, we have the following result: increasing land cultivated by 10 percent would induce a 2.7 percent increase in output as a direct effect. However, the 10 percent increase in land cultivated also induces an approximately 14.5 percent reduction in total biomass (in fact, the average value for $x/\bar{x}$ in the 10 villages analyzed is about 0.31). A 14.5 percent reduction in biomass in turn would cause

---

[9]In doing this, we are assuming that the system is in long-run equilibrium. To consider situations outside long-run equilibrium, the specification of the empirical and theoretical models needs to be much more complicated and requires a much larger data set than what we have (see López 1993).

according to the estimates in Column 3, a 2.5 percent decrease in agricultural output. Thus, the net effect of expanding area cultivated on agricultural output is still positive, but of the order of 0.2 percent, many times smaller than the direct effect. The first row of Table 2-3 shows the net effect of expanding the area cultivated by 10 percent using the estimates from Table 2-1. In general, the net effects on output of expanding land cultivation are positive, but very small.

The second row of Table 2-3 shows the net effect of land cultivated on net farm income rather than on output under each scenario. Net farm income is defined as the gross value of output less land clearing costs and less (plus) the value of the biomass decrease (increase). That is, since expanding land cultivated requires investing labor and other resources in first clearing and preparing the land, a more appropriate analysis of the impact of expanding cultivated land on farm income should account for the costs embodied in expanding land into cultivation (since the system is rotational, these clearing costs are recurrent rather than once-and-for-all). In making their land allocation decisions, however, farmers affect their level of biomass assets as well. Hence, total agricultural income is

$$Y_A = pF(L, x, z, \theta) - cx + u\eta \tag{5}$$

where p is output price, L is total labor used, x is land cultivated, z are other inputs used, c is the per acre land clearing cost, η is defined in (2), and u is the shadow price of the stock of biomass density,

$$u(t) = \int_t^\infty p(\bar{x} - x)F_\theta(L, x, z, \theta) \\ e^{-r(\upsilon - t)}\, d\upsilon,$$

where r is the discount rate and $F_\theta \equiv \partial F/\partial \theta$. It can be shown that in steady state

$$u = \frac{(\bar{x} - x)F_\theta}{r + x/\bar{x}},$$

in which case the effect of expanding cultivated land on national income is

$$\frac{d \ln Y_A}{d \ln x} = \left[\frac{\partial \ln F}{\partial \ln x} + \frac{(1 + r)x/\bar{x}}{r + x/\bar{x}} \right. \\ \left. \frac{\partial \ln F}{\partial \ln \theta} \frac{d \ln \theta}{d \ln x} \right] - s_c \tag{6}$$

where $s_c \equiv \dfrac{cx}{Y_A}$ is the share of land clearing cost in net revenue. The first right-hand term in Equation (6) captures the direct effect of expanding land cultivation, which is positive. The second right-hand term accounts for the present value of the future effects on income of reducing biomass associated with the land cultivated expansion. (Note that this term is negative because $d\ln\theta/d\ln x$ is negative.) The last right-hand term accounts for the direct costs involved in expanding land cultivation. The expression in square brackets in the right-hand side of (6) is evaluated by using the coefficients in Table 2-1 and an evaluation of Equation (4). According to information obtained in the field, it was estimated that the share of land clearing cost in net revenues is between 12 percent and 17 percent. We use the lower bound estimate and thus assume that $s_c = 0.12$. Using this, one can calculate the total effect of increasing cultivated land by 10 percent on net farm revenues. These estimates are provided in the second row of Table 2-3. As can be seen, expanding cultivated land has a negative effect on farm income despite that we use the most conservative estimates of land clearing costs. If we assume that $s_c = 0.16$ rather than 0.12, the effect of expanding land cultivate on income becomes substantially more negative, reaching a value of -0.75 percent when the OLS estimates are used and -1.0 percent when the Instrumental Variables estimates are used. Thus, the empirical evidence suggests that too much land is cultivated and that any further expansion of the cultivation level is detrimental for village income once a full account of the indirect effects is considered. Table 2-3A provides estimates of the degree by which land is over-cultivated and the income losses implied by such cultivation. As can be seen, despite the use of conservative estimates, the income losses are quite large, reaching almost 3 percent when our best econometric estimates are used.

Labor demand aspects

In the policy analysis, we also need estimates for the agricultural labor demand elasticities. Given the estimates of the production function and the land equation the labor elasticities are indeed implicitly defined. Using the production function estimates of Table 2-1, Column 3, and the land equation estimates reported in Table 2-2, Column 2, it can be shown that the implicit labor demand elasticity is about -1.26.[10] By directly estimating a labor demand equation, we obtain estimates somewhat higher. Thus, it appears that demand for labor in western Ghana agriculture is highly elastic.

General Equilibrium Simulations

In this section, we evaluate the impact on national income of various government policies. The policies analyzed are the following: (a) a net reduction of agricultural export taxes, (b) a decrease in tariff protection to the industrial sector, (c) a decrease in government employment as a measure to control the fiscal deficit, and (d) a decrease in public sector wages as an alternative to reduction of public employment. We perform the analysis using two general equilibrium models, one that postulates a tight and competitive labor market, and another that assumes urban unemployment or subemployment in the Harris-Todaro tradition. The main feature of the Harris-Todaro model is that rural and urban wages for identically skilled workers are not equalized.[11] The first model assumes a competitive labor market which leads to equal wages for given skill levels. Both models assume a small open economy with exogenously given border prices.

Environmental distortions in a Harris-Todaro model

To specify a general equilibrium model we first need to specify the land clearing cost (c) in terms of real factor use. We assume that land clearing requires labor in fixed proportion. We specify that γ days of labor are necessary to clear one acre of land. In this case, $c = \gamma w$ and the agricultural production function need to be modified slightly to account for this, $F(L - \gamma x, x, \theta)$. This specification accounts directly for the cost of clearing land. An increase in x has a direct positive effect on output and two indirect negative effects, decreasing θ and decreasing the amount of labor that is effectively devoted to production.

National income for a small economy evaluated at the opportunity cost of resources needs to be specified in terms of world prices rather than at domestic prices. Thus, national income can be defined as

---

[10]See Annex 2-B for a derivation of this result.

[11]*Editors' note:* This is in contrast to the standard assumption that wages equalize with competition and labor mobility. The Harris-Todaro framework recognizes the role of imperfect information, limited labor mobility and institutional constraints, leading to significant differences in wages in distinct sectors of the economy. See, for example, Todaro (1989).

$$Y^* = p^* F(L - \gamma x, x, \theta) + q^* G(L_N; K_N)$$

$$+ \alpha L_g + u\eta \qquad (7)$$

where p^* and q^* are the international prices of agriculture and the urban goods, respectively, $G(\cdot)$ is the production function of the urban goods, L_N is labor, and K_N is other factors of production used in production of the urban good. L_g is government employment, α is labor productivity in government, and thus αL_g is production of government services (we have normalized the price of government services to one).

The other components of the model are the profit maximization conditions for farmers that determine L and x,

$$(1 - \tau) p^* F_1(\cdot) = w \qquad (8)(i)$$

$$F_2 - \gamma F_1 - \lambda \eta F_3 \frac{1 + r}{r + x/\bar{x}} \frac{\partial \theta}{\partial x} = 0 \quad (8)(ii)$$

where τ is the ad valorem tax rate affecting agriculture production $((1 - \tau) p^* \equiv p$ is, therefore, the domestic price of the agricultural goods), and $0 \leq \lambda \leq 1$ is an efficiency parameter determining the extent by which the effect of changing cultivated area on biomass is taken into consideration in the land allocation decisions. Subscripts in the function indicate first derivative with respect to the corresponding term. Note that γF_1 is the real cost (deflated by $(1 - \tau)p^*$) of clearing land (what was called c before). From Equations (8)(i) and (8)(ii)), one can solve for $x((1 - \tau)p^*, w)$ and $L((1 - \tau)p^*, w)$.

The level of employment in the urban private sector, L_N, is determined by the level of the urban wage rate, $\bar{w}$, which in a Harris-Todaro model is different from w,

$$(1 + t) q^* G_1(\cdot) = \bar{w} \qquad (9)$$

where t is the ad valorem tariff rate that protects the nonagricultural sector (note that the domestic price of the nonagricultural good is $q \equiv (1 + t)q^*$). Thus, from (9), employment in the private urban sector is $L = L((1 + t)q^*, \bar{w})$. The relationship between $\bar{w}$ and w is given by the well-known equilibrium condition that the wage in the rural sector is equal to the expected wage in the urban sector,

where L is the total labor force. The expression

$$w = \left[\frac{L_g + L_N}{\bar{L} - L} \right] \bar{w} \qquad (10)$$

sion in square brackets corresponds, therefore, to the rate of employment in the urban sector. Since $\bar{w}$ is given exogenously by government regulations regarding public sector wages, wage indexation, minimum wages and fringe benefits, in general there is (urban) unemployment or underemployment. This implies that the term in square brackets in (10) is less than one and hence, $w < \bar{w}$. The level of unemployment or underemployment (U) is determined by

$$U = \bar{L} - L_g - L_N((1 + t)q^*, \bar{w})$$

$$- L((1 - \tau)p^*, w) \qquad (11)$$

We assume that L_g is determined by the government exogenously. This implies that U is determined recursively after w, L, and L_N are solved from the rest of the model.

With the above specification, we can illustrate the possible effects of the following policies on national income, Y^*, and the environmental resource, θ.

(a)   Decreasing the degree of taxation of agriculture, i.e., decreasing τ or equivalently increasing p for a given p^*.

(b) Reducing protection to the industrial sector or trade liberalization, i.e., reducing t (or, equivalently, increasing q for a of given q^*).

(c) Government wage policies that reduce labor regulations and public sector wages, i.e., a reduction in $\bar{w}$.

(d) Reducing public sector employment, i.e., a cut in L_g.

(The detailed derivations are presented in Annex 2-D.)

The main distinctive feature of using this model for analysis is that we explicitly account for the interactions between the rural environmental distortion documented in the section, *Policy Issues in Ghana*, and the conventional distortions, including trade protection, labor market regulations, and oversized government. The policy analysis focuses on the consequences of reducing the conventional distortions for national income, real wages and the rural environmental stock.

We compare the effects of the policies under each one of the maintained assumptions regarding the labor market, i.e., the Harris-Todaro and the competitive labor market assumptions. Although the level of open unemployment recognized in government statistics is very low (2–3 percent), there are indications that these statistics considerably underestimate the actual level of unemployment. Moreover, it appears that the level of disguised unemployment is quite high in Ghana. Also, the available sectoral wage data suggests that rural wages tend to be significantly lower than urban wages in sectors that use levels of skills that are comparable to those in agriculture (i.e., wholesale, restaurants). Finally, there is some evidence that the public sector still tends to lead the urban private sector in wage adjustments.

All these would be consistent with a Harris-Todaro model where the urban wage rate determination is significantly affected by nonmarket forces and is for this reason higher than in the rural areas. However, the urban-rural wage dispersion, although significant, is not too large (smaller than in many other developing countries) and open urban unemployment is small compared to other developing countries even if one assumes considerably downward biases in the available statistics. This decreases our confidence that the Harris-Todaro hypothesis is clearly better than the competitive labor market hypothesis. For this reason, we report here the policy evaluations obtained using both models. The idea is to determine how the results may vary under alternative assumptions.

To evaluate the policies considered, we need information on basic parameters pertaining to the agricultural sector, as well as the private urban and government sectors. The agricultural sector parameters are all obtained from our own econometric estimates reported in the section, *Estimating Production Functions and Land Allocation Decisions*. The nonagricultural parameters are mostly derived from recent World Bank publications. The exceptions are the elasticities of labor demand in the urban private sector, which are not available for Ghana. We use instead elasticities reported for other African countries in a study by Riveros (1992).

Table 2-4 presents the parameter values used to evaluate the expressions derived in Annex 2-D. Some limitations of these data are worthwhile to emphasize. The parameters for the agricultural sector are reliable and consistent given that have been obtained from a single source. However, the sample used to estimate these parameters is not necessarily representative of the country as a whole because, as discussed before, the entire database corresponds to the Bron-Ahafo, Ashanti, and Western regions of Ghana. These are important agricultural areas, but the degree of representativeness of these three regions for the country's agriculture is not clear. The data required for the nonagricultural sector is not too demanding, consisting mostly of shares of the different sectoral outputs and sectoral employment in the economy. Data on labor demand elasticities for the nonagricultural sector are also needed. Unfortunately, there is no estimate of these elasticities for Ghana, and thus we have assumed "reasonable" values for them. We performed sensitive analysis to see how the results are affected by changing these values.

The results of the policy simulations are presented in Table 2-5. The policy changes simulated are not very large because the estimated elasticities are valid only as local measures. That is, the elasticities are valid only within the range of the exogenous variables for which they were estimated. As the exogenous variables (i.e., policy variable) change, the elasticities and other parameters used also change, thus increasing the error of the simulation. Thus, we postulate relatively gradual policy adjustments of the order of 5 percent.

More important than the actual quantitative estimates reported in Table 2-5 is the qualitative pattern of response to policy changes. The major patterns observed in Table 2-5 are the following:

1. The effects of the policy adjustment on national income are small in both the Harris-Todaro and in the competitive models (see Row 1). This is, of course, not surprising. Most analyses typically find that the income or welfare effects of removing even large distortions is very small, less than 1 percent of GDP. In the case of Ghana, the remaining distortions are not very large, and we simulate its partial, not total, removal. Moreover, accounting for the environmental distortion tends in general to decrease the magnitude of the policy changes on national income.

2. Under the assumption of competitive labor markets, the effects of trade liberalization (i.e., of reducing taxation to agriculture and decreasing tariff protection to the industrial sector) on national income are negative once the environmental distortion is accounted for. In the Harris-Todaro specification, the effect of reducing agricultural taxation is positive while that of liberaliz-

ing imports is negative. In the presence of unemployment (Harris-Todaro case), any reform (such as decreasing of agricultural implications) that increases output prices will contribute to decrease unemployment and thus to induce larger gains. On the contrary, policies that reduce output prices, such as import liberalization, cause higher unemployment, which, in turn, reduces the income gains. The level of unemployment is increased by price increases because urban wages are set in nominal terms, and thus any increase in output price implies a de facto reduction of the real wage distortion (i.e., by reducing real wages) and any output price reduction causes and increase in the real wage and thus a greater distortion. This employment effect of trade reform is strong enough to change the signs of the competitive labor market effects (Table 2-5, Row 1). This explains the positive income effect of reducing agricultural taxation and the negative effect of reducing tariff protection. By contrast, in the absence of wage distortions (i.e., in the competitive labor market case) decreasing agricultural taxation reduces income because the worsening of the environmental distortion that such a policy induces more than offsets the gains from eliminating the price distortion. Similar reasoning explains the negative effects of import tariff reductions on national income both with and without wage distortions.

3. Both trade reforms have positive income effects in the absence of wage and environmental distortions (see numbers in brackets in Table 2-5). In the absence of environmental distortions, but with wage distortions, the agricultural tax reduction also has a positive effect on income, but decreasing tariff protection induces a negative effect. The reasons for this are similar to those discussed in paragraph 2 above.

4. Somehow surprisingly, public sector employment policies affect income in the same direction whether wage distortions

exist or not. The effect, however, is more strongly positive in the competitive case. The fact that labor productivity is higher in the private than in the government sector is responsible for the positive effect on national income of reducing public employment. This effect is, however, much more remarkable in the case of competitive labor markets where the rest of the economy competes for labor directly with the government. In the wage distortion case, the existence of unemployment considerably dampens the effects of changes in government employment on private sector employment. In this case, the government competes for labor with the private sector only in an indirect way.

5. As indicated before, the environmental distortion is sufficiently strong to render the effect of trade liberalization perverse in the competitive labor market case.

6. Perhaps the most important result of this section is that, although the effects of the reforms on national income vary in direction and magnitude depending on the labor market assumption used, their effects on the rural environmental stock are consistently negative regardless of the model used. All four reforms cause a decrease in biomass ranging from 3 percent for agricultural price liberalization to 1 percent for public sector wage reductions. The implications of this are very serious, suggesting that even mild additional reforms are likely to cause a significant loss of forest and biomass. This is important given that biomass and other forest resources have value beyond their contribution to national income. For example, biomass contributes to welfare beyond the Ghanaian economy such as biodiversity preservation and carbon sequestration. The combined net effect of a series of reforms to further liberalize goods and labor markets and to reduce the size of the government without tackling the environmental distortion may be mildly positive for national income, but at the cost

of devastating the remaining biomass resources of the rural areas.

Conclusion

The major findings emerging from this paper are the following:

1. Biomass is an important factor of production in Western Ghana. Its contribution to agricultural output ranges from 15 percent to 20 percent of the value of output. This means that the contribution of the biomass factor of production to national GDP ranges between 7.5 percent and 10 percent.

2. The empirical evidence suggests an overexploitation of biomass through a more than optimal level of land cultivated. Or, equivalently, fallow periods appear to be too short and thus the stock of the environmental resource is below the socially optimum levels. In this chapter, we have defined the social value of biomass quite narrowly, considering only its contribution to agricultural output. We have excluded further roles of biomass that transcend the Ghanaian economy, such as its contribution to biodiversity and carbon sequestration.

3. The quantitative importance of agricultural prices, rural wages, and population pressure as a source of biomass degradation has been clearly demonstrated.

4. The evaluation of a deepening of the structural reforms in Ghana suggest that, in general, their impact on national income is rather small once the existence of the rural environmental distortion is considered. The effects of furthering trade liberalization (decreasing implicit tax to agriculture or reducing tariff protection) is in general ambiguous. The possibility of adverse effects is present for agricultural tax reduction, depending on the characteristics of the labor market. Import liberalization has a negative effect on national income regardless of whether or not a wage distortion exists. The effects of reducing the fiscal deficit through either lowering public em-

ployment or lowering public wages, however, are unambiguously positive for national income regardless of the performance of the labor market.

5. Without parallel efforts to address the environmental distortion, the impact of a deepening of trade liberalization on biomass depletion may be quite adverse. Further losses of biomass of the order of 5–10 percent by completing the trade liberalization process are not unlikely. Decreasing public sector employment and public wages, on the other hand, also causes a negative impact on the biomass stock, but their quantitative impacts are more moderate than those linked to trade liberalization.

The above implications are obtained using parameters estimated by exploiting cross-sectional and time variability during the 1988–89 years in western Ghana. A key empirical result underlying the policy simulations is that the main source of supply response in agriculture is the expansion of the cultivated area rather than agricultural intensification. If agricultural price responsiveness relied less on land expansion and more on intensification, the policy evaluation of trade liberalization would probably be more favorable. Currently, Ghana is gradually improving its agricultural research and extension services which could in the future allow for greater reliance on yield increases. On the other hand, it is plausible to assume that as long as (forest) land is available for cultivation, a significant component of the supply response is likely to continue to be based on agricultural area expansion. To the extent that land is a normal factor of production (and there are no reasons to question this), any increase in real output prices is likely to induce a greater demand for land. This, in turn, will be manifested in an expansion of the agricultural frontier as long as more land is available.

Table 2-1: Production Function, Ghana, 1988–89

	(1) OLS	(2) Instrumental variable	(3) Instrumental variable and village-specific dummies
Constant	9.44 (13.30)	9.08 (13.6)	9.31 (13.6)
Land cultivated	0.27 (3.16)	0.22 (2.65)	0.27 (3.12)
Total labor	0.25 (2.47)	0.30 (2.89)	0.25 (2.51)
Village biomass	0.15 (1.86)	0.20 (2.56)	0.17 (2.22)
Tools	0.28 (3.13)	0.29 (3.20)	0.26 (2.99)
Dummy cocoa producers	0.62 (4.37)	0.58 (4.13)	0.60 (4.31)
Dummy 89	-0.57 (-3.14)	-0.30 (-1.71)	-0.61 (-3.30)
Dummy size A[1]	-0.25 (-1.23)	-0.40 (-2.02)	-0.51 (-1.66)
Dummy size B[2]	-0.46 (-1.50)	-0.86 (-2.79)	-0.25 (-1.32)
Village dummies (several)	no	no	yes
N	139	139	139
R^2	0.46	0.40	0.46
R^2	0.43	0.36	0.42
F	9.60	10.70	10.20

1. Dummy size A is equal to one for extremely small farm size (less than 5 acres) and zero otherwise.
2. Dummy size B is equal to one for extremely large farm size (greater than 100 acres) and zero otherwise.

Note: a. t-statistics are in parentheses.

       b. Double-log specifications were used.

       c. The dependent variable is the log of real agricultural output per household.

Table 2-2: Land Equation, Western Ghana, 1988–89 (double-log specification)

	(1)	(2)
Constant	7.10 (2.66)	8.85 (4.0)
Family members	0.37 (2.33)	–
Wage/agricultural output price	-1.01 (-2.19)	-1.26 (-3.13)
Tools	0.27 (1.94)	0.42 (3.32)
Percentage of fallow land over total land	-0.19 (-0.91)	–
Dummy for cocoa producer	0.89 (4.37)	0.86 (4.34)
Dummy for Ashtanti-Bron	-0.57 (-2.44)	-0.69 (-2.97)
Dummy 89	1.49 (5.77)	1.44 (6.57)
N	139	139
R^2	0.54	0.51
R^2	0.51	0.49
F	21.67	27.94

– = Endogenous variables.

Note: 1. t-statistics are in parentheses.

2. The dependent variable is the log of the area cultivated by each household.

Table 2-3: Net Effect of Increasing Cultivated Land by 10 Percent (percent)

	Measures based on OLS estimates[1]	Measures based on instrumental variables/village dummy estimates[2]
On output Level	0.5	0.2
On net farm income[3,4]	-0.4	-0.65

1. Obtained using estimates in Table 2-1, Column 1.
2. Obtained from estimates in Table 2-1, Column 3.
3. Net farm revenue is defined as value of output net of land clearing costs. It was assumed that the share of land clearing costs in net revenues was 8 percent (this is the absolute lowest boundary according to field estimates in western Ghana).
4. A 10 percent discount rate is assumed.

Table 2-3A: Extent of Overcultivation and Income Losses (percent)

	Based on OLS estimates	Based on instrumental variable/village dummy estimates
Excess land cultivated	26	45
Income loss	0.96	2.7

Table 2-4: Basic Parameters and Elasticities Used in the Simulations

Agricultural sector		Rest of the economy	
$S_L = 0.25$	$\partial \ln x / \partial \ln p = 1.26$	$\partial \ln L_N / \partial \ln q = 0.40$	$\beta = 0.66$
$S_x = 0.27$	$\partial \ln x / \partial \ln w = -1.26$	$\partial \ln L_N / \partial \ln w = -0.40$	$Y_A^*/Y^* = 0.48$
$S_\theta = 0.17$	$\partial \ln L / \partial \ln p = 1.36$	$L_N/L = 0.33$	$t = 0.17$
$S_c = 0.08$	$\partial \ln L / \partial \ln w = -1.36$	$\varepsilon = 1.14$	$S_{LN} = 0.30$
$\tau = 0.05$	$d \ln L / d \ln \theta = -1.45$	$L_N/L_e = 1.33$	$Y_N^*/Y^* = 0.25$

Note: All parameters for the agriculture sector, with the exception of τ, are derived from the estimated production function and land cultivated equation. Parameters for the rest of the economy are obtained or derived from various World Bank sources. The implicit ad valorem net tax rate for agriculture (τ) was estimated as a weighted average rate.

Table 2.5: Effects of Various Policies (percent)

	Net reduction of agricultural implicit tax[1]		Decrease tariff protection to industry[2]		Decrease government employment[3]		Decrease public sector wages[4]	
	Harris-Todaro Model	Competitive model	Harris-Todaro Model	Competitive model	Harris-Todaro Model	Competitive model	Harris-Todaro Model	Competitive model
National Income	0.21 (0.27)	-0.02 (0.91)	-0.17 (-0.13)	-0.02 (0.91)	0.07 (0.10)	0.20 (0.03)	0.22 (0.24)	–
Agricultural Wages	3.36	4.55	-0.99	-1.341	-0.71	-0.83	-0.56	–
Environmental Resource Level	-3.03	-1.67	-1.83	-2.45	-1.32	-1.52	-1.05	–

– = not applicable.
1. A 5 percent increase in agricultural prices due to the elimination of implicit tax to agriculture.
2. A 5 percent decrease in nonagricultural sector prices due to halving the level of tariff protection.
3. Five percent reduction in public employment.
4. Five percent cut in public wages.
Note: Numbers in parentheses correspond to the effect of the policies on national income when the environmental distortion is ignored.

Annex 2-A: Derivation of a Land Demand Equation

If farmers maximize profits, the level of cultivated land and the amount of labor would be chosen so as to satisfy (ignoring by the time the discount rate) the following:

$$F_L(L, x, z, \theta) = w/p \qquad \text{(a)}$$

$$F_x(L, x, z, \theta) + \lambda \, F_\theta \, \frac{\partial \theta}{\partial x} = c/p \qquad \text{(b)}$$

where L is labor, x is area cultivated, θ is village biomass, w is the wage rate, p is agricultural output price, c is the cost per acre of clearing land, and z is other input endowments. Subscripts in the $F(\cdot)$ function reflect marginal products of the respective input. The parameter $0 \le \lambda \le 1$ is an efficiency parameter that reflects the extent to which the effect of land cultivation decisions on biomass are taken into consideration. A value $\lambda = 1$ implies full account of the externality and, thus, community efficiency. Since F_θ is mostly an external effect, the value of λ will depend on the community controls over individual land cultivation decisions. Note that since $\frac{\partial \theta}{\partial x} < 0$, a higher λ implies that farmers cultivate less land.

Equations (a) and (b) solve simultaneously for L and x, where $L = L(\frac{w}{p}, \frac{c}{p}, z)$ and $x = x(\frac{w}{p}, \frac{c}{p}, z)$. Note that land clearing costs are mostly labor and hence, c can be written as a function of the wage rate. If γ units of labor are needed to clear an acre of land, then $c = \gamma w$ and $L = L(\frac{w}{p}; z)$, $x = x(\frac{w}{p}; z)$. Table 2-2 reports the estimates of x based on this specification.

Annex 2-B: Derivation of a Labor Demand Specification

The first order condition for labor allocation is

$$pF_L(L, x(p,w), \theta, z) = w,$$

where $x(p,w)$ is evaluated at the estimated level. Totally differentiating this with respect to w, explicitly using the fact that x depends on w as well, we obtain

$$\frac{\partial L}{\partial w} = \frac{1 - pF_{Lx}\, \partial x/\partial w - pF_{L\theta}\, \partial\theta/\partial w}{pF_{LL}},$$

where F_{ij} indicates second order derivative with respect to arguments i and j. The above equation can be represented in log form,

$$\frac{\partial \ln L}{\partial \ln w} = \frac{1 - s_x\, \partial \ln x/\partial \ln w - s_\theta\, \partial \ln \theta/\partial \ln w}{s_L - 1}$$

The estimates of the production function directly yield the values for s_x, s_θ, s_L. Moreover, from the estimate of the land equation we evaluate $\partial \ln x/\partial \ln w$ and using Equation (4), we can also measure

$$\partial \ln \theta/\partial \ln w = \frac{d \ln \theta}{d \ln x} \frac{\partial \ln x}{\partial \ln w}.$$

Annex 2-C: Data Sources and Definition of Variables

The data used come from the Living Standards Survey (LSS) conducted in Ghana in 1988 and 1989 (World Bank 1993). These panel data include a wide range of information such as labor force activity, individual characteristics, consumption, and production at the household level, as well as wages at the village level. The sample used consists of all observations repeated in 1988–89 for which information on agricultural revenue, land cultivated, hours worked by family members and hired labor exists.

Statistics on fallow, forest, and agricultural land and biomass density for each village were provided by a special study done for this project by EARTHSAT, based on satellite images that cover the western region of Ghana for the years 1988 and 1989. The total number of villages considered was sixteen—all in the western region of Ghana. The villages are New Bansakrom, Yankye, Akantamwa, Tanoso, Sireso, Bibiani, Asunsu, Doduoso, Nsuatre, Susuanso, Dormaa, Apronsie, Kenyasi, Ewisa, Boasi, and Wenchi.

The Living Standards Survey (LSS) and the EARTHSAT data were matched to obtain a unique data set that includes the usual individual characteristic variables with information on natural resources at the village level. The total number of households considered is 139.

Variables

Real Agricultural Output per Household

Total Output in Cedis 1988. It is the sum of total sales to the market, payments in kind to hired labor, seeds kept, home consumption, and home production.

Wage/Agricultural Output Price

Average wage per village earned per day by a male working in the fields, divided by the average price of agricultural output at the village level.

Family Members

Number of family members older than ten years and younger than sixty years of age.

Total Labor

Total number of days worked in the field by family members or hired labor.

Land Cultivated per Household

Land cultivated by each farmer (in acres).

Tools

Total number of tools owned by each farmer.

Percentage of Fallow over Total Land

LFALLOW/(LFALLOW + LAGRIC), where LFALLOW is total land under fallow in each village and LAGRIC is total land cultivated in each village. *Source:* EARTHSAT.

Village Biomass

LFALLOW*iFALLOW/(LFALLOW + LAGRIC), where IFALLOW is the average biomass density in each village. *Source:* EARTHSAT.

Annex 2-D: Effects of Policy Adjustment on National Income

Policy simulations in a Harris-Todaro economy

Reducing taxation to agriculture

As indicated in the main text, lowering τ is equivalent to increasing p, keeping p^* constant. Thus, the effect of such policy on Y^* can be estimated by differentiating totally Y^* in Equation (7) with respect to p, (maintaining p^* constant):

$$\frac{dY^*}{dp} = p^* F_1 \frac{\partial L(p,w)}{\partial p} + p^* \left(F_2 - \gamma F_1 + \eta F_3 \right)$$

$$\frac{1+r}{n+x/\bar{x}} \Bigg) \frac{\partial x(p,w)}{\partial p} + \left[p^* F_1, \frac{\partial L(p,w)}{\partial w} \right.$$

$$+ p^* \left(F_2 - \gamma F_1 + \eta F_3 \frac{1+r}{n+x/\bar{x}} \right)$$

$$\frac{\partial x(p,w)}{\partial w} \Bigg] \frac{dw}{dp} \qquad (12)$$

Thus, the effect of p on Y^* can be decomposed into three effects: (a) an increase in p causes greater use of farm labor, i.e., a rise in L which, in turn, increases agricultural output; (b) a higher p also leads to an expansion in cultivated areas, which will affect agricultural production negatively if an environmental distortion exists (i.e., if the term in parentheses is negative); (c) the rise in p also induces higher wages which, in turn, affect both the level of agricultural employment and cultivated land. The first right-hand term in Equation (12) corresponds to effect (a), the second one to effect, (b) and the third one to effect (c).

Expressing Equation (12) in percentage or logarithmic form yields

$$\frac{d\ln Y^*}{d\ln p} = \left\{ s_L \frac{\partial \ln L}{\partial \ln p} + \left(s_x - s_c + \frac{x}{\bar{x}} \frac{1+r}{r+x/\bar{x}} \right. \right.$$

$$s_\theta \frac{d\ln\theta}{d\ln x} \Bigg) \frac{\partial \ln x}{\partial \ln p} + \left[s_L \frac{\partial \ln L}{\partial \ln w} \right.$$

$$+ \left(s_x - s_c + \frac{x}{\bar{x}} \frac{1+r}{r+x/\bar{x}} s_\theta \frac{\partial \ln\theta}{\partial \ln x} \right)$$

$$\frac{\partial \ln x}{\partial \ln w} \Bigg] \frac{d\ln w}{d\ln p} \Bigg\} \frac{Y_A^*}{Y^*} \qquad (13)$$

where $s_L \equiv \dfrac{F_1 L}{F} = \dfrac{\partial \ln F}{\partial \ln L}, s_x = \dfrac{\partial \ln F}{\partial \ln x}$, $s_\theta \equiv \dfrac{\partial \ln F}{\partial \ln\theta}$, and $Y_A^* = p^* F(\cdot)$ is agricultural output valued at world prices. From the micro analysis of the previous section, we obtain estimates for s_L, s_x, s_θ, $\dfrac{\partial \ln\theta}{\partial \ln x}$, $\dfrac{\partial \ln x}{\partial \ln p}$, $\dfrac{\partial \ln x}{\partial \ln w}$. Also the effects of p and w on employment are implicit in the production function. The effect of agricultural output prices on the wage rate w, however, has to be obtained by solving the general equilibrium model. Logarithmically differentiating Equation (10) we obtain

$$\frac{d\ln w}{d\ln p} = \frac{\partial \ln L(p,w)/\partial \ln p}{\beta - \partial \ln L/\partial \ln w} \qquad (14)$$

where $\beta \equiv \dfrac{\bar{L}-L}{L}$ is the ratio of urban labor force relative to rural employment. The effect of p on w is positive, given that L is increasing in p and decreasing in w. Note, however, that this effect is always less than one.

Thus, the microestimates of the previous

section, Equation (14), and information on the share of agricultural income in national income evaluated at world prices (Y_A^*/Y^*), are all the information needed to evaluate the effect of decreasing agricultural taxation on national income. Similarly, one can obtain an expression to evaluate the general equilibrium effect of raising agricultural prices on the environmental resource. From Equation (1'), it is clear that $\theta = \theta[x(p,w), \bar{x}]$. Thus, logarithmic differentiation of θ with respect to the price of the agricultural goods yields

$$
\frac{d\ln\theta}{d\ln p} = \frac{d\ln\theta}{d\ln x}\left[\frac{\partial\ln x(p,w)}{\partial\ln p}\right.
$$
$$
\left. +\frac{\partial\ln x(p,w)}{\partial\ln w}\frac{d\ln w}{d\ln p}\right] \quad (15)
$$

where $\dfrac{d\ln\theta}{d\ln x}$ is defined in Equation (4). The first term in square brackets corresponds to the partial equilibrium effect, while the second reflects the indirect wage effect. Given that $\dfrac{d\ln\theta}{d\ln x}<0$, we have that the direct effect is always negative (note that $\dfrac{\partial\ln x(p,w)}{\partial\ln p}>0$), while the indirect wage effect is positive, given that $\dfrac{\partial\ln x}{\partial\ln w}<0$ and $\dfrac{d\ln w}{d\ln p}>0$. Since $\dfrac{d\ln w}{d\ln p}<1$, however, the direct negative effect must dominate the indirect effect. Thus, Equations (12), (14), and (15) provide the basis for the evaluation of the effects of reducing taxation to agriculture on national income, agricultural wages and the environmental resource stock.

Note that, since in the context of a Harris-Todaro model, the agricultural sector does not directly compete with the urban sector, there is no real reduction in output in urban activities. Indeed, the expansion of agricultural employment is entirely attained by reducing the level of unemployment or underemployment in the urban centers. Thus, what reducing agricultural taxation does is to induce a better utilization of the pool of labor in the economy and, at the same time, a more intensive utilization of land. The tradeoff, however, is that it also causes a reduction in the environmental resource, which was already at levels below the social optimum. Which one of the two forces dominate is an empirical matter depending on the actual values of the various parameters that conform Equations (12), (14), and (15).

Trade liberalization via reduced protection to urban activities

Decreasing trade protection to urban activities implies a reduction in tariffs t, or equivalently, a reduction in q for a given level of q^*. Logarithmic differentiation of Y^* as defined by Equation (7) with respect to q (keeping q^* constant) yields

$$
\frac{d\ln Y*}{d\ln q} = \frac{Y_A^*}{Y^*}\left\{s_L\frac{\partial\ln L}{\partial\ln w}\frac{d\ln w}{d\ln q} + \left(s_x - s_\cdot\right.\right.
$$
$$
\left.\frac{(1+r)x/\bar{x}}{r+x/\bar{x}}s_\theta\right)\frac{d\ln\theta}{d\ln x}\right)\frac{\partial\ln x}{\partial\ln w}
$$
$$
\left.\frac{d\ln w}{d\ln q} + \frac{L_N}{L}\epsilon\frac{(1-\tau)}{1+t}\frac{\partial\ln L_N}{\partial\ln q}\right\} \quad (16)
$$

where $\epsilon \equiv \dfrac{\bar{L}-L}{L_N+L_g}$ is the inverse rate of urban employment. We note that in deriving Equation (16), we have used Equations (8(i)), (9), and (10). Combining these three equations, we get $G_1(\cdot)=\epsilon\dfrac{1-\tau}{1+t}F_1(\cdot)$. Note also that we have normalized the world prices to one, i.e., $p^+ = q^* = 1$, which implies no loss of generality, given that these prices are exogenous (in fact, we can always pick the units of measurement of the agricultural and nonagricultural goods so that each unit is worth US$1.00).

The effect of changes in the protection level of the nonagricultural goods can be decomposed into three effects: (a) an increase in q will reduce employment in agriculture because of its wage effect thus negatively affecting agricultural production and national income (first right-hand term in Equation (16)); (b) the increase in agricultural wages induced by increasing q also leads to a fall in cultivated land which, given an environmental distortion, will have a positive effect on agricultural output and national income (second right-hand term in Equation (16)); and (c) the increase in q causes an expansion in employment in the protected sector (third right-hand term in Equation (16)). This effect is also positive to the extent that it decreases unemployment. However, its magnitude will crucially depend on the degree of relative protection of the nonagricultural sector $\left(\dfrac{1-\tau}{1+t} \right)$.

The larger is the tariff protection level t and the agricultural tax τ, the smaller will be effect (c) in this paragraph. Indeed, this reflects a tradeoff between decreasing unemployment, which is positive for national income and for increasing employment and output in the protected sector, which is detrimental for national income.

In order to evaluate Equation (16) we need to determine the effect of changes in the price of the nonagricultural goods on the agricultural wage rate, $\dfrac{d\ln w}{d\ln q}$. From Equation (10) we get that

$$\frac{d\ln w}{d\ln q} = \frac{\partial \ln L_N / \partial \ln q}{\beta - \partial \ln L / \partial \ln w} \qquad (17)$$

Of course, if labor in the urban sector is a normal input $(\partial n L_N / lnq > 0)$ we have that Equation (17) is necessarily positive.

Finally, the effect of q on the environmental stock comes entirely through its effect on cultivated land:

$$\frac{d\ln \theta}{d\ln q} = \frac{d\ln \theta}{d\ln x} \left[\frac{\partial \ln x(p,w)}{\partial \ln w} \frac{\partial \ln w}{\partial \ln q} \right] \qquad (18)$$

An increase in q will induce higher agricultural wages which, in turn, reduce cultivated land and thus generate a positive effect on the level of the environmental resource. Thus, Equations (16) through (18) allow us to evaluate the effect of import liberalization (i.e., of reducing q) on national income, agricultural wages, and the environmental resource, given information on the relevant parameters and elasticities.

Wage and public employment policies

A decrease in government intervention in urban wage settlements (i.e., more lax regulations on wage indexation, reducing public wages, discarding minimum wages) can be represented by a reduction in $\bar{w}$. A change in $\bar{w}$ on Y^* can be analyzed directly from Equation (7) by differentiation:
where S_{LN} is the share of labor costs in the private urban sector. An increase in $\bar{w}$ will

$$\frac{d\ln Y^*}{d\ln \bar{w}} = \left\{ s_L \left(\frac{\partial \ln L(p,w)}{\partial \ln w} \frac{d\ln w}{d\ln \bar{w}} \right) \right.$$

$$+ \left(s_x - s_c + \frac{(1+r)x/\bar{x}}{r + x/\bar{x}} s_\theta \frac{d\ln \theta}{d\ln x} \right)$$

$$\left. \frac{\partial \ln x(p,w)}{\partial \ln w} \frac{d\ln w}{d\ln \bar{w}} \right\} Y_A^* / Y^*$$

$$+ s_{LN} \frac{\partial \ln L_N}{\partial \ln \bar{w}} Y_N^* / Y^* \qquad (19)$$

change w (not necessarily in the same direction, as we shall see) which, in turn, will affect agricultural employment (first right-hand side term in Equation (19)) and land cultivated (second right-hand side term in Equation (19)). Also, the higher $\bar{w}$ reduces employment in the private urban sector, which is detrimental for national income (third right-hand term in Equation (19)).

The effect of the regulated urban wage on the agricultural wage can be derived directly from Equation (10):

$$\frac{d\ln w}{d\ln \bar{w}} = \frac{\bar{w}L_N}{wL} \frac{1 + \partial \ln_N / \partial \ln \bar{w}}{\beta - \partial \ln L / \partial \ln w} \qquad (20)$$

Clearly the sign of Equation (20) will be determined by the elasticity of labor demand in the urban sector. If demand for labor in the nonagricultural private activity is inelastic (i.e., $\partial \ln_N / \partial \ln \bar{w}$ is less than unit elastic), the agricultural wage will increase; but, if it is elastic, it would cause a fall in the agricultural wage. The intuition behind this is clear: An increase in $\bar{w}$ reduces employment in the urban sector which, in turn, reduces the rate of urban employment rate, or equivalently, reduces the probability of finding employment in the urban sector. The lower probability of finding employment has a negative effect on rural wages because fewer farm workers would be willing to migrate. But the increase in $\bar{w}$ has the opposite effect. Which effect dominates depends on the extent by which the rate of urban employment falls. If the demand for labor in urban activities is more than unit elastic, the probability of finding an urban job will dominate and vice versa if the demand for labor is inelastic.

Similarly, the effect of $\bar{w}$ on the environmental resource can be represented through the effect on cultivated land:

$$\frac{d\ln \theta}{d\ln \bar{w}} = \frac{d\ln \theta}{d\ln x} \left[\frac{\partial \ln x(p,w)}{\partial \ln w} \frac{d\ln w}{d\ln \bar{w}} \right] \qquad (21)$$

Thus, if an increase in $\bar{w}$ increases, the agricultural wage land cultivated will decline, and the environmental resource will improve. In general, however, the effect of regulated urban wages on the rural environmental stock would be ambiguous.

The implications of changes in public sector employment can be analyzed in a simi-

lar way. Actually, the effect of L_g on agriculture takes place entirely via the level of the rural wage:

$$\frac{d\ln Y^*}{d\ln L_g} = \left\{ s_L \left(\frac{\partial \ln L(p,w)}{\partial \ln w} \frac{d\ln w}{d\ln L_g} \right) \right.$$

$$+ \left(s_x - s_c + \frac{(1+r)x/\bar{x}}{r + x/\bar{x}} s_\theta \frac{d\ln \theta}{d\ln x} \right)$$

$$\left. \frac{\partial \ln x(p, w)}{\partial \ln w} \frac{d\ln w}{d\ln L_g} \right\} \frac{Y_A^*}{Y^*}$$

$$+ \alpha L_g / Y^* \qquad (22)$$

A change in L_g does not have any direct effect on the urban sector to the extent that there is urban unemployment. It does affect the agricultural wage, however, by changing the rate of urban employment. The effect of this on agriculture is captured by the first and second right-hand term in Equation (22). The third right-hand term reflects the fact that workers in the public sector are productive (possibly with a very low productivity), which has an effect on national income. Thus, in the context of a fixed urban wage, the tradeoffs of a government employment policy occurs between the public sector and the agricultural sector rather than the urban activities.

From Equation (10) it can be shown that the effect of L_g on rural wages is

$$\frac{d\ln w}{d\ln L_g} = \frac{\bar{w}L_g}{wL} \frac{1}{\beta - \dfrac{\partial \ln L}{\partial \ln w}} \qquad (23)$$

which is positive, as could be expected. Finally, the effect of L_g on the environmental factor is

$$\frac{d\ln \theta}{d\ln L_g} = \frac{d\ln \theta}{d\ln x} \left(\frac{\partial \ln x(p,w)}{\partial \ln w} \frac{d\ln w}{d\ln L_g} \right) \qquad (24)$$

The sign of Equation (24) is necessarily positive given that the agricultural wage rate increases. Thus, public sector employment expansion is beneficial for the rural environment if urban wages are fixed.

Environmental distortions in a tight and competitive labor market

The definition of the national income Y^* (Equation (7)) and the profit maximizing conditions Equation (8) remain unchanged, while the profit maximizing condition Equation (9) for the urban sector changes in a trivial manner,

$$(1 + t) q^* G_1(\cdot) = w \qquad (9')$$

where the only change (with respect to Equation (9')) has been to use w instead of $\bar{w}$. Now wages faced by both sectors are equalized.

Since competitive labor markets imply full employment, Equation (10) is now replaced by the labor market clearing condition:

$$\bar{L} = L_g + L_N((1 + t) q^*, w)$$

$$+ L((1 - \tau) p^*, w) \qquad (10')$$

Differentiating Equation (7) using Equations (8), (9'), and (10'), we can now obtain expressions for the effect of changes in agricultural taxes on national income:

$$\frac{d \ln Y^*}{d \ln p} = \frac{Y_A^*}{Y^*} \Bigg\{ \frac{t + \tau}{(1 - \tau)(1 + t)} s_L$$

$$\left(\frac{\partial \ln L(p, w)}{\partial \ln p} + \frac{\partial \ln L(p, w)}{\partial \ln w} \right.$$

$$\left. \frac{d \ln w}{d \ln p} \right) + \left(s_x - s_c + \frac{(1 + r) x / \bar{x}}{r + x / \bar{x}} \right.$$

$$s_\theta \left. \frac{d \ln \theta}{d \ln x} \right) \left(\frac{\partial \ln x(p, w)}{\partial \ln p} \right.$$

$$\left. + \frac{\partial \ln x(p, w)}{\partial \ln w} \frac{d \ln w}{d \ln p} \right) \Bigg\} \qquad (25)$$

It can be shown that since wages are flexible, the Lerner's symmetry condition applies. This implies that the effect of q on national income

is identical, but of opposite sign to the effect of p, i.e., $d \ln Y^* / d \ln q = - d \ln Y^* / d \ln p$. Now there are only two distortions, namely, the trade distortion associated with the tariffs and export tax and the environmental distortion. Thus, the effect of changing p or q can also be decomposed into two effects: (a) The changes in p or q induce a reallocation of labor between the two sectors (first right-hand side terms in Equation (25)). This change causes income to increase when p is raised because the agricultural sector is initially discriminated against due to both the agricultural tax and the tariff protection to the nonagricultural sector (that is, agricultural production is below the socially optimal level and the nonagricultural sector is producing above such level). When q increases, the effect is unambiguously negative. (b) The environmental effect is captured by the second right-hand side in Equation (25). This effect is due to the fact that changes in p or q affect the level of cultivated area.

To be able to evaluate Equation (25), we need to provide an expression for the wage effects. From the labor market clearing condition it follows that

$$\frac{d \ln w}{d \ln p} = - \frac{\partial \ln L(p, w) / \partial \ln p}{\left(\dfrac{L_N}{L} \right) \dfrac{\partial \ln L_N}{\partial \ln w} + \dfrac{\partial \ln L(p, w)}{\partial \ln w}} \qquad (26)(i)$$

$$\frac{d \ln w}{d \ln q} = - \frac{\partial \ln L_N(q, w) / \partial \ln q}{\dfrac{L_N}{L} \dfrac{\partial \ln L_N(q, w)}{\partial \ln w} + \dfrac{\partial \ln L(p, w)}{\partial \ln w}}$$

$$(26)(ii)$$

Under the assumption that labor is a normal input in both the rural and urban sectors we have that both an increase in p and q induce higher wages.

The effects of government employment policies can be analyzed in a similar way, by differentiating Equation (7):

$$\frac{d\ln Y^*}{d\ln L_g} = \frac{Y_A^*}{Y^*} \left\{ \frac{t+\tau}{(1-\tau)(1+t)} \, s_L \, \frac{\partial \ln L(p,w)}{\partial \ln w} \right. \tag{27}$$

$$\frac{d\ln w}{d\ln L_g} + \left(s_x - s_c + \frac{(1+r)x/\bar{x}}{r+x/\bar{x}} \right.$$

$$\left. s_\theta \, \frac{d\ln\theta}{d\ln x} \right) \frac{\partial \ln x(p,w)}{\partial \ln w} \, \frac{d\ln w}{d\ln L_g} \right\}$$

$$+ \frac{\alpha L_g}{Y^*} - \frac{Y_N^*}{Y^*} s_{LN}$$

The increase in government employment induces higher wages which, in turn, cause a fall in employment in both the urban private sector and the agricultural sector. At the same time, the increased wage rate leads to a reduc-tion of cultivated area which has a positive rural environmental effect. Also, government services increase. Given that the marginal contribution of public employment to national income is possible very low, the net effect of increasing L_g is likely to be negative.

Also from Equation (10′), it is clear that

$$\frac{d\ln w}{d\ln L_g} = -\frac{1}{\left(\frac{L_N}{L_g}\right)\frac{\partial \ln L_N}{\partial \ln w} + \left(\frac{L}{L_g}\right)\frac{\partial \ln L}{\partial \ln w}} \tag{28}$$

which is positive given that demand for labor in both sectors is downward sloping. Finally, the effect of L_g on the environmental resource is identical to the Harris-Todaro case, except that now we use Equation (28) instead of Equation (23) to evaluate $d\ln w/d\ln L_g$.

Bibliography

African Development Bank (ADB), Economic Commission for Africa (ECA), and Organization of African Unity (OAU). 1984. "The African Food Crisis and the Role of African Development Bank in Tackling the Problem." A paper presented jointly by the staff of the ADB, ECA, and OAU to the Symposium on the future of ADB and the Food Crisis of Africa. Tunis, Tunisia, May.

Allen, J. 1985. "Wood Energy and Preservation of Woodlands in Semi- and Developing Countries: The Case of Dodoma Region, Tanzania." *Journal of Development Economics* 19:59–84.

Dasgupta, P., and K.-G. Mäler. 1990. "The Environment and Emerging Developing Issues." World Bank Annual Conference on Development, Washington, D.C.

Deacon, R. 1992. "Controlling Tropical Deforestation: An Analysis of Alternative Policies." Working Paper No. 1029. Country Economic Department, World Bank, Washington, D.C.

Feder, G., T. Onchan, Y. Chalamwong, and C. Hongladarom. 1988. *Land Policies and Farm Productivity in Thailand.* World Bank, Johns Hopkins University Press, Baltimore, Md.

Food and Agriculture Organization (FAO). 1986. "Natural Resources and Human Environment for Food and Agriculture in Africa." Environment and Energy Paper No. 6. Rome.

Glantz, M. 1977. *Desertification: Environmental Degradation in and around Arid Lands.* Boulder, Colo.: Westview Press.

Larson, B., and D. Bromley. 1990. "Property Rights, Externalities, and Resource Degradation." *Journal of Development Economics* 33:235–62.

López, R. 1993. "Resource Degradation, Community Controls and Agricultural Productivity in Tropical Areas." University of Maryland, College Park, unpublished.

López, R., and M. Niklitschek. 1991. "Dual Economic Growth in Poor Tropical Areas." *Journal of Development Economics* 36:189–211.

Perrings, C. 1989. "An Optimal Path to Extinction? Poverty and Resource Degradation in the Open Agrarian Economy." *Journal of Development Economics* 30:1–24.

Riveros, Luis A. 1992. "Labor Costs and Manufactured Exports in Developing Countries: An Econometric Analysis." *World Development (U.K.)* 20:991–1008.

Sinn, H. 1988. "The Sahel Problem." *KIKLOS*, May, 41.

Todaro, M. 1989. *Economic Development in the Third World*, 4th edition. New York: Longman.

World Bank. 1993. "Ghana Living Standards Survey (GLSS), 1987-88 and 1988-89: Basic Information." World Bank, Poverty and Human Resources Division, Washington, D.C.

3

Economic Policies
for Sustainable Resource Use in Morocco

Ian Goldin and David Roland-Host

WATER IS A DISTINCTIVE RESOURCE because it constitutes a direct input to almost every economic activity, drawing a continuous thread from ordinary use in agriculture, through manufacturing, and into the myriad of service sectors. Despite a long economic history, water allocation stands out as one of the most significant cases of market failure in both developing and developed economies. The institutional arrangements that have governed water allocation, from prehistory to the present day, have fostered serious resource misallocation, technological choice that is neither statically nor dynamically efficient, and an array of negative economic and environmental externalities that propagate through downstream linkages to the rest of the economy.

This chapter is based on a paper presented in a conference on Sustainable Economic Development: Domestic and International Policy, convened by the Centre for Economic Policy Research and the Organisation for Economic Co-operation and Development (OECD) Development Center, May 24–25, 1993, Paris.

Historically, the relative abundance and regenerative nature of water resources have fostered inefficient water use.[1] In modern times, the clear delineation of regional boundaries limiting migration, population growth, and rising living standards have combined to intensify water use in agriculture and elsewhere, and the sustainable practices for utilizing this essential resource are receiving greater scrutiny. It is only a matter of time until the reforms in water allocation, already initiated in a number of countries, are more widely applied. The essential issue is how to devise reforms that have the efficiency and incentive properties to be economically and politically sustainable. To answer this question, which is a pressing concern for many developing countries, we consider the case of Morocco. Our choice of Morocco has been facilitated by the fact that it possesses relatively sophisticated data resources and shares many common characteristics with water-scarce economies. We thus anticipate results from this case to have wider applicability.

In this chapter, we draw on Morocco to illustrate the linkages between trade and macroeconomic policies and sustainable resource use.[2] To this end, we evaluate the current state of water distribution in Morocco, distinguishing between relatively arid and moist farming regions and between rural and urban households. The available evidence suggests that the existing allocation system fosters suboptimal and unsustainable patterns of water use and that inefficiencies arising from inappropriate pricing at the micro level have been compounded by distortions in relative prices resulting from macroeconomic and trade policies. Our analysis supports the conclusion that increased marketability of water can realize substantial static and dynamic efficiency gains in agriculture, including greater conservation. The development of an appropriate incentive framework, which includes the implementation of water tariffs that more closely approach marginal costs, is expected to contribute to demand management and conservation in irrigation where subsidies are greatest. The adjustment of relative prices in favor of sustainable resource use will be greatly facilitated by trade reforms. These currently provide protection to agriculture; in the absence of trade reform, higher water charges would be passed through to output paces, seriously limiting efficiency gains.

In order to focus discussion of the general economic principles of sustainable resource use, we have developed a computable general equilibrium (CGE) model of Morocco. This captures sufficient detail in agriculture to evaluate alternative water allocation schemes. The model provides a convenient vehicle for identifying the components of domestic economic adjustment in response to various resource management policies, and allows us to assess the implications for Morocco's trade position. Conversely, the CGE model is also used to evaluate the implications of alternative trade policies for agriculture in general and water use in particular. Our results indicate that the static benefits of more efficient water allocation would be considerably magnified if the country pursued more outward-oriented trade practices.

The next section presents an overview of Moroccan water use and policy. The section, *Methodological Issues*, contains a general conceptual discussion of efficient and sustainable water allocation. The section, *The Moroccan CGE Model*, presents the Moroccan CGE model and the data that were used to calibrate it. This is followed in the section, *Simulation Results*, with a series of simulation results evaluating the efficacy and interrelationships between water policies and trade policies. The last section is devoted to concluding remarks.

---

[1] Relative abundance is of course a de facto result of human settlement where traditional farming practices were sustainable.

[2] The analysis of Morocco presented in this chapter is illustrative and preliminary and is an initial stage of a major research project which includes construction and estimation of a detailed database on the country's economy and water use.

Practical Issues
in Moroccan Water Allocation

Owing to a limited resource base and recurrent droughts, water is a scarce commodity in many parts of Morocco. The main sources of fresh water are found in the mountains, at considerable distances from urban and irrigated areas. This geographic situation necessitates storage dams and long transmission facilities, with high average cost and marginal cost rising steeply as increasingly sparse water resources are developed. The country's population is growing at more than 2.6 percent annually and is expected to exceed 43 million by the year 2020. Rapid increases in water demand by agriculture, industry, and urban households are anticipated by the government. Urban migration and rising incomes are expected to lead to a 4.2 percent annual growth in urban household demand, and rapid economic growth is predicated on an anticipated 5 percent annual increase in industrial demand. Meanwhile, the National Irrigation Program aims to extend the area under irrigation by 30 percent in the next decade. Irrigation currently accounts for 92 percent of the demand for water, urban households 5 percent, and industry only 3 percent.

The availability of adequate water resources is a prerequisite for meeting the country's economic targets. Water resources are already becoming scarce in certain areas, and initial projections for the year 2020, based on expected economic growth, current relative prices, and related water demand, clearly point to the emergence of an economywide water deficit. While the water balance today is largely positive in most of the north (Loukkos, Mediterranean, Sebou, and Oum Er R'bia basins), it is generally negative in the south (Souss, Zia, Rheris, and Guir basins). Although there is currently an annual overall water surplus of 1.1 billion cubic meters (amounting to some 15 percent of all renewable water resources), the anticipated annual growth in demand of 4 percent is expected to lead to overall water shortages in the medium term. In addition, serious water management problems are already evident in some parts of the country. These include a severe deterioration in water quality, depletion of nonrenewable groundwater resources, the increasing exploitation costs for marginal water sources, and the failure of the existing system to supply more than 10 percent of the rural population with potable water. Despite the fact that nearly all urban dwellers have safe water supplies, half the country's population is rural. Thus, over 45 percent of the population lack secure water supplies.

By the year 2020, assuming current trends continue, water will still be in surplus in the Loukkos, Sebou, and Mediterranean basins in the north, but all other river basins will have negative balances. Moreover, without significant water demand management, the overall water balance will become negative (in excess of 200 million cubic meters annually before 2020), which means that even nationwide water transfers (assuming they are economically feasible) could not meet regional water deficits. The case for timely and judicious government intervention is therefore compelling. On the demand side, this might include policies to promote conservation and improved demand management in irrigation and among urban and industrial consumers. On the supply side, greater attention needs to be paid to water quality and development of additional water resources. The latter possibilities include improved secondary water capture, treatment, and recycling, decentralization of brackish and sea water, and sustainable groundwater mining.

Appropriate pricing and incentive policies are the keys to resolving Morocco's water dilemma. A continuation of current practices implies not only growing distortions in the allocation of an increasingly scarce resource, but also an increasingly unsustainable fiscal burden. Public investments in the water sector already account for more than 25 percent of the government's investment budget and, by

2020, are expected to account for up to 60 percent, reflecting the escalating costs associated with interbasin transfers and exploitation of marginal resources.[3] Meanwhile, recurrent costs are mounting with the aging of the existing water supply, irrigation, and sanitation systems. Irrigation water charges currently cover less than 10 percent of the long-run marginal cost of delivering water to agriculture, while urban water tariffs contribute less than half the cost of urban and industrial supplies.[4]

Subsidies have had a particularly distortionary effect in the agricultural sector. Low water charges (coupled with low effective collection rates on these charges) have artificially promoted production of water-intensive crops. Sugar cane (which uses approximately 10,000 cubic meters per hectare) and lucerne (15,000 cubic meters per hectare) have particularly low value added per unit of water use. The existing incentive framework does not encourage production of crops with high returns on water use. These include wheat (4,000 cubic meters per hectare) and vegetables (3–4,000 cubic meters per hectare).[5]

The consequences of higher water charges on patterns of production and the rural-urban terms of trade are examined in this chapter. Our primary focus is on the general equilibrium effects of water policy on relative prices and resource allocation between agricultural and nonagricultural activities. In Morocco, these sectoral effects will be intertwined with those of macroeconomic adjustment policies that are being pursued concurrently. In particular, water prices are expected to be increased at a time when output prices and other input prices are being affected by macroeconomic reforms and trade liberalization. This calls for the analysis of water pricing issues in a framework which simultaneously includes possible changes in output and other relative prices.

Significant structural reform is currently under way in Morocco. This is expected to lead to the gradual reduction in import protection, which currently maintains the prices of sugar, cereals, oilseeds, meat, and dairy products well above their opportunity cost on world markets. Gradual and broad-based agricultural trade reform is envisaged in the context of structural adjustment agreements with the World Bank. These reforms would be accelerated following a General Agreement on Tariffs and Trade (GATT) agreement. The simultaneous introduction of trade and water pricing reforms would imply increased input prices and a decline in output prices. The impact on the highly subsidized sugar cane, cereals, cotton, and oilseeds subsectors could be particularly serious as factor price increases are passed through to agricultural commodities. The government budget is affected negligibly. Thus, the static effects of the policy appear to be detrimental, but a silver lining appears in the results for water use as the economy moves decisively toward greater sustainability. In the rural sectors, water use falls by about one third, and even urban water use is also driven down slightly by declining aggregate demand. Trade liberalization has more salutary effects on the static efficiency of resource use.

Methodological Issues

In this section, we discuss the Moroccan water distribution question from three perspectives.[6] The first of these concerns static efficiency of water allocation in Moroccan

---

[3] Authors' estimates based on current trends.

[4] Authors' estimates based on average current water charges.

[5] These estimates of water use are derived from field estimates in Morocco. They are simply indicative averages. In practice, water use varies from area to area and intensity of production, and inter alia, depends on the rainfall, soils, and time of planting.

[6] As was emphasized in the previous section, trade reform also plays an important role in our empirical policy analysis. The theory and methodology on this topic are well known, however, and we omit reviewing them in this section.

agriculture. We argue that a publicly managed system of water distribution, if it is coupled with economic incentives, could significantly improve the efficiency of water use in the country, increasing real output and incomes in the process. Second, we discuss how reforming agricultural water distribution can improve the intertemporal efficiency or sustainability of water use and expand the growth prospects for Moroccan agriculture. Third and finally, we discuss the important issue of how to allocate the country's water resources between rural and urban areas. Guaranteeing equitable quantities and qualities of water for household and economic use in both parts of the country will inevitably determine the political sustainability of Moroccan water policy.

Static efficiency

Historical water rights conventions represent one of the most serious market failures in traditional agriculture. As Easter (1986) and others have observed, the water rights mechanism results in a queuing allocation, where those with the original endowment use the resource at zero marginal cost and pass the remainder on to successive rights holders at zero marginal revenue. The absence of a market for water thus removes any incentive for conservation or transfer activity which might increase overall output and income. It is now widely acknowledged that some kind of institutional intervention, between the two extremes of public appropriation with uniform redistribution and completely privatized water sales, can provide the missing incentives to use water more efficiently.

Consider a simple case with two agricultural producers, identical except for their water endowments, calling one arid (A) and the other moist (M). Under the traditional scheme, M uses free water until its marginal product equals zero, while A is constrained by insufficient water. Since A's marginal product for water is inevitably higher than that of M, any reallocation of water between the two would raise national agricultural output. All

arguments for improving static efficiency rest on this basic productivity disparity; what remains is the incentive properties of different allocation schemes.

Assume for convenience only that water can be transferred without conveyance losses or quality degradation. If water is simply appropriated and redistributed, M and A are still unlikely to use the resource efficiently even though aggregate output rises. If, on the other hand, water were bought from M and sold to A, any price would begin to exert rational efficiency considerations on their production decisions. Water now has a real opportunity cost for M, who might change the mix of other inputs or even invest to innovate and reduce water use with minimal effects on marketable output. By the same token, a price for water would also allow A to expand factor use in the appropriate mix to most profitably use the newly available water.

Clearly, water reallocation can increase output, and market pricing of water can improve efficiency. What then is the role of the public sector, apart perhaps from providing education and initial financing. The failure of water markets is not simply due to ignorance, but results from significant problems of enforcement. Any distribution scheme of reasonable scope will cover many private holdings and perhaps even regional or national jurisdictions. It is quite difficult to guarantee the integrity of transfer agreements over such distances and with so many intervening third parties. Thus, the public sector must assume a lasting supervisory role to make such an allocation scheme work. As we shall see below, public oversight may also be necessary to correct for other externalities arising in water use and allocation.

Dynamic efficiency

Water is a renewable resource, but its recurrent supply is relatively constant over the long term. Once the recurrent supply is fully utilized, the only potential for growth in the economy will come from innovations which reduce the water intensity of agricultural production. To avoid a period of stagnation and forced adjustment, Morocco could begin now to foster the innovations that will reduce the intensity of its water use and raise its growth potential.

The literature on economic growth is replete with examples of how the correction of market failures can guide resource allocation and use to more sustainable paths. Dasgupta and Heal (1979) and, more recently, Grossman and Helpman (1991), are two prominent examples of approaches that seek to elucidate sufficient conditions for improving dynamic efficiency. Both emphasize the importance of market incentives to invest and innovate as a means of raising the sustainable trajectories of output and real income growth. It is clear, for example, that the reforms proposed above to improve static efficiency of water allocation would also improve dynamic efficiency by promoting both conservation and shifts to other inputs, including new technologies. Bringing water "into the market" will also facilitate intertemporal appraisal of its asset value and contribute to dynamic efficiency.

Rural-urban water allocation

The growth of urban areas has occasioned water reallocation since well before Roman times. In the last century, however, the problems of urban water insufficiency have intensified as these areas have rapidly grown in size and density and become focal points for industrial activity. In terms of public health and economic modernization, assuring adequate quantity and quality in water supplies is one of the most serious challenges facing some developing countries.[7]

In Morocco, the challenge of balancing water use between urban and rural constituencies is complicated by the rapid growth of agriculture.[8] Agriculture has been the major consumer under the traditional rights system and the current administered system of water distribution at controlled prices. On the other hand, agricultural water use diminishes not only the quantity, but the quality of water available for other uses. Water use in farming occasions a number of negative externalities, including loading of water with high mineral concentrations, fertilizers and their organic derivatives, and pesticide residues. These potential shortcomings must be weighed against the economic benefits of increased farm output and exports.

From the perspective of the urban sector, water is already an economic commodity, although its price rarely measures its production or opportunity cost with any meaningful degree of precision. Urban households in developing countries also have incomplete information about water quality, and intervention is usually necessary to protect the public interest. These considerations argue for a carefully designed and comprehensive approach to national water policy, one which relies on a balance between regional interests, as well as between market forces and regulatory responsibility.

The Moroccan CGE Model

The conceptual approach of the previous section was intended to clarify some basic issues. In this section, we provide a tool for policy analysis in the form of an empirical model of the Moroccan economy. As an example of its use, we report some simulation results in the section, *Simulation Results*, which evaluate the kind of water reforms discussed above.

Our Moroccan model is typical of most individual country models in the CGE litera-

---

[7]Ninety percent of all fatal childhood diseases in Africa are waterborne.

[8]Half the country's population lives in rural areas and these are generally the poorest segment of the population. Agriculture constitutes 15 percent of gross domestic product (GDP), 40 percent of employment, and 30 percent of export earnings.

ture. It simulates price-directed resource allocation in commodity and factor markets, with endogenous determination of domestic consumption and production decisions. We assume that Morocco is a small importer and exporter relative to the rest of the world, and thus world prices are taken as exogenous to the model. In a given sector, demand for domestic goods and imported substitutes is characterized by a standard constant elasticity of substitution (CES) specification of product differentiation. Likewise, domestic producers supply output to constant elasticity of transformation (CET) differentiated domestic and export markets.

The formal structural equations of the Moroccan CGE model are presented in Annex 3-A. They are typical of one-country models of this type, except for the treatment of regional and sectoral factor allocation.[9] The agriculture sector is decomposed into two (generic) regions, and Irrigated, according to method of water use. Each agricultural subsector chooses its factor mix and output level individually, subject to endogenous domestic prices for output, intermediate inputs, labor, and property. Property or capital is assumed to be immobile within and between agricultural sectors and mobile between other sectors. This leads to imperfect factor price equalization across sectors, but we assume that land is essentially dedicated to agricultural activities, and that its irrigation status remains constant over the time horizon of the simulations. Firms are assumed to be perfectly competitive, with average cost pricing under constant returns to scale.

Water is a factor of production in this model, and its use is determined by neoclassically derived factor demand criteria. We assume that water is costless in Rainfed agriculture (see the social accounting matrix in Annex 3-B). Water transfer between Rainfed and Irrigated agriculture, as well as between rural and urban areas, is assumed for our simulations to be effected at prices fixed by the government, and that water redistribution is costless. To model market-directed water transfer between agricultural activities and also between rural and urban activities, a two-stage transformation frontier might be specified between Rainfed and Irrigated and between rural and urban, respectively. The nonmarket allocation mechanism used here most closely resembles current Moroccan policy, however, so we focus on this in the simulations below.[10]

Like the social accounting matrix (SAM) to which it is calibrated, the CGE model distinguishes three types of final demand: household, investment, and government demand. In all the simulations reported below, we assume that the latter two are held constant in terms of the numeraire. We report a variety of aggregate and household-specific results to give an indication about how real output, resource use, and general purchasing power are affected by the policies considered.

Both increased water prices and reduced tariffs have direct fiscal implications, of course. In the case of water, we specify that the net change in water revenue is redistributed to households in proportion to their incomes. Otherwise, we have chosen to hold the numeraire levels of government consumption constant to minimize distortions in final demand. This leaves the government financing gap endogenous, and we assume this would be reconciled with nondistortionary taxes or transfers.

The model is calibrated to a 1985 social accounting matrix for Morocco, and herein lie two of its distinguishing features. First, the Moroccan SAM distinguishes between urban and rural income groups. This is essential to

---

[9]See, e.g., de Melo and Tarr (1992) for a more detailed exposition on models of this type.

[10]The results of most of our simulations entail water savings (less transfer) and increased water revenue vis-à-vis the status quo. This mitigates the severity of the water mobility assumption and means the fiscal implications of the policies examined are generally positive.

evaluate the issue of social efficiency in water distribution. Second, the SAM details value added for three factors of production, labor, capital, and water. This decomposition of factors is particularly important to the modeling of agricultural sectors. The original SAM detailed twenty agricultural sectors, but for the present simulations, we have chosen a three-sector aggregation to facilitate more intensive discussion of the general policy issues. The three-sector SAM is presented in Annex 3-B.

To completely calibrate the model, the above data on observed economic activity must be combined with estimates of structural parameters. These include elasticities of demand (Equation 3.5 in Annex 3-A), factor substitution (Equation 3.7), and transformation between domestic and export markets (Equation 3.9). Table 3-1 details the values used in the all the simulations reported in the next section. Even in an aggregate model such as this one, results are sensitive to these parameters, and we report on this in Annex 3-B.

Simulation Results

In this section, we report on the results of a few policy simulation experiments with the Moroccan CGE model. These experiments are intended to illustrate simulation methodology in the context of two important general economic issues currently facing the country, trade orientation and sustainability of water resources. In particular, we conducted three experiments to evaluate generic policies of trade liberalization and water price reform. We find that the results of each policy are interesting in their own right, but that when they are implemented in concert, the economy reaps the benefits of each policy without the serious negative side effects of either.

Table 3-2 presents the aggregate results of the three experiments. In Experiment 1, prices for rural irrigation water, which cover 92 percent of the country's marketed water use, are doubled from 8 to 16 percent of their urban counterpart. Experiment 2 is a trade policy simulation, entailing a complete re-

moval of nominal Moroccan tariffs, which in 1985 *averaged* 21 percent across the economy and 32 percent in agriculture. The third and final experiment combines the water price and liberalization policies of the first two simulations.

The aggregate results indicate that, other things being equal, reforming water prices in the agriculture sectors will have a contradictory effect on the economy. This is to be expected, since the price increase is basically taking the form of a distortionary tax against a leading sector of the economy. Incomes and real consumption of both rural and urban households decline slightly, and real consumption falls somewhat more as increased factor prices are passed through to agricultural commodities. The government budget is affected negligibly. Thus, the static effects of the policy appear to be detrimental, but a silver lining appears in the results for water use as the economy moves decisively toward greater sustainability. In the rural sectors, water use falls by about one third and even urban water use is also driven down slightly by declining aggregate demand.

Trade liberalization has more salutary effects on the static efficiency of production and real incomes. Economywide real GDP rises only slightly since the main factors, labor and capital, are fixed in total supply. Despite this, household incomes and real consumption post significant gains substantial import barriers are reduced, domestic purchasing power rises, exports become more competitive, and resources are allocated more efficiently across the economy. While this typical neoclassical result supports greater initiative for Moroccan trade reform, two drawbacks are readily apparent. First, the government has foregone an important sources of revenue by eliminating tariffs, and a gap of about 35 percent emerges in the public budget. Second, the expansionary influence of liberalization has increased domestic water use substantially. Thus, the economy is on a more growth-oriented, but less sustainable, trajectory.

The last experiment combines the first two, and it is apparent that combining trade and water reform would confer substantial advantages on the economy, both in the medium and long term. The expansionary effects of trade liberalization are largely retained, but reforming water prices still induces substantial reductions in agricultural (and economywide) water use. Although this conservation is partly offset by expanding demand in urban sectors, the net result for the economy is less water consumption. Thus, the higher growth path under the combined policy is more sustainable than was the status quo. The government budget still declines appreciably with tariff revenues, but this might be offset by alternative, nondistortionary source of revenue.

More detailed results for sectoral adjustments in the three reform experiments are given in Table 3-3. Note first that agriculture in general and irrigated agriculture in particular suffer output declines in the two water price increase experiments. In Experiment 1, agriculture obviously suffers from factor taxation, but in Experiment 3, the expansionary effects of trade reform fail to offset this because agriculture is the most protected of the three sectors. Irrigated agriculture, where the water price increase is directly incident, contains both the most protected (e.g., sugar) and most export-oriented crops (e.g., tree crops), and in this case, the export expansion offsets most of the combined contractionary effects of tariff removal and higher water taxes.[11] Irrigated farming is induced to cut water use almost 50 percent in the first experiment, and more than one third in the combined trade and water reform experiment. In the case of Experiment 2, the benefits of export expansion outweigh the costs of increase import competition, and irrigated agriculture expands slightly when water prices are

constant. Rainfed agriculture manages to attract labor and expand production in both water price experiments, but loses a little ground in the balance between expanding exports and increased import penetration in the trade reform only experiment.

The other two sectors behave in predictable ways. Increased water prices and reduced real incomes reduce demand for Manufactures. Since Manufactures are more intensive in agricultural intermediates and therefore experience more water price transmission, both their domestic and external demand are reduced. Services thus become relatively more competitive, but the effect is barely significant. When Morocco eliminates tariffs in Experiment 2, the more tradeable sectors expand output, the less so (Services) contracts in the presence of economywide constraints on labor and capital. In the combined experiment, the results of larger magnitude in the individual experiments prevail. In other words, Agriculture and Services contract for the different reasons, and Manufacturing expands. Indeed, the results of the two policies for nonagricultural sectors are almost additive.

Conclusions

Like many other developing countries, Morocco faces serious water resource constraints. The continuation of current water use practices into the next century threatens to sharply attenuate the development process. A more sustainable approach to development therefore requires that appropriate mechanism for water production and allocation be introduced. In this chapter, we evaluate direct and indirect economic policies to influence water use patterns, including changes in water: pricing and trade reform. Our results indicate that there is considerable scope of substitution between water and other factors of production and that economic incentives to promote this can move Moroccan resource use decisively toward a more sustainable path of economic development.

---

[11] It would be desirable to disaggregate this and other sectors to trace the more detailed effects of these policies. This is the subject of work in progress, which includes the estimation of a 125-sector SAM for the country.

To assess the country's water use policy in an economywide setting, we chose a CGE model. The modeling methodology is still under development, and the data we have been able to assemble thus far are highly aggregated and preliminary; our results should be interpreted accordingly. Despite this, the conclusions that emerge from the general equilibrium analysis are robust to reasonable parameter variations. Most importantly, it is apparent that increases in water paces, particularly in agriculture, can realize substantial resource savings.

The general equilibrium results suggest that agricultural water use, which constitutes 92 percent of Morocco's total use, could be reduced by more than a third if rural water prices were doubled (even though in this case they would still only reach about 16 percent of urban water prices). Taken in isolation, such a policy would secure a more sustainable basis for future income growth, but would reduce medium term real rural incomes and Moroccan GDP. If water price reform were undertaken in concert with more comprehensive Moroccan trade reform, the medium-term effects on incomes would be more than offset, with rural, urban, and aggregate real income rising substantially while still achieving substantial water savings. Thus, the combined policies move the economy onto a path that is at once more prosperous and sustainable.

While more precise quantitative estimates await refinement of the model and more intensive data gathering, our preliminary results demonstrate that a combination of economywide and sectoral policies are necessary to secure a sustainable basis for the country's future. Our results indicate that piecemeal approaches are unlikely to achieve the combined objectives of static efficiency and dynamic sustainability. The potential efficiency gains and resource savings from integrated, economywide policy reform are substantial and, despite the short-term adjustments they might occasion, they can increase medium-term real incomes and facilitate sustainably high real growth in the future.

Table 3-1: Estimates of Structural Parameters

	Agriculture	Manufactures	Services
CES demand elasticity	0.9	1.4	1.4
CET supply elasticity	1.4	1.4	1.4
CES factor elasticity	0.6	0.9	1.1

Table 3-2: Aggregate Simulation Results (percentage changes from base)

	Experiment 1	Experiment 2	Experiment 3
Real GDP	-.65	.79	.11
Rural			
Income	-.92	8.69	8.48
Real consumption	-1.21	8.97	8.23
Urban			
Income	-.92	8.58	7.77
Consumption	-1.02		7.07
Government balance*	-.59		
Water use			
Rural	-34.28	1.64	-34.48
Urban	-1.23	9.20	8.02
TOTAL	-28.66		-4.12

* Change in the government budget balance as a percentage of the overall budget.

Table 3-3: Sectoral Simulation Results (percentage changes)

Experiment 1	Output	Exports	Labor	Capital	Water	Imports
Agriculture						
Rainfed	23.84	17.36	28.23			
Irrigated	-25.40	-29.30	-22.76		-49.33	
TOTAL	-3.24	-8.30	.19	.27	-34.28	1.75
Manufactures	-.59	-.63	-.60	-.47	-1.46	-.55
Services	.01	.64	00	.16	-1.05	-.67
Experiment 2						
Agriculture						
Rainfed	-.18	12.66	-.78			
Irrigated	.34	13.24	-.77		3.65	
TOTAL	.10	13.19	-.78		1.64	17.46
Manufactures	4.01	23.25	4.18	2.96	11.23	9.32
Services	-1.05	11.27	-.95	-2.38	7.30	-12.96
Experiment 3						
Agriculture						
Rainfed	1.03	7.22	4.57			
Irrigated	-7.36	-1.69	-4.82		-34.75	
TOTAL	-3.58	-.79	-.60		-15.64	18.71
Manufactures	3.54	22.76	3.65	2.65	9.80	8.73
Services	-1.03	12.16	-.97	-2.13	6.26	-13.70

Annex 3-A: Model Equations

Formal Structure of the Morocco Model

Domestic demand

$$Q_i^C = LES(PQ_i, Y_h) = \gamma_i + \frac{\eta_i}{PQ_i}(Y - \sum_{j=1}^{n} PQ_j \gamma_j) \qquad 3.1$$

$$Q_i^G = s_i^G \overline{Q}^G \qquad 3.2$$

$$Q_i^I = s_i^I \overline{Q}^I \qquad 3.3$$

$$Q_i^V = \sum_{j=1}^{n} a_{ij} X_j \qquad 3.4$$

Demand Allocation Between Domestic and Imported Goods

$$Q_i = CES(D_i, M_i, \overline{\lambda}_i), \quad Q_i = Q_i^C + Q_i^V, \qquad 3.5$$

$$\frac{M_i}{D_i} = \left[\left(\frac{\alpha_i}{(1-\alpha_i)} \right) \left(\frac{PQ_i}{PM_i} \right) \right]^{\lambda_i} \qquad 3.6$$

Production Technology and Factor Demands

$$X_{ik} = CES(L_{ik}, K_{ik}, W_{ik}, \overline{\rho}_{ik}) \qquad 3.7$$

$$F_{ik} = \left(\frac{X_{ik}}{AX_{ik}} \right)^{(1-\rho_{ik})} \left[\beta_{Fik} \frac{TC_{ik}}{W_{Fik}} \right]^{\rho_{ik}}, \quad F=L, K, W \qquad 3.8$$

Supply Allocation by Destination of Commodities and Services

$$X_{ik} = CET(S_{ik}, E_{ik}, \tau_{ik}) \qquad\qquad 3.9$$

$$\frac{E_{ik}}{S_{ik}} = \left[\left(\frac{\delta_{ik}}{(1-\delta_{ik})} \right) \left(\frac{PS_{ik}}{PE_{ik}} \right) \right]^{-\tau_k} \qquad\qquad 3.10$$

Composite Domestic Prices

$$PQ_i Q_i = PD_i D_i + PM_i M_i \qquad\qquad 3.11$$

$$PS_i S_i = \sum_k PS_{ik} S_{ik} \qquad\qquad 3.12$$

Foreign Prices

$$PM_i = (1 + t_{Mi}) PWM_i R \qquad\qquad 3.13$$

$$PE_i^k = (1 + t_{Ei}^k) PWE_i R \qquad\qquad 3.14$$

Domestic Market Equilibrium

$$S_{ik} = D_{ik} \qquad\qquad 3.15$$

$$PS_{ik} = PD_i \qquad\qquad 3.16$$

$$\sum_{i=1}^{n} \sum_{k} F_i^{\,k} = \bar{F}_s, \quad F=L, K \tag{3.17}$$

$$\bar{w}_w = w_w \tag{3.18}$$

$$K_i^{\,k} = \bar{K}_i^{\,k}, \quad i=Agriculture \tag{3.19}$$

Cost

$$TC_{ik} = a_{ik}^{-1} X_{ik} \left[\sum_{F=L,K,W} b_{Fik}^{\,p_{ik}} w_{Fik}^{\,1-p_{ik}} \right]^{\frac{1}{1-p_{ik}}} + \sum_{j=1}^{n} a_{ij} PQ_j X_{ik} \tag{3.20}$$

$$w_{Fik} = w_F \bar{w}_{Fik} \quad, \quad i \neq Agriculture, \quad F \neq W \tag{3.21}$$

Pricing

$$PX_{ik} = AC_{ik} \tag{3.22}$$

Private and Public Income

$$Y_h = \sum_{i=1}^{n} \sum_{F=L,K,W} \theta_{hiF} \sum_{k} w_{Fik} F_{ik} + R\bar{r}_h + Y_G - \bar{Q}_G \tag{3.23}$$

$$Y_G = \sum_{i=1}^{n} \sum_{k} t_{ik} PX_{ik} X_{ik} + R\sum_{i=1}^{n} \left[t_{Mi} PWM_i M_i - \sum_{k} t_{Eik} PWE_i E_{ik} \right] + \sum_{i=1}^{n} \theta_{gIW} \sum_{k} w_{Wik} W_{ik} \tag{3.24}$$

Balance of Payments

$$\sum_{i=1}^{n}\left[\sum_{k} PWE_i E_{ik} - PWM_i M_i\right] = \bar{B}$$

3.25

Numéraire

$$\frac{\sum_{i=1}^{n} PD_i D_i}{\sum_{i=1}^{n} \bar{PD}_i \bar{D}_i} = 1$$

3.26

Variable and Parameter Definitions

AC_{ik}	Average cost of firm type k in sector i
B	Net foreign savings
D_i	Total domestic demand for output in sector i
E_i	Total exports in sector i
E_{ik}	Exports of firm type k in sector i
F_i	Total demand for factor F in sector i
F_{ik}	Factor F demand by firm type k in sector i
FC_{ik}	Fixed cost of firm type k in sector i
F_S	Economywide factor F supply
M_i	Total imports in sector i
N_{ik}	Number of firms of type k in sector i
P_{Di}	Domestic demand price for output in sector i
P_{Ei}	Export demand price for output in sector i
P_{Eik}	Export demand price for output of firm type k in sector i
P_{Mi}	Import price in sector i
P_{Qi}	Composite demand price in sector i
P_{Si}	Domestic supply price in sector i
P_{Sik}	Domestic supply price for firm type k in sector i
PW_{Eik}	World export demand price for output of firm type k in sector i
P_{Xi}	Ouput price in sector i
P_{Xik}	Output price of firm type k in sector i
PW_{Mi}	World import supply price in sector i
Q_{iC}	Composite (domestic and imported) domestic demand for output of sector i

Q_i	Composite consumption demand for output of sector i
Q^I	Aggregate real investment demand
Q^G	Aggregate real government demand
Q_i^V	Composite intermediate demand for ouput of sector i
R	Exchange rate
r_h	Remittance income accruing to household h
S_i	Total domestic supply in sector i
S_{ik}	Domestic supply of firm type k in sector i
t_{Eik}	Export subsidy rate for output of firm type k in sector i
t_{Mi}	Tariff rate in imports in sector i
TC_{ik}	Total cost of firm type k in sector i
t_{ik}	Sectoral producer or indirect tax rates
VC_{ik}	Variable cost per unit output
w_F	Economywide average price of factor F
w_{Fik}	Price of factor F paid by firm type k in sector i
W_{ik}	Water demand by firm type k in sector i
x_i	Total ouput in sector i
x_{ik}	Output of firm type k in sector i
x_i	Output of sector i
Y	Aggregate domestic income
Y_G	Government income
Y_h	Household income

Parameters

μ_i	CES elasticity of substitution between product varieties in sector i
δ_{ik}	Base share of exports in value of output of firm type k in sector i
ρik	Factor substitution elasticity of firm type k in sector i
θ_{giW}	Share of water revenue going to government
θ_{hiF}	Share of factor F income from sector i going to household h
α_i	Base share of imports in domestic demand for sector i
λ_i	CES elasticity of substitution between imports and domestic goods
η_i	Marginal budget share for consumption of good i
γ_i	Subsistence consumption of good i
τ_{ik}	CET elasticity of transformation between domestic and export markets
β_{Fik}	Factor F share in value-added of firm type k in sector i
AD_i	Calibrated intercept parameter for demand

a_{ij}	Intermediate demand share for good i by sector j
AX_{ik}	Calibrated intercept parameter for production

Subscripts

i	Sectors of production—Agriculture, Manufactures, Services
k	Subsectors, in the case of Agriculture only, where the two subsectors are Rainfed and Irrigated
F	Factors of production—Labor, Property, and Water
h	Households—Rural and Urban

Note: Variables are denoted by English letters, and structural parameters by Greek letters. An overstrike denotes a base value in the case of a variable and an exogenously specified value in the case of a parameter. More than one pricing rule is specified above, although they are mutually exclusive in the simulations.

Annex 3-B: Social Accounting Matrix (SAM) for Morocco, 1985

Social Accounting Matrix for Morocco, 1985 (millions of current DH)

	AgRain-Fed 1	AgIrrig 2	Manufact 3	Services 4	Labor 5	Capital 6	Water 7	Tariff 8	ExpTax 9	IndTax 10	HHRural 11	Hurban 12	Govt 13	CapAcct 14	Row 15	Total
1. AgRainFed	199	244	2829	15	0	0	0	0	0	0	3062	4277	0	1430	134	12190
2. AgIrrig	348	298	3458	18	0	0	0	0	0	0	3062	5227	0	1748	613	14771
3. Manufact	1318	1611	47376	22625	0	0	0	0	0	0	11074	23273	0	13273	12186	132737
4. Services	525	642	9516	11542	0	0	0	0	0	0	7591	24851	16399	23500	3785	98352
5. Labor	1555	1901	11219	43258	0	0	0	0	0	0	0	0	0	0	0	57933
6. Capital	5125	6264	11599	14437	0	0	0	0	0	0	0	0	0	0	0	37425
7. Water	590	722	1497	1863	0	0	0	0	0	0	0	0	0	0	0	4672
8. Tariff	598	731	7719	0	0	0	0	0	0	0	0	0	0	0	0	9047
9. ExpTax	9	10	314	0	0	0	0	0	0	0	0	0	0	0	0	333
10. IndTax	55	68	2683	463	0	0	0	0	0	0	0	0	0	0	0	3269
11. HHRural	0	0	0	0	7782	12832	0	0	0	0	0	0	306	0	8589	29509
12. HHUrban	0	0	0	0	50151	24583	0	0	0	0	0	0	436	0	1200	76379
13. Govt.	0	0	0	0	0	0	4672	9047	333	3269	583	6420	31	806	663	25823
14. CapAcct.	0	0	0	0	0	0	0	0	0	0	4137	12331	3020	0	21269	40757
15. ROW	1867	2281	34527	4131	0	0	0	0	0	0	0	0	5631	0	0	48437
TOTAL	12190	14771	132737	98352	57933	37425	4672	9047	333	3269	29510	76379	25823	40757	48437	

Annex 3-C: Results of Sensitivity Analysis

Because the Morocco model is calibrated to an equilibrium SAM dataset, most of its information requirements are met from direct observation of the economy under study. Although this small model is rather parsimonious, a number of its structural parameters must still be specified with indirect information, using econometric estimates from other sources and judgment about values which might reasonably be expected to apply. Of particular interest in the present simulations is the elasticity of substitution between productive factors in the agricultural sectors. This CES parameter (ρ in Equation 3.7 above) is a key determinant of the adjustment in irrigated water use resulting from a price increase. Table 3C-1 summarizes the results of nine simulations we conducted to assess the CGE model's sensitivity to this parameter. We replicated each of the policy scenarios reported in section five (experiments 1–3) with three alternative values to bracket the experiment outcomes. Substitution elasticities in agriculture are generally conceded to be rather low, and we chose a central case of .6 as a reference.[12]

Note that, with only two exceptions in thirty-six, the results are qualitatively consistent, and the exceptions are within a reasonable neighborhood of zero in any case. As one would expect, the magnitudes of the results are monotone in the elasticity, indicating that greater flexibility in factor substitution yields more dramatic adjustment. Despite this, the essential endogenous variables summarized here vary much less than the elasticity parameter. From these comparisons we infer that our general conclusions about the three policies are robust. In particular, the efficacy of combined trade and water reforms, in terms of water conservation and real income growth, is consistently supported.

Another way to appraise the sensitivity of the model is to experiment with a wider range of exogenous shocks. Table 3C-2 reports the results of a variety of alternative water price increases, including increases of 1.5, 2, and 4 times current rates for irrigated agriculture. The last case corresponds roughly to an equalization of rural and urban water prices. There are six replications, three each for experiments 1 and 3, experiment 2 being omitted since it entails only tariff reductions. The qualitative results are fully consistent within and across experiments, and their magnitudes vary in the expected direction and by about the same relative magnitude of the shock. From this we infer that water price reforms of any reasonable degree would yield significant conservation, and that a concerted effort to reform water policy and trade would achieve agricultural water saving with increased rural income.

---

[12]Recall that, in light of capital immobility in agriculture, this elasticity is actually restricted to substitution between labor and water.

Table 3C–1: Results for Varying Factor Substitution Elasticity

| | Experiment 1 | | | Experiment 2 | | | Experiment 3 | | |
| | *Low* | *Central* | *High* | *Low* | *Central* | *High* | *Low* | *Central* | *High* |
	.3	*.6*	*1.2*	*.3*	*.6*	*1.2*	*.3*	*.6*	*1.2*
All agricultural output	-2	-4	-5	.1	.1	.3	-2	-4	-5
Irrigated ag output	-5	-8	-12	-.1	.3	.8	-5	-7	-11
Irrigated ag water use	-22	-37	-58	2	4	8	-20	-35	-55
Rural income	-.1	-.1	.3	9	9	9	8	9	9

Table 3C–2: Results for Varying Water Prices

| | Experiment 1 | | | Experiment 3 | | |
| | *Low* | *Central* | *High* | *Low* | *Central* | *High* |
	1.5x	*-2x*	*4x*	*1.5x*	*2x*	*4x*
All agricultural output	-2	-4	-8	-2	-4	-8
Irrigated ag output	-4	-8	-17	-4	-7	-17
Irrigated ag water use	-24	-37	-67	-21	-35	-60
Rural income	0	0	0	8	7	6

Bibliography

Arrow, K. J., and R. C. Lind. 1970. "Uncertainty and the Economic Evaluation of Public Investment Decisions." *American Economic Review* 60:364–78.

Boggess, W., R. Lacewell, and D. Zilbeiman. 1993. "Economics of Water Use in Agriculture." In M. Osborne (ed.), *Agricultural and Environmental Resource Economics*. Clarendon, U.K.: Oxford University Press.

Burness, H., and J. Quirk. 1979. "Appropriative Water Rights and Efficient Allocation of Resources." *American Economic Review* 69:25–37.

Caswell, M., E. Lichtenberg, and D. Zilberman. 1990. "The Effects of Pricing Policies on Water Conservation and Drainage." *American Journal of Agricultural Economics* 72:883–90.

Chakravorty, U., and J. Roumasset. 1991. "Efficient Spatial Allocation of Irrigation Water." *American Journal of Agricultural Economics* 73:165–73.

Clarke, C. W. 1976. *Mathematical Bioeconomics: The Optimal Management of Renewable Resources*. New York: John Wiley and Sons.

Dasgupta, P., and G. H. Heal. 1979. *Economic Theory and Exhaustible Resources*. Cambridge, U.K.: Cambridge University Press.

de Melo, J., and D. Tarr. 1992. *A General Equilibrium Analysis of U.S. Foreign Trade Policy*. Cambridge, Mass.: MIT Press.

Dinar, A., and D. Zilberman. 1991. *Economics of Management of Water and Drainage in Agriculture*. Norwell, Mass.: Kluwer Academic Publishers.

Easter, K. W. 1986. *Irrigation, Investment, Technology, and Management Strategies for Development*. Boulder, Colo.: Westview Press.

Fisher, A. C. 1981. *Resource and Environmental Economics*. Cambridge, U.K.: Cambridge University Press.

Gibbon, Diana. 1987. *The Economic Value of Water*. Washington, D.C.: Resources for the Future.

Grossman, G. M., and E. Helpman. 1991. *Innovation and Growth in the Global Economy*. Cambridge, Mass.: MIT Press.

Hotelling, H. 1931. "Economics of Exhaustible Resources." *Journal of Political Economy* 39:137–75.

Nobe, K. C., and P. K. Sampath. 1986. *Irrigation Management in Developing Countries: Current Issues and Approaches*. Boulder, Colo.: Westview Press.

OECD. 1989. *Water Resource Management: Integrated Policies*. Paris: OECD.

Parlin, B., and M. Lusk. 1991. *Farmer Participation and Industrial Organization*. Boulder, Colo.: Westview Press.

Pearce, D. W., and R. K. Turner. 1990. *Economics of Natural Resources and the Environment*. Baltimore, Md.: Johns Hopkins University Press.

Postel, Sandra. 1992. *Last Oasis: Facing Water Scarcity*. New York: Norton.

Reigner, Marc. 1990. *Overtapped Oasis: Reform or Revolution for Western Water*. Washington, D.C.: Island.

Reinert, K-A., and D. W. Roland-Host. 1991. "Structural Parameter Estimates for Trade Policy Modeling." Discussion Paper, U.S. International Trade Commission, Washington, D.C.

Tuluy, H., and B. L. Salinger. 1989. "Trade, Exchange Rate Policy, and Agricultural Pricing Policies in Morocco." Comparative Studies in the Political Economy of Agricultural Pricing Policy, World Bank, Washington, D.C.

World Bank. 1989. "World Bank Experience with Irrigation Development," Volume III: Morocco, Report 7876. World Bank, Washington, D.C.

4

Poverty, Migration, and Deforestation in the Philippines

Wilfrido Cruz, Herminia Francisco, and Gregory Amacher

IT IS NOT AN ACCIDENT that assessments of problems of environmental degradation invariably bring up concerns about poverty. In many instances, the worst effects of environmental pollution or natural resource degradation are borne by the poor. In both urban and rural areas and in various occupations, they are the ones who can least afford to protect themselves from environmental degradation. The poor spend long hours in polluted factories; they are exposed to agricultural chemicals; and services that are taken for granted by those who are better off, such as clean water and waste disposal, are normally unavailable in slums and rural areas (World Bank 1992; WCED 1987).

The authors are grateful to Ma. Concepción J. Cruz, Jeremy Warford, Gershon Feder, Stein Hansen, William Hyde, Imelda Zosa-Feranil, and Shreekant Gupta for their comments and suggestions. Murty Kamilbady provided valuable research assistance in implementing the migration model. The authors are, of course, solely responsible for the views in this chapter.

Poverty also often turns out to be an underlying reason for households or communities to degrade resources. For example, short decisionmaking time horizons, associated with poverty, prevent many farmers from investing in soil conservation techniques that may be necessary for sustainable agriculture but whose payoffs are not immediate (Mink 1993).

While the links between poverty and environment are many, this chapter has the limited scope of focusing solely on one particular component of the poverty problem: _the large number of rural poor_. It also focuses attention on a particular aspect of environmental degradation: _the conversion of forest land to unsustainable agriculture_. Both these issues constitute pressing problems for developing countries. In the rural areas of many countries of the developing world, too many people depend on too few resources for their livelihood, resulting in persistent rural poverty and creating pressures to exploit even fragile resources, such as forest lands.

The goal of this study is to examine the role of poverty and population pressure in deforestation through the conversion of forest lands to agriculture. A second, related objective is to determine the potential for combining poverty alleviation reforms with environmental goals in the area of forest land management. To accomplish this, the study builds on previous work on estimating the extent and causes of increasing population pressure on Philippine uplands (M. C. Cruz, Zosa-Feranil, and Goce 1988). An empirical migration model is then constructed, based on the most recent Philippine census, to focus explicitly on the role played by economic, environmental, and demographic factors in motivating migration from lowland communities to forest lands. The limitations of this modeling exercise must be noted. The lack of economic and demographic data that differentiate between lowland and forest sites was a formidable obstacle, and a major investment in time was necessary to generate new information for this study. Even with this information it was necessary to substantially simplify the application of the migration model; future work is clearly required in this area. In this context, the policy implications identified in the last section should be viewed as a limited, though important step to improve current understanding of poverty, migration, and deforestation interactions.

Deforestation, Upland Population Growth, and the Role of Policy Failures

In this section, we describe the deforestation trend in the Philippines, focusing on land use changes. We then argue that, together with commercial logging, the growth of upland population has been a key part of the process of deforestation since increasing conversion of land to agriculture has effectively prevented forest renewal. Finally, we discuss the range of sectoral and macroeconomic policies (or policy failures) that have contributed to the incentives motivating this pattern of migration from lowlands to forest lands. Because these disincentives to environmentally sound behavior arise not from externalities but from misguided policies, their effect has been referred to as "policy failures" (Pearce and Warford 1993).[1]

Deforestation

Recent assessments have documented the rapid decline of forest resources in the Philippines, the growth of forest land communities, and the expansion of cultivated areas in marginal areas. Between 1970 and 1985, the Bureau of Forest Development (1985) reported a deforestation rate of 85,000 hectares a year. A higher estimate of 95,000 hectares per year in the same period was cited in FAO

---

[1]In contrast to the term "market failure," which applies to the environmental disincentives arising from externalities.

(1983). More recently, the Philippines Natural Resource Accounting Project (1992) in the Philippines has estimated an average reduction in forest cover of 210,000 hectares per year for 1970–89. This process of deforestation and the subsequent conversion of forest land into nonsustainable agriculture are perhaps the most costly forms of resource degradation in the Philippines.

Actual forest cover declined from more than 34 percent to about 24 percent during the last two decades. Table 4-1 provides the current land use in the Philippines, based on the estimates made by the Swedish Space Corporation. By 1988 the forest cover had declined to only 24 percent with areas devoted for extensive and intensive cultivation comprising 72 percent of land cover. The areas under extensive cultivation are made up of plantation areas and grasslands, which are usually deforested lands and are degraded by slash-and-burn farming.

Upland population and conversion of forest land to agriculture

Soils and the natural resources directly associated with land use can be generally classified as *land* resources. This incorporates various characteristics, such as fertility, topography, and vegetative cover that result in substantial land quality and productivity distinctions. In most countries, the lands suitable for intensive agriculture are generally the lowlands. (Two notable exceptions are the hill regions of Nepal before the eradication of malaria in the Terai and the Altiplano of Bolivia.)

In the Philippines, the term *lowlands* generally corresponds to land officially classified as "alienable and disposable"—that is, suitable for privatization. The technical criterion used for alienable and disposable lands is whether their slope is less than 18 percent. Lands with 18 percent or greater slopes are deemed inappropriate for agriculture and are kept in the public domain. They are referred to as *uplands* or *forest lands* (whether or not they are actu-

ally forested). With this classification, about 14.1 million hectares, or close to half of the land area of the whole country, are forest lands and under the jurisdiction of one government department. Private users are formally excluded from these resources or allowed access only as concessionaires, under government jurisdiction. The pattern of timber felling and the permanent conversion of forest lands to agriculture is directly affected by this resource management approach. This approach makes the assumption that centralized regulation of such vast areas is feasible. However, the incentives governing the behavior of forest users undermine this management approach.

Both the commercial loggers and the farmers who have settled illegally on forest land contribute to the deforestation process. With respect to the logger's structure of incentives, low timber cutting charges make him undervalue the true worth of the forest as a renewable resource. He therefore worries only about maximizing the returns to his investment from harvesting the resource. This perspective leads him to harvest more than if he were made to appreciate the much greater value of the forest. The latter would be possible only if both the market and environmental value of the trees were charged to him and if a long enough planning horizon is provided so that he may appreciate the long-term returns to forest management. As it is, the private logger harvests considerably more trees and at an age earlier than would be appropriate from a social decisionmaking perspective.

From the perspective of upland farmers, the continuing conversion of public lands to agriculture is an inevitable result of the lack of alternative livelihoods in lowland agriculture and in industry. Although crops can be grown in marginal or even in forest lands, doing so generates substantial environmental externalities. For example, soil erosion can damage irrigation and power facilities downstream in the "lowlands," reduce water quality, and aggravate seasonal flooding. Erosion also reduces soil productivity in the uplands. In this case, agriculture is not sustainable or can be maintained only with increased inputs of capital and labor.

The decisionmaking perspective of the upland farmer explains this propensity for degradation. For him, the absence of secure claims to his upland plot creates a decisionmaking perspective where the long-term worth of the land is disregarded in favor of harvesting or growing as much as may be possible in the short term. The primary economic constraint that he perceives is the amount of labor that his household can generate to exploit the land. At the same time, the upland farmer is not concerned with the downstream externalities generated by his activities. The results are on-site land resource degradation and off-site damages through soil erosion.

There have been attempts to distinguish between deforestation from commercial logging and from encroachment, and to identify the "primary" source of deforestation (e.g., Kummer 1990). This distinction, however, is not very fruitful for resource management concerns. Deforestation is often associated with both commercial logging and encroachment of migrants into the uplands. These two are interrelated in the sense that commercial logging by building roads and reducing forest clearing costs often paves the way for migrants who engage in shifting cultivation. Since logging by itself will not necessarily lead to a permanent change in land use, it is the growth of forest land population that is the effective cause of land conversion.

The difficulty, of course, is in estimating the population in forest lands. Both because of the geographic extent of the problem as well as its lack of official recognition until recently, there is no direct source of information on migration to forest lands. We therefore use the methodology developed by M. C. Cruz, Zosa-Feranil, and Goce (1988) to modify census categories of residence according to environmental maps. Conventional census

information is classified according to administrative jurisdictions (with municipalities as the basic unit for data processing) and not according to environmental boundaries. To make such information relevant for environmental assessment, it is necessary to reclassify administrative categories into environmental ones. Cruz et al. (1988) have used the official classification system for "forest land" (based primarily on slope) to devise a conservative method for identifying municipalities and the proportion of their population that inhabit forest lands. This system identifies 709 municipalities as forest land municipalities, representing 47 percent of all municipalities and more than half of the country's total land area of 30 million hectares.

Using this method and census data from various years, M. C. Cruz et al. (1992) have estimated the increasing number of people inhabiting forest lands from 1950 to 1990. (see Table 4-2). It was estimated that forest land population has been increasing and accounted for as much as 30 percent of total population in 1980 (M. C. Cruz, Zosa-Feranil, and Goce 1988). Together with population increase in forest lands, recent assessments of Philippine land use conclude that large areas previously forested have already been converted into farms. Extensive agriculture continues to expand in forest lands, resulting in soil erosion (World Bank 1989a). In the 1960s cultivated area in the uplands amounted to only 10 percent of lowland cropped area. By the 1980s it had increased to about 40 percent. This means that the growth of upland cultivated area had averaged 7 percent or more per year for the past three decades (W. Cruz and Repetto 1992) (see Figure 4-1).

What Motivates Increasing Upland Population?

Our analysis of the link between poverty and deforestation focuses on the role of upland migration. This extends work done in three important areas: (a) analyzing the systematic relationship among problems of population pressure, agricultural stagnation, and environmental degradation (what has been referred to as the population-agriculture-environment nexus); (b) the identification of migration to forest lands as a direct mechanism relating poverty in rural lowlands to the exploitation of marginal resources; and (c) the recognition of the contribution of macroeconomic policy distortions to the problem of persistent rural poverty and subsequently to upland migration and deforestation.

The population, poverty, and degradation nexus

Various studies have considered the systematic relationship between rapid population growth, rural poverty, and environmental degradation. Boserup (1965) identified the problem of population pressure leading to intensification of agriculture. Although she recognized the questionable impact of intensification on quality of life as more labor is utilized per unit of land, she did not explicitly address the environmental degradation associated with the decline of the fallow and the increased dependence on chemical inputs.

More recent concern with environmental aspect of increasing population pressure on limited agricultural resources has led to a broader appreciation of the nature and the extent of the problem. Cleaver and Schreiber (1991), assessing the conditions of agriculture in Sub-Saharan Africa, focused on what they called the "nexus" effect, linking land degradation with high population growth, limited agricultural lands, and the difficulty of adapting traditional techniques and institutions to rapidly changing conditions. Shifting cultivation and grazing activities, appropriate in low population density conditions, give way to more intensive land uses. Agricultural intensification, however, cannot keep pace with population pressure, and resources are subsequently overexploited and become unproductive. Low productivity leads to economic stagnation, and the resulting poverty delays the demographic transition, thus closing a cycle of poverty, population pressure, and environmental degradation.

The role of internal migration

While absolute increases in population have crucial long-run implications, the immediate problem of population pressure on degraded resources is directly related to the geographical distribution of population. Traditional assessment of migration has focused on the attraction of cities and patterns of rural to urban movements (Yap 1977; Williamson 1988). However, economic stagnation in industry and traditional agriculture has led growing numbers of households to migrate from traditional, lowland agriculture to marginal forest lands in search of alternative livelihoods. Thus, internal migration, from lowland to upland sites, has been the main mechanism linking conditions in lowland communities to the problem of rapid population growth in uplands (M. C. Cruz, Zosa-Feranil, and Goce 1988).

The role of macroeconomic and sectoral policies

The factors that lead to pervasive problems of rural poverty, as well the factors that encourage migrants to occupy (and overexploit) forest lands are all affected by economywide and sectoral policies. W. Cruz and Gibbs (1990) focus on tenurial insecurity regarding resources as a major source of inadequate investment. Poverty from lack of access to agricultural resources and unemployment lead landless rural households to exploit marginal, open access resources. In turn the lack of property rights leads to overexploitation, reduced incomes, and persistent poverty.

Beyond these sector-specific institutional factors is a more pervasive but less apparent set of misguided development policies (such as industrial protection and exchange rate overvaluation) that has led to economic stagnation in general and have penalized the agricultural sector in particular (Krueger,

Schiff, and Valdes 1991). Such policies create pervasive distortions that significantly contribute to economic stagnation and rural poverty. Thus, efforts to reduce deforestation pressures will require not only sector-specific policy changes, but also macroeconomic reforms (Hansen 1990, W. Cruz, and Repetto 1992). Indeed in a recent study on the Philippines and Costa Rica, it has been proposed that attempts to address the deforestation problem will entail a combination of demographic, economic, and resource management policies (M. C. Cruz et al. 1992).

The role of policy failures: postwar to early 1980s

This section describes how misguided policies—from the 1950s until reforms were implemented in the 1980s—have led to economic stagnation and pervasive poverty. Absolute poverty measures based on minimum food requirements or basic needs show that there has been some progress in alleviating poverty in the Philippines. In the early to mid-1970s, 50–60 percent of the population fell below the poverty threshold (World Bank 1985). By the early 1980s the percentage fell to about 40 percent. However, throughout the 1970s and 1980s, a greater proportion of rural households fell below the poverty threshold (World Bank 1988). Table 4-3 shows that poverty incidence, defined as the number of households falling below the income needed for basic consumption, is substantially larger in the rural sector.

The macroeconomic source of persistent poverty in the Philippines was the generally poor historical performance of the economy, from the postwar period until reforms were initiated in the mid-1980s. Gross national product (GNP) grew at respectable rates of close to 8 percent annually during the early 1950s, but growth in the 1960s and 1970s declined to less than 6 percent per year. There was some improvement in the 1970s, but this was undermined by the economic crisis that resulted in net economic decline in the first

half of the 1980s. In spite of efforts at economic reforms with the change in administration in 1986, economic recovery has been quite tentative, resulting in barely positive average growth rates for the 1980s. (Refer to Intal and Power 1991 for a detailed description of the main phases of economic policies.)

The policy regime also had important implications for unemployment. Capital-intensive industrialization was encouraged indirectly by the protection system and directly by the investment incentives program. During the 1970s, the system of tariffs made capital and intermediate input use relatively cheap. Similarly, Board of Investment subsidies encouraged the expansion of capital and energy-intensive industries, such as pulp and paper, petrochemicals, and steel and copper. While the trade and investment policies promoted capital-using activities, foreign exchange policy discouraged the development of labor-using export industries. The result was a long-term lagging capacity to generate employment. The expected process of industry siphoning off labor from the agricultural sector was arrested. The average annual growth of the labor force from 1970–88 was 3.6 percent, but total employment for the same period grew by only 3.3 percent (NEDA 1990).

Beyond the general effect of sluggish economic growth on poverty incidence and unemployment, some studies have analyzed the specific impacts of government policies on agriculture. These have proposed that the net effect of government policy in many poor countries has been to penalize agriculture in order to subsidize an inefficient industrial sector. Due to specific subsidies in agriculture, such as irrigation and credit support, it is often believed that policies of poor country governments generally favor agricultural activities and therefore incomes. However, Krueger, Schiff, and Valdes 1991 have demonstrated in a comparative study involving 18 developing countries that government policies, in fact, generally penalize agriculture, while protecting the industrial sector.

The studies showed that the direct incentive effect for the key agricultural exports of these 18 countries, measured as the proportional difference between a commodity's producer price and border price, was negative, averaging -8 percent during the last 25 years. On top of this incentive bias versus agriculture, the indirect effects of the overvaluation of the local currency and the impact of industrial protection on the price of agricultural relative to industrial goods was even greater, averaging -20 percent. Thus, macroeconomic policies that were designed to promote industrialization had the unanticipated effect of undermining agricultural incentives and therefore rural incomes.

This intercountry finding has been studied in the detail in the Philippines (David et al. 1986; Intal and Power 1991). Focusing on the four most important agricultural crops in the Philippines, Intal and Power found that the total nominal protection rates for these crops, from 1960–86, were mostly negative (refer to Table 4-4).

Migration from Lowlands to Forest Lands

This section builds on the discussion of historical patterns of increasing upland population and the role of macroeconomic and sectoral policies in motivating migration to forest lands. The role of economywide determinants is analyzed together with environmental and demographic factors in upland migration. This allows us to undertake an empirical assessment of the key variables affecting migration to forest lands, and to identify relevant areas for policy interventions.

Migration model

While there have been many propositions regarding the factors affecting population movements to forest areas, this represents only one of a small number of efforts to undertake a quantitative analysis, using actual migration data.[2] To analyze the mechanism linking economic conditions in lowland areas to the process of environmental degradation in forest lands, we focus on migration streams (M) from lowland origins (i) to forest land destinations (j).[3]

Migrants in lowland urban or rural areas face a large set of potential upland (forest land) destinations. To capture the decision-making process implicit in this process, we utilize an econometric procedure that accommodates the many choices facing the potential migrant: a multinomial discrete choice framework. In this approach, it is explicitly recognized that the individuals' decision to move involves a complex comparison of (known) utility the individuals receive at their origin, and the utility they expect to receive at potential destinations.

Since each individual can physically move to only one site at one time, the potential destinations form a discrete set of alternatives. Each migrant in the same location faces the same alternative set. The aggregation of similar choices made by individuals at an origin makes possible the application of the discrete choice framework to typical data sets, where migration streams (e.g., the number moving from one location to another location) rather than individual data are available.[4] Also, note that the model does not address the initial decision on whether or not to move. Incorporating this aspect would require much more data than are available. (Refer to Annex 4-A for the formal presentation of the migration model.)

In the Philippine upland migration case, the

---

[2]See also M. C. Cruz, Zosa-Feranil, and Goce 1988 and M. C. Cruz et al. 1992.

[3]Although the migration streams are derived from municipality-to-municipality data, they are aggregated into provincial streams for the purpose of this analysis.

[4]That is, the polychotomous choices faced by each individual are translated into similar "choices" for migration streams.

multinomial discrete choice model is essential for two reasons. First, there are over 70 provinces spread over a large geographic area. Each province provides a potential opportunity for upland exploitation by willing migrants in any other province. Second, forest lands vary widely in quality and suitability for agriculture across provinces, making the decision to move to a particular province dissimilar with the decision to move to any other province.[5]

Migration measures and determinants

Using the 1990 census, migration streams from lowland to forest lands, M_{ij}, were determined based on whether current (1990) residents in forest land municipalities had resided in lowland municipalities five years before (1985). The basic data source for the M_{ij}'s was a municipality-by-municipality migration matrix, obtained from the census office. The migration streams into the 709 forest land municipalities from lowland municipalities were aggregated into provincial lowland to forest land streams. This resulted in 77 destinations (the forest land municipalities grouped into the 77 provinces in the country) and 77 origins (lowland municipalities grouped similarly by province). The 77 X 77 matrix yielded 5,929 observations on M_{ij}'s. The frequency distribution of these streams is presented in Table 4-5. Note that most of these M_{ij}'s were either 0 or less than 500.

Determinants of upland migration

As indicated in the previous sections, migration to forest lands constitutes an important factor leading to deforestation. In this section, we describe the various factors affecting forest land migration. Within the forestry sector, conditions of access to forest resources

are the key factors that could affect migration into forest lands. These include timber concession rules and delineation of government forest reserves. In addition to forest sector factors, economic incentives and a rapidly growing population constitute external factors that contribute to pressures for migration into forest lands. The economic factors affecting migration include poverty, income and employment, and agricultural tenure conditions that influence economic security. Finally, demographic variables (e.g., population density and conditions of urbanization) also play important roles in the migration decision.

As was the case with upland migration stream, information on the determinants for the regression model is not readily available. One of the most difficult to obtain was information on income, which had to be differentiated between lowland and forest land areas in the regression model. The use of average household income in the origin and destination provinces (available from the Family Income and Expenditure Surveys) cannot be interpreted as indicative of the level of lowland and upland income. This is because average income measures in any given province include both the income of households in lowland and forest land municipalities (within the province).

The data used to construct the variables for lowland and forest land average household incomes were based on a national "benchmark" survey undertaken by the Institute of Agrarian Studies (IAST) of the University of the Philippines (IAST 1990a,b). This survey, involving 8,935 households was commissioned by the Department of Agrarian Reform and had a sampling frame that was explicitly designed to capture lowland versus upland socioeconomic differences. The villages (or *barangays*) in the study sample were grouped by ecological zones (lowland, forest land, and coastal). The major limitation of the survey was that not all provinces were included in the sample. Data for the other determinants in the model were taken both from published na-

---

[5]The use of a geographically broad data set also allows assessment of economy-wide policies and the role of the environment, unlike other recent studies that have focused on a small group of migrants, or on a specific urban area.

tional surveys and from records of government departments. Table 4-6 describes in detail the definition of the variables, their sources, and their hypothesized relationship to the migration streams, M_{ij}. (See Annex 4-B for a description of the data.)

Data transformation and estimation

Some transformations of the data were required to accommodate the econometric specification. First, the municipalities comprising the Metropolitan Manila area were combined into one "province," reducing the number of provinces to 74. Second, 6 of the 74 provinces do not contain upland forest areas, so no migration could be observed into these provinces. Therefore, these provinces were dropped as potential destinations; however, they were still included as origins for migration streams. Since the goal of the migration analysis is to predict lowland to upland migration trends, dropping these provinces is not problematic and is consistent with our model. Some of the data regarding attributes of each province were also missing, and affected provinces had to be dropped from the model prior to computing migration proportions, leaving us with 31 possible origin provinces and 52 possible destination provinces.[6] The total number of observations for this reduced data set is 3,898. The missing data problem was particularly important for the upland and lowland income variables.

Table 4-7 presents maximum likelihood estimates of the effect of the various explanatory variables on the choice of migration. All variables were converted into log form. These estimates reflect the effect of the explanatory variables on the destination decision of the

migration stream, or equivalently, on each representative individual in a particular origin. Eleven of the explanatory variables are significantly different from zero, including many economic and environmental quality indicators. Most of the variables have expected signs, except where they are not statistically different from zero.

The first set of results, on socioeconomic determinants in Table 4-7, demonstrates that economic incentives exert substantial influence in the migration decision. Among the socioeconomic factors, the cost of migration has the largest effect on choice of destination, based on the index of cost of long-range migration.[7] Most of the income-related variables are also important, although other related socioeconomic factors, such as farm tenancy rates and provincial unemployment, do not significantly affect the migration decision.

Both average provincial income and the incidence of poverty have significant effects on migration. Higher household incomes make upland sites in the province more attractive to migrants. In addition, the more poverty there is (the more households fall below the poverty line in a destination province), the more migrants want to go to other places.

Aside from province-level determinants, the economic factors also include more site-specific income variables. The results on these variables suggest that further refinement of income variables—so that they directly relate to upland versus lowland destinations within a province—can contribute to the analysis of migration. Our current results suggest that such "targeted" income variables have different effects on migration. Average upland income clearly increases the likelihood that the upland site will be chosen by migrants, although its effect on destination choice is not

---

[6]Dropping observations effectively means that the model represents fewer choices. However, dropping choices does not affect the estimation with respect to any of the other choices, under the independence of irrelevant alternatives assumption required of the multinomial discrete choice model (e.g., Amemiya 1985, pp. 300–301).

[7]The index took the value of 0 when migrants to upland municipalities remained within their origin province, or the value of 1 when they moved to municipalities in other provinces.

as large as those of provincial income and poverty incidence (its coefficient is smaller). By contrast, if income gains occur in purely lowland municipalities, these do *not* significantly affect migration destination.

Environmental variables (including agricultural resources) comprise another set of factors important to the migration decision. Arable land and crop land in lowland areas serve as indicators of the predominance of lowland agricultural resources in a province. If the main rural opportunities are dominated by agriculture, these provinces would be less important as upland migration destinations. This is supported by our econometric results, showing that provinces with larger crop land areas have less upland migration. The size alone of arable land is not a significant factor, indicating that what is more important is the ongoing use of these resources.

The proportion of cultivated land to total land area could be positively or negatively linked to upland migration. As noted in Table 4-6, a high percentage of land being intensively or extensively cultivated could indicate crowding in the province, thus discouraging migrants. Alternatively, it could indicate more developed markets and land accessibility, which means increased opportunities for upland migrants. In the estimation results, the proportion of intensively cultivated land leads to more migration, while extensively cultivated land does not appear as a significant factor in the model.

The group of environmental factors in the model that are directly related to physical characteristics of forest land include the percentage of land actually under forest cover (forest land), and the proportion which is steeply sloping (with greater than 30 percent slope). Public forest land, however, follows an administrative classification: not all public forest land is forested, and not all are steeply sloping. These are lands that have been kept in the public domain and are administered by the forestry agency. As noted in the discussion in the previous section, historically it has been

very difficult for government to exclude settlers from these lands, and in many areas they are *de facto* open access lands.

The econometric results show that the purely physical attributes of forest land resources (both extent of land that is forested and slope characteristics) are not significant determinants of migration. By contrast, proportion of public forest land is significantly associated with upland migration. In addition, road density in forest land significantly contributes to migration. These results imply that the forest sector factors most relevant to migration are not the physical conditions of uplands. Instead, the focus should be on indicators of accessibility to resources: tenure or land allocation systems in the case of public forest lands and physical accessibility in terms of road density in the upland sites.

The last group of variables in the model includes the demographic determinants of migration. Lowland population turns out to be a positive influence on migration. Large upland population, controlling for upland population density, also leads to more migration. However, upland population density itself did not have a significant effect on migration. Finally, growth rate of population, as an indicator of general expansion of the community, was positively linked to migration.

Conclusion

Previous studies have already linked the continuing conversion of forest land to agriculture with increasing upland population, but the role of economywide factors motivating population movements to forest lands has not been previously studied in detail. It had been suggested that economywide and sectoral economic policies (e.g., those promoting logging) and institutional conditions (e.g., the open access nature of forest lands) are the cause of increasing forest land population.

In this chapter, we have integrated economywide considerations with both sectoral and environmental factors, in a model focusing on the choice of upland migration destinations. We hypothesized the role of economic factors, specifically poverty and income, as the key determinants of migration. To assess this empirically, lowland to upland migration data were constructed, a database on a range of economic, environmental and demographic factors was assembled, and the migration model was implemented using a multinomial discrete choice framework.

The most important result was to demonstrate empirically the role of economywide incentives motivating upland migration decisions. Poverty incidence and perceived income in potential destinations have significant impacts on migration destination, essentially supporting the view that improved economic conditions constitute the key attraction to migrate to an upland destination. This suggests that economic incentives also operate on the origin side, in a complementary manner—i.e., higher poverty incidence motivates out-migration.[8]

In addition to this result on economywide economic factors, location-specific income data allow an assessment of the role of more "targeted" policy instruments. From the migration model results, improving incomes in existing upland communities (a good goal) leads to more upland migration (an unwelcome effect). To respond to this apparent dilemma, it is important to incorporate the environmental factors in the evaluation of economic policy options. For example, the analysis of environmental factors in the model

demonstrates that public forestry management (or lack of it) aggravates migration. Thus, in this case reforms or programs to improve upland income reforms or alleviate poverty need to be implemented with complementary forest land tenure and management reforms. In addition, economywide reforms that target more directly lowland income gains, and improved lowland opportunities could lead to income improvements without increasing migration incentives.

Finally, focusing on the role of environmental management, policy-relevant instruments need to be developed. While the physical characteristics of forest lands (e.g., slope) or existing population density are not affected by policy (at least in the short term), the property rights governing forest lands can be modified substantially. Regarding forest land management reforms, our results support current discussions on the need to devolve forest land management, from central government to community or user groups. This would change the open access conditions in many areas and would contribute to reducing migration pressures on these lands. This analysis is relevant for articulating an agenda for effective reforms. The results confirm that forest sector-specific efforts to create alternatives to ineffective centralized management and to provide technological support in stabilizing agriculture in steep lands should continue to be pursued. However, because of the extent of external pressures on forest lands, economic incentives—both economywide and sectoral—underlying migration pressures on forest lands must similarly be addressed.

---

[8]Because our migration model focuses on the choice among alternative upland sites (and not on whether or not to migrate), the results do not allow us to make direct conclusions on the role of poverty and income in the decision to migrate.

Table 4-1: Land Use Classification in the Philippines, 1988

Land use/cover	Area (000 ha)	Percent of total
A. Forest	7,226	23.92
Pine	81	0.27
Mossy	246	0.81
Dipterocarp	6,629	21.94
Closed	2,435	8.06
Open	4,194	13.88
Mangrove	149	0.49
Other	121	0.40
B. Extensive cultivation	11,958	39.58
Open in forest	30	0.09
Grassland	1,813	6.00
Mixed grass, brush plantation, etc.	10,114	33.49
C. Intensive cultivation	9,729	32.58
Plantation	5,336	17.67
Coconut	1,133	3.75
Other	91	0.30
Coconut, cropland	3,748	12.40
Other cropland	365	1.20
Cropland	4,392	14.54
D. Fishponds	205	0.67
Fishpond from mangrove	195	0.64
Other fishponds	10	0.03
E. Nonvegetated Areas	101.4	0.34
Eroded areas	0.7	0.002
Quarries	8.0	0.02
Riverbeds	81.0	0.27
Other barren land	10.0	0.03
F. Other	439	1.45
Built-up areas	131	0.43
Marshy areas	103	0.34
Lakes	205	0.68
G. Unclassified	546	1.80
TOTAL	30,205	99.96

Table 4-2. Philippine Forest Land Population, 1950–85

Census years	Forest land population (thousands)	Annual growth rate between census years (percent)
1950	5,868	—
1960	8,192	3.39
1970	11,169	3.15
1975	12,702	2.61
1980	14,440	2.60
1985	17,513	3.39

Source: M. C. Cruz et al. (1992).

Table 4-3: Incidence of Poverty in the Philippines, 1971–88 (percent)

Year	Urban	Rural
1971	38	58
1985	42	58
1988	48	60

Note: The income threshold for the mid-1980s was estimated to be P4,764 per person per year in 1978 prices.
Source: 1971 and 1985 estimates from World Bank 1988; 1988 estimate from the Family Income and Expenditure Survey (1988).

Table 4-4: Nominal Protection Rates for Main Agricultural Commodities, 1960–86 Averages (percent)

Crop	Direct NPR	Indirect NPR	Total
Rice	8	-25	-17
Corn	39	-33	6
Sugar	-18	-19	-37
Coconut	-12	-21	-33

Note: Direct nominal protection rate (NPR) measures the proportional difference between a commodity's producer price and the border price due to direct government price subsidies or taxes. Indirect NPR measures the difference due to the indirect effect of industrial protection and local currency overvaluation.

They then estimate the implication of total disincentives to *total real income effects* on the households dependent on these crops, for 1971–84. This indicator measures the impact of output and input price policies on value added of a sector, also incorporating the effect of price policies on cost of living. For the four crop sectors, the real income effects were all negative (even for corn-producing households), ranging from -2.49 to -3.61 percent. These were negative and large since agricultural disincentives meant that farmers not only earned less, but also had to pay relatively more for protected industrial goods (Intal and Power 1991).

Thus, the effects of policy failures have meant pervasive poverty and economic stagnation. In particular, lowland agriculture was penalized heavily, causing a distinct rural bias in poverty incidence. Traditional agricultural communities suffered most. Coupled with rapid population growth, these conditions of poverty and unemployment have contributed to incentives for migrants to move to forest lands, in search of alternative livelihoods.

Table 4-5: Frequency Distribution of Migration Streams, M_{ij}'s, 1990 Census

M_{ij}	Frequency	Percent	Cumulative frequency	Cumulative percent
0	2,638	44.5	2,638	44.5
1–500	3,128	52.8	5,766	97.3
500–900	94	1.6	5,860	98.8
> 1,000	69	1.2	5,929	100.0

Note: M_{ij}'s refer to individuals in forest land municipalities in 1990 who resided in lowland municipalities in 1985.

Table 4-6: Description of Migration Determinants and Hypothesized Link to Migration

Description of upland migration factors	Expected sign of migration effect
Socioeconomic factors:	
Average household income. Mean household income in province. *Source:* NEDA 1988.	[+] Higher provincial income levels tend to make a destination more attractive to upland migrants.
Poverty incidence (%). Proportion of households falling below poverty line. *Source:* National Statistical Coordination Board 1985.	[-] The more poverty there is, the more likely upland migrants will choose other locations.
Average upland income. Mean income of households in upland municipalities in the province. *Source:* IAST 1990a,b.	[+] Higher income in upland sites attract more migrants.
Average lowland income. Mean income of households in lowland municipalities in the province. *Source:* IAST 1990a,b.	[-] Higher income in lowland sites in the province makes upland sites less attractive.
Unemployment rate. Percentage of labor force that is unemployed in the province. *Source:* NEDA 1985.	[-] More unemployment will discourage upland migration.
Percent of population employed in agriculture. *Source:* NCSO 1980.	[+/-] The importance of agricultural employment may affect migration destination.
Farm area tenancy/lease rate. Percent of farm area under tenancy or lease. *Source:* Bureau of Agricultural Economics 1980.	[-] High rate of tenancy or leasing indicates tenurial insecurity and will discourage upland migration.
Index of cost of long-range migration. Index = 1 if migration is to municipality in other province, 0 otherwise. *Source:* NCSO 1990.	[-] Within province, movements are less costly; this encourages migration to upland sites within the province.
Urbanization rate (%). Percent of Urban to Total Population. *Source:* NCSO 1980.	[+] Urbanization is associated with greater economic opportunities and social services, thus attracting migration.

Description of upland migration factors	*Expected sign of migration effect*
Literacy rate (%). Percentage of population that is literate. *Source:* NEDA 1990.	[+] High literary rate is an indicator of socio-economic well-being and increases likelihood that site will be chosen by migrants.

Environmental factors:

Cropped area (sq km). Total cropland in province in 1987. *Source:* NEDA 1987.	[-] Indicator of lowland agricultural orientation of province, thus less attractive as upland migration destination
Arable land (sq km). Total arable land in province, 1987. *Source:* NEDA 1987.	[-] Indicates importance of lowland resources versus uplands in the province.
Percent of land under extensive cultivation. Extensively cultivated land includes: cultivated and other open areas, grass land, cultivated area mixed with brush and grass land. *Source:* World Bank 1989b.	[+/-] A high percentage of extensively cultivated land could indicate crowding in the province, thus discouraging migrants, in general. Alternatively, it could indicate more developed markets and land accessibility, which means increased opportunities for upland migrants.
Percent of land under intensive cultivation. Intensively cultivated land includes: coconut and other plantations, cereal crop and sugar lands, combination of crop land and coconut/other plantations.	[+/-] Presence of intensive cultivation could discourage more migrants. However, it could also mean more accessibility and developed markets.
Percent forested land. Proportion of provincial area under forest cover. *Source:* World Bank 1989b.	[+] Greater proportion of land under forest will attract more upland migrants.
Land area with greater than 30 percent slope (%). Calculated from data provided by the Bureau of Soils and Water Management.	[-] Steeply sloping lands will tend to be less productive and will discourage upland migrants.
Public forest land (% of provincial area). Includes all land, whether forested or not, classified as public forest. *Source:* Forest Management Bureau 1989.	[+] Proportion of land area governed as public forest land. Because of ineffective public management, such lands are mostly de facto open access and attract migrants.
Road Density in Upland Area (km/sq km). Kilometers of roads per square kilometer of area of upland municipality. *Source:* Department of Public Works and Highways, National Statistics Office 1987.	[+] Presence of roads in forest land indicates easier access and improved profitability of farming, thus attracting migrants.

Demographic factors:

1980 lowland population. Provincial population less upland population in 1980. *Source:* 1980 Census and estimates of 1980 upland population from M. C. Cruz, Zosa-Feranil, and Goce 1988.	[+/-] Having large lowland population may increase attraction of upland destination, but it could also have a negative crowding effect.

Description of upland migration factors	*Expected sign of migration effect*
1980 upland population. Population in municipalities classified as upland. *Source:* M. C. Cruz, Zosa-Feranil, and Goce 1988.	[+] Large upland population indicates presence of established communities, which attract migrants.
Upland population density. Upland population per square kilometer of upland municipalities, 1980. *Source:* M. C. Cruz, Zosa-Feranil, and Goce 1988.	[-] High upland density would limit land available to new migrants.
Population growth rate 1980–90. Calculated from 1980 and 1990 Censuses.	[+] Perceived growth in potential destination would attract migrants.

Table 4-7. Multinomial Discrete Choice Estimates of Determinants of Upland Migration

Migration factors (expected link to upland migration)	Coefficients	Standard errors
Economic factors:		
Average household income	3.97**	1.465
Poverty incidence (%)	-3.74**	1.216
Average upland income	0.208**	0.058
Average lowland income	-0.038	0.067
Unemployment rate (%)	18.87	20.68
Percent of population employed in agriculture	-1.966	2.137
Farm area tenancy/lease rate	0.11	0.26
Index of cost of long-range migration	-33.03**	1.01
Urbanization rate (%)	-0.32	0.427
Literacy rate (%)	-11.53	20.49
Environmental factors:		
Cropped area (sw km)	-1.54*	0.922
Arable land (sq km)	0.519	0.614
Percent of land under extensive cultivation	0.494	0.416
Percent of land under intensive cultivation	1.081**	0.438
Percent forested land	0.906	0.77
Land area with greater than 30 percent slope (%)	0.352	0.255
Public forest land (% of provincial area)	1.05**	0.322
Road density in upland area (km/sq km)	1.27**	0.468
Demographic factors:		
1980 lowland population	3.55*	1.929
1980 upland population	0.78**	0.302
Upland population density	-1.63	1.20
Population growth rate 1980–90	1.37**	0.34

* denotes significance at 0.10 level.

** denotes significance at 0.05 level.

Notes: Log likelihood is -292.39; F statistic is 0.0033. All variables refer to destination province, unless noted otherwise. Index of Long-range Migration = 1, if upland migration is to another province; 0, if within province.

Figure 4-1: Expansion of Agriculture in Lowlands and Forestlands, 1960–87

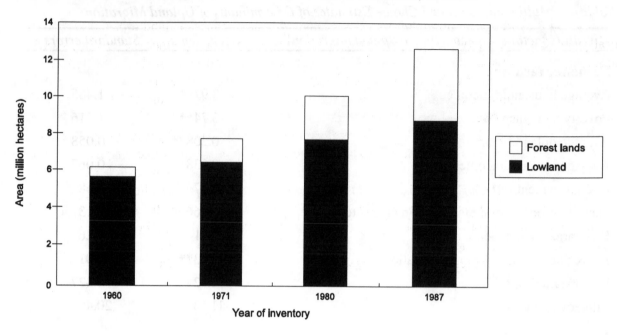

Annex 4-A: Multinomial Discrete Choice Model of Upland Migration

Our discussion of upland migration suggests that individuals in either lowland urban or lowland rural provinces face a large set of potential upland forest destination provinces. However, some migration occurs between upland provinces for households displaced from their illegal land claims, or that leave after their land becomes unproductive. In this section, we describe an econometric procedure that accommodates the many choices facing the potential migrant, and we show how the model can apply to observed migration streams.

An individual's decision to move is a complex comparison of (known) utility the individual receives at his origin, and the utility he expects to receive at potential destinations. Since each individual can physically move to only one site at one time, the potential destinations form a discrete set of alternatives. Each migrant in the same location thus faces the same alternative set. The aggregation of similar choices made by individuals at an origin makes possible the application of the discrete choice framework to typical data sets, where migration streams (e.g., the number moving from one location to another location) rather than individual data are available.[9]

Assume there is a representative individual, person i, residing in province i, who receives the following utility:

$$V_i(X_i;\Omega_i) = V_{i0}, \tag{1}$$

where V_{i0} is individual i's known utility at his/her location, X_i is a vector of variables specific to province i, and Ω_i are demographic characteristics of individual, as well as important environmental variables that affect utility. We assume $\partial V(X_i;\Omega_i)/\partial X_i \geq 0$ and $\partial^2 V(X_i;\Omega_i)/\partial X_i^2 \leq 0$.

This ith individual will migrate from province i to province j only if j is preferred to all other m alternatives:[10]

$$V_i(X_j;\Omega_j) > E\{V_i(X_m;\Omega_m)\}, \ \forall m \neq j. \tag{2}$$

where $E\{V_i(X_m;\Omega_m)\}$ represents utility the ith individual expects to receive at site m, and the total number of possible destinations is denoted by N. If the individual chooses to stay in location i and not move, then

$$V_i(X_i;\Omega_i) > E\{V_i(X_k;\Omega_k)\}, \ \forall k \neq i. \tag{3}$$

If the choices in Equations (2)–(3) are observed for each individual in destination i, then a "migration stream" can be defined that describes aggregate migration. The migration stream from origin site i to destination site j, denoted M_{ij}, is the number of individuals in province i for whom condition (2) is true. By aggregating these individuals into a common stream of migrants, we necessarily assume that they are "identical"; that is, each migration stream can be described by the decision facing a representative individual. This representative individual assumption is conventional

---

[9]That is, the polychotomous choices faced by each individual are translated into similar "choices" for migration streams.

[10]The assumes the individual moves to only one location at a time.

in discrete choice models like (1)–(2), where individual-based data is not available (Ben-Akiva and Lerman 1985).[11]

Any environmental, income, or demographic variables that make an individual's expected utility higher at a given location will determine their destination site choice. Moreover, if each individual moves only once in the time frame covered by the model, then the arguments of the utility function can be defined so that they vary only over destinations. In other words, for each M_{ij}, the origin variables become constant for all individuals composing M_{ij}, thus allowing aggregation.

To obtain an estimable form of the migrant's decision, we must convert expected utilities into random utilities. Using random utilities accommodates the fact that each migrant's expectations of their utilities at the destination as well as their origin are known to the individual but not to the researcher. Random utilities are obtained by appending error terms to the site-specific utility functions in (1)-(3). Following convention, we assume that random utility for each individual is monotonic and separable in its variables (McFadden 1987; Hausman and McFadden 1984), so that for any potential destination m for the ith individual:

$$V_i(X_m; \Omega_m) + \epsilon_m = \alpha_0 + \beta_1 X_{1m} + ...$$
$$+ \beta_k X_{km} + \gamma_1 \Omega_1 + ... + \gamma_k \Omega_k \tag{5}$$

where X_{lm} are destination specific variables, ϵ_i is a utility-specific error term with probability density function, f_e, Ω_l are demographic indicators, and $\beta_1,..,\beta_k, \gamma_1,... \gamma_k$ are constants to be estimated. Note that by appending the demographic variables in a linear fashion, we approximate their effect in the utility function, as others have suggested (e.g., Pudney 1989).

Using (5) in (1)–(3), the probability that migration from i to j occurs for the ith individual is

$$P_{ij} = pr\{V_i(X_j; \Omega_j) + \epsilon_j > V_i(X_i; \Omega_i) + \epsilon_i\} \tag{6}$$

This probability can be estimated using either individual data, where choices are represented as (0,1) binary variables, or using sample proportions.[12] Sample proportions are especially well suited for large-scale population studies where individual decisions are not observed or aggregated (Ben-Akiva and Lerman 1985, other cites).

In the above model, the sample proportion defines the frequency distribution of migration patterns.[13] The proportion is computed for each origin i and destination j:

$$p_{ij} = M_{ij}/\sum_j M_{ij}. \tag{7}$$

Using p_{ij}, the choices in (6) are represented as frequencies that must sum to one when added over choices for each migration stream.

---

[11]The representative individual assumption is essential in this chapter given the scale of the problem we investigate and the availability of data. For example, we later estimate migration for over 5,000 possible choices and 10,000 migrants. Like other countries where such data are compiled, the census data available for such a study in the Philippines is not individual-based.

[12]The assumption required is that individuals making the same choice can be summarized by a representative individual.

[13]This assumes, as is the case for our data, that observations are collected randomly.

The error in (6) has an extreme value distribution. Assuming ϵ_i are iid normal random variables, a maximum likelihood procedure can be used to determine how the probability of observing a migration pattern from site i to destination j depends on the vector of explanatory variables in the utility function, (5). From the maximum likelihood estimates, one can then determine how migration patterns are affected by the explanatory variables using the standard marginal effects computation.[14]

The random utility decision together with (1) and (4) comprise a "multinomial discrete choice model" (Amemiya 1985). An important feature of discrete choice models is that they accommodate decisions made simultaneously about multiple destination sites. Statistical tests can also be conducted regarding the relevance of explanatory variables that determine the observed migration patterns.

---

[14]In particular, $\partial P_{ij}/\partial X_{ki} = ...\beta_k...$ where β_k is the *ML* estimate of the coefficient associated with X_{ki} from (5).

Annex 4-B: Descriptive Statistics of Explanatory Variables in the Migration Model

Table 4B-1: Descriptive Statistics of Explanatory Variables in the Migration Model

Variable Xi	MEAN	STD	DEV	MIN	MAX
Percent upland migration	Y	0.23	0.17	0.04	0.79
Upland population density	X1j	38.41	6.74	6.60	73.96
Arable land in *i* (sq km)	X2i	1,148.44	467.25	247.00	2,363.00
Percent land area with 30 percent slope in province *j*	X3j	38.70	18.14	5.79	69.19
Land area classified as public forest (ha) in *j*	X4j	328,097.00	216,105.00	40,422.00	1,041,850.00
Percent land under extensive cultivation in *j*	X5j	38.85	12.43	16.00	66.00
Percent of total farms in *i* under tenancy/leasehold	X6i	24.75	11.37	2.48	50.43
Unemployment rate in province *i* (%)	X7i	6.16	2.75	2.00	11.90
Percent literacy rate in *i*	X8i	89.60	8.30	59.77	97.84
Urbanization in *j*	X9j	0.32	0.22	0.06	0.99
Lowland income in *i*	X10i	40,078.00	20,126.00	11,722.00	94,763.00
Upland income in *j*	X11j	25,919.00	12,382.00	6,518.00	60,042.00

Bibliography

Amemiya, T. 1985. *Advanced Econometrics.* Cambridge, Mass.: Harvard University Press.

Ben-Akiva, M., and S. Lerman. 1985. *Discrete Choice Analysis: Theory and Application to Travel Demand.* MIT Press Series in Transportation Studies. Cambridge, Mass.: MIT Press.

Boserup, E. 1965. *The Conditions of Agricultural Growth.* London: Allen and Unwin.

Bureau of Agricultural Economics. 1980. *Agriculture Census.* Manila: Bureau of Agricultural Economics, Department of Agriculture.

Bureau of Forest Development. 1985. Manila: Department of Environment and Natural Resources.

Cleaver, K. and G. Schreiber, 1991. *The Population, Environment and Agriculture Nexus in Sub-Saharan Africa*, Africa Region Technical Paper, World Bank, Washington, D.C.

Cruz, M. C., C. A. Meyer, R. Repetto, and R. Woodward. 1992. *Population Growth, Poverty, and Environmental Stress: Frontier Migration in the Philippines and Costa Rica.* Washington, D.C.:World Resources Institute.

Cruz, M. C., I. Zosa-Feranil, and C. L. Goce. 1988. "Population Pressure and Migration: Implications for Upland Development in the Philippines." *Journal of Philippine Development* XV(l).

Cruz, W., and C. Gibbs. 1990. "Resource Policy Reform in the Context of Population Pressure: The Philippines and Nepal." *American Journal of Agricultural Economics* 72(5).

Cruz, W., and R. Repetto. 1992. *The Environmental Effects of Stabilization and Structural Adjustment Programs: The Philippines Case.* Washington, D.C.: World Resources Institute.

David, Cristina, W. Cruz, and associates. 1986. *Agenda for Action for the Philippine Rural Sector.* Manila: Philippine Institute for Development Studies.

Family Income and Expenditure Survey (FIES). Manila: National Economic and Development Authority.

Food and Agriculture Organization (FAO). 1983. *Tropical Forest Resources Assessment Project Forest Resources of Tropical Asia.* Rome: Food and Agriculture Organization.

Forest Management Bureau. 1989. *Philippine Forestry Statistics.* Quezon City: National Economic and Development Authority.

Hansen, S. 1990. "Macroeconomic Policies and Sustainable Development in the Third World." *Journal of International Development* 2(4).

Hausman, J., and D. McFadden. 1984. "Specification Tests for the Multinomial Logit Model." *Econometrica* 52(5):1219–1240.

Intal, P., and J. Power. 1991. "Trade, Exchange Rate, and Agricultural Pricing Policies in the Philippines." In A. Krueger, M. Schiff, and A. Valdes, *The Political Economy of Agricultural Pricing Policies.*

Institute of Agrarian Studies (IAST). 1990. *Terminal Report: Benchmark Survey of Potential CARP Areas.* Los Baños, Laguna, Philippines: University of the Philippines at Los Baños.

————. 1990. Unpublished information based on a survey conducted in 1990. Los Baños, Laguna, Philippines.

Krueger, A., M. Schiff, and A. Valdes. 1991. *The Political Economy of Agricultural Pricing Policies.* Baltimore: Johns Hopkins University Press for the World Bank.

Kummer, David. 1990. "Deforestation in the Post-War Philippines." Ph.D. diss., Boston University.

McFadden, D. 1987. "Method of Simulated Moments for Estimation of Discrete Response Models with Numerical Integration." Massachusetts Institute of Technology, Department of Economics. Working Paper No. 464 (August), pp. 1–47.

Mink, S. 1993. "Poverty and the Environment." *Finance and Development* 30(4): 8–10.

National Census and Statistics Office (NCSO). 1980, 1990. *Census of the Population of the Philippines.* Manila: National Economic and Development Authority.

———. 1985. *Barangay Census.* Manila: National Economic and Development Authority.

National Economic and Development Authority (NEDA). 1985, 1987, 1988, 1990. *Philippine Statistical Yearbook.* Manila: National Census and Statistics Office.

National Statistical Coordination Board (NSCB). 1985. *Philippine Statistical Yearbook.* Manila.

The Philippines Natural Resources Accounting Project. 1992. Technical Resources Program, Project No. 498-0432. Prepared by the International Resources Group, Ltd., in association with the Mandala Agricultural Development Corporation and Edgevale Associates under Contract No. 492-0432-C-00-1015-05 with USAID Philippines, Manila.

Pearce, D. W., and J. J. Warford. 1993. *World Without End: Economics, Environment and Sustainable Development.* Washing-ton, D.C., and New York: World Bank and Oxford University Press.

Pudney, S. 1989. *Modelling Individual Choice: The Econometrics of Corners, Kinks, and Holes.* Oxford, U.K., and New York: Blackwell.

Williamson, J. 1988. "Migration and Urbanization." In H. Chenery and T. N. Srinivasan (eds.), *Handbook of Development Economics*, Vol. 1. New York: Elsevier Science Publishing Co., pp. 424–65.

World Bank. 1985. *The Philippines: Recent Trends in Poverty, Employment and Wages.* Washington, D.C.: World Bank.

———. 1988. *The Philippines: The Challenge of Poverty.* Washington, D.C.: World Bank.

———. 1989a. *Philippines: Environment and Natural Resource Management Study*, Washington, D.C.: World Bank.

———. 1989b. *SPOT Satellite Surveys 1987 of the World Bank.*

———. 1992. *World Development Report 1992: Development and the Environment*, New York: Oxford University Press.

World Commission on Environment and Development (WCED). 1987. *Our Common Future.* Oxford, U.K.: Oxford University Press.

Yap, Lorene. 1977. "The Attraction of Cities: A Review of Migration Literature." *Journal of Development Economics* 4:239–64.

5

Economywide Policies and the Environment: A Case Study of Poland

Robin Bates, Shreekant Gupta, and Boguslaw Fiodor

Overview

IN EXAMINING THE LINKAGES between economywide policies and environmental degradation in formerly planned economies, we focus on Poland for two reasons. First, Poland is representative of the challenges that all former socialist countries of Central and Eastern Europe (CEE) face as they attempt to restructure their economies. Not only was it one of the pioneers in the dramatic changes we now witness in CEE, but Poland also has now had substantial experience with the transition toward a market economy.

CEE comprises Bulgaria, the Czech and Slovak Federal Republic (CSFR), the former German Democratic Republic, Hungary, Poland, Romania, and the former U.S.S.R. In the subsection, *Energy intensity and the environment in Poland*, references to CEE exclude the German Democratic Republic.

In addition, Poland demonstrates clearly the disastrous environmental legacy of central planning: in 1988–89 it was the third largest emitter of sulfur dioxides (SO_2) and nitrogen oxides (NO_x) in Europe (after the former Soviet Union and Germany); with regard to particulate emissions it ranked second (Nowicki 1993); and SO_2 and NO_x emissions per dollar of GNP were highest among all countries of CEE, including the former Soviet Union (WRI 1992).

With respect to air quality, the concentrations of SO_2, NO_x, and particulates were significantly higher than permissible standards in all big Polish cities (Nowicki 1993). In the heavily polluted Katowice region, for instance, in 1989 average annual concentrations of SO_2 and NO_x exceeded permissible standards by a factor of two, while particulates exceeded standards by a factor of four (Bates, Cofala, and Toman 1994)—well beyond the guidelines proposed by the World Health Organization (WHO).[1]

The primary focus of this case study is on the impact of energy production and consumption on air pollution, although more efficient production and consumption of energy will have a beneficial impact on other media as well. The section, *Environmental Effects of a Centrally Planned Economy: A Retrospective View*, examines historically the ways in which central planning led to environmental degradation in Poland, in order to isolate the policy changes that are necessary in the future. Given the fundamental role played by a perverse incentive system, the section, *Environmental Effects of the Transition to a Market Economy: Challenges for the Future*, discusses how Poland is restructuring economic incentives in general, and analyses the impact on the energy sector and air pollution in particular.

We believe that the Polish experience contains important lessons for all centrally planned economies that are making the transition toward a market economy. It also reinforces the more general lesson—that competitive markets and clear property rights can lead to substantial environmental benefits.

Environmental Effects of a Centrally Planned Economy: A Retrospective View

General features of a socialist economy

Until the 1980s, the Polish economy was dominated by central planning, and shared the main features of other socialist economies: extensive state ownership of the means of production, and a centralized mechanism for the allocation of scarce resources. Such economies have been analyzed by Kornai and others,[2] who argue that these economies are resource constrained, in contrast to capitalist economies, which are demand constrained. Resource constraints arise due to the simultaneous existence of taut plans and soft budgets. A taut plan implies physical targets that are rigid or binding enough to force the firm to hit a resource constraint. Thus, in the Kornai framework, a firm would produce more output if additional inputs were available. At the same time, budgets are soft, i.e., if inputs are available, funds to buy them can usually be obtained. Any financial losses are covered through subsidies, and firms are never bankrupt.

The softening of budget constraints implies a basic change in the system of managerial incentives, compared with a market-based economy, since profit-seeking and cost-minimizing behavior are not rewarded. Two consequences in particular are underlined here: the lack of responsiveness to input prices, and the

---

[1]The permissible annual average concentration in Poland for SO_2 is 32 $\mu g/m^3$, and for NO_x and particulates, it is 50 $\mu g/m^3$ each. The WHO guidelines suggest upper limits for SO_2 and particulates of 60 and 90 $\mu g/m^3$, respectively (UNEP 1992).

[2]Kornai's analysis was articulated in *Economics of Shortage* (1980). It has since been refined and restated by Kornai and others. For a review, see Kornai (1992).

creation of excess demand. With respect to the former, a downward-sloping demand curve by the firm for its inputs presupposes the existence of a hard budget constraint. However, the softer the budget constraint, the weaker the compulsion to adjust demand to relative prices. In the extreme case of a perfectly soft budget constraint, own-price elasticity of demand is zero: the demand curve is vertical, i.e., determined by other explanatory variables and not by the price. It is important to note that this is not merely a matter of a firm reacting less elastically to some particular price or the other. "The softness of the budget constraint blunts responsiveness to every price" (Kornai 1992, p. 146). For example, if one of two inputs that are perfect substitutes becomes cheaper, it is far from certain that the firm will consider this in selecting its input mix: it is not price, but other considerations, such as output maximization, that drive the demand for inputs. The implication of this in the context of excessive energy use in Poland is that price reform in itself may not achieve a reduction in energy use: it has to be accompanied by a hardening of the budget constraint, i.e., enterprise reform or privatization.

Second, a combination of soft budgets and taut plans results in persistent shortage or excess demand. Firms in a resource constrained economy are not cost minimizers, but rather output and resource-use maximizers. If the budget constraint were hard, demand for inputs would be limited, since expenditures on purchasing inputs would be conditional on revenues generated by the sale of output, which in turn is constrained by the demand for the firm's output. Further, output maximization is the firm's paramount goal, since it is usually the only criterion by which its performance is judged. Thus, it tries to stockpile inputs in order to be able to produce without interruption. The only constraint is the actual availability of inputs.

Empirical evidence on the material intensity of socialist economies is provided by Gomulka and Rostowski (1988). They com-

pute various measures of material intensity for eleven capitalist and four socialist countries and find the latter to be considerably more material intensive, in particular, more energy intensive.[3] In another cross-country study, Slama (1986) also finds higher energy intensity of production in socialist countries. More recently, Moroney (1990) simultaneously considered energy and physical capital as aggregate inputs. He concluded that CMEA countries as a group consumed, on an average, approximately twice as much energy per unit of capital and per unit of real GDP as the economies of Western Europe. Further, while both sets of countries relied on capital accumulation and increased energy consumption as sources of economic growth, the CMEA countries relied to a greater extent on energy.

In the case of Poland, the material intensity inherent in all socialist systems has been exacerbated by abundant and cheap availability of coal, resulting in particularly high levels of energy intensity. In contrast, in a market economy like Australia's, which exports three times as much coal as Poland (U.S. EIA 1990), coal accounted for only 44 percent of primary energy supply (British Petroleum Company 1992). Thus, it appears that an abundant energy supply is necessary but not sufficient for high energy intensity: a resource-intensive economic system has to exist as well.

Energy intensity and the environment in Poland

The energy sector plays a major role in the economy of Poland. With primary energy supply in excess of 100 metric tons of oil equivalent in 1990, it was the second largest energy sector among the countries of CEE, after the former Soviet Union. It is also one of

---

[3]Aggregate energy consumption per unit of value added in the industrial sectors of the seven European CMEA countries was found to be 40–134 percent higher than that in the 15 Organisation for Economic Co-operation and Development (OECD) countries.

the largest sectors of the Polish economy. In 1990 it contributed 13 percent of gross domestic product (GDP), employed 5 percent of the labor force, and between 1986 and 1990 accounted for 30 percent of the total investment in industry (World Bank 1993b, Vol. 1).

While several cross-country comparisons bear out the energy intensity of the Polish economy (defined as energy consumed per unit of output),[4] two problems with national income data need to be kept in mind. The first is that official figures for centrally planned economies suffer from conceptual limitations and poor accuracy. Second, since official exchange rates for these economies are arbitrary, comparable estimates of national income are calculated either by using commercial exchange rates, or by using a Purchasing Power Parity (PPP) approach. Since the latter results in income figures that are higher, using PPP measures of national income reduces energy intensity statistics.

Table 5-1 reports energy intensity of national income, based on PPP. In addition to the level of energy intensity, an important aspect is its behavior over time. Thus, while energy intensity in Poland has declined, the rate of decline has not been as rapid as in other countries. Moreover, the rate of decline has slowed down over time (Table 5-1).[5]

With respect to energy intensity, it is important to note, however, that Poland is not an outlier compared with other parts of CEE. Table 5-2 shows energy intensity per unit of output for CEE (relative to OECD) and also for the five smaller CEE countries as a group, excluding the former Soviet Union (CEE5).

---

[4]See for instance, Bates and Moore (1992), Table 4, and IEA (1990), Figure 2.

[5]This is confirmed by fitting a quadratic time trend to annual energy intensity data from 1960–91. While the coefficient on the trend variable was negative and significant, the coefficient on the square of the trend variable was positive and significant. Thus, energy intensity has declined, but the rate of decline has slowed down over time. Results are available from the authors on request.

Note that the figure for Poland is close to the CEE5 mean of 2.0. What is notable about Poland, however, is the dominance of coal (often referred to as the "coal monoculture") in the consumption of primary and final energy. In addition, coal accounted for over 95 percent of domestic primary energy production in Poland in 1990. Finally, Poland was the world's fourth largest exporter of hard coal, and coal exports accounted for 12 percent of export earnings in 1990 (World Bank 1993b, Vol. 2). Thus, the major environmental problems in Poland are those connected with energy in general, and the excessive use of coal in particular, which is a dirty fuel to mine and to burn.

Energy production and use in Poland in 1990, by stationary sources (mainly for producing electricity and heat), accounted for 70–80 percent of the emissions of particulate matter (PM) and SO_2, and nearly 50 percent of the emissions of NO_x (Bates, Cofala, and Toman 1994). Within the energy sector, coal contributed 82 percent of PM, 90 percent of SO_2, and 46 percent of NO_x emissions (Bates, Cofala, and Toman 1994). An important source of this contribution to PM is the "low-stack" sector, i.e., households, commerce, and services, which, in 1987, relied on coal for more than 60 percent of its total fuel use (Hughes 1991). This figure is high, not only in comparison to Western European countries, but also other parts of CEE (see, for instance, Hughes 1991, Figure 7).

The low-stack sector includes district heating[6] enterprises, which "use coal as their primary energy source, consuming 24 million tons of coal products—13 percent of the country's output—in 1989, and creating 11 percent of national sulfur dioxide emissions, 10 percent of particulate fallout, and 8 percent of

---

[6]District heating is formally defined as "a heating system that transmits and distributes heat from one or more energy source to, among others, residential, industrial and commercial consumers for space heating, cooking, hot water and for industrial purposes" (IEA 1992, p. 378).

nitrous oxide emissions. Because so many of the sources of that pollution are low-stack, small boilers in urban areas, the subsector has a disproportionate impact on local air quality" (World Bank 1993b, Vol. 5, p. 2). Localized emissions from the low-stack sector cause greater health and property damage than power station emissions, which are dispersed from high stacks.

Other pollutants related to the mining and use of coal include solid waste from coal mines and fly ash disposed on land, and salted mine water discharged into rivers. Other ecological impacts of coal mining consist of depletion of ground water, subsidence of land, and loss of topsoil through strip mining.

Patterns of energy use

Using 1990 data, the primary energy supply in Poland went to the following uses (see Figure 5-1): 32 percent went to the transformation and energy sector, where it was converted into heat and electricity. Direct consumption of primary energy by final consumers accounted for 62 percent, and the remaining 6 percent was nonenergy use (based on World Bank 1993b, Vol. 1, Fig. 2).[7] The final consumers of primary energy, in turn, were dominated by industry (38 percent), and commercial and agricultural uses (50 percent), with the residential and transport sectors accounting for 6 percent each. Of the total primary energy used by the transformation and energy sector, the breakdown was (a) district heat 15 percent, (b) combined heat and power generation 56 percent, (c) own use and losses 25 percent, and (d) gas and oil production 4 percent.

For an understanding of the causes of energy intensity in Poland, the breakdown of energy use is better grouped into two analytical categories. The key attribute for defining

these categories is whether an economic entity is public or private. The crucial difference between the two is that the latter have relatively hard budgets. From this perspective, the nature of economic activity undertaken by these entities is not particularly relevant. Thus, households and private firms are both classified as private entities, since both face hard budgets. In socialist countries, however, private entities contribute a relatively insignificant share of total output: in Poland, the public sector, broadly defined to include government, accounted for more than 80 percent of national output in 1985 (Milanovic 1989). Also with respect to employment, the public sector accounted for more than 70 percent of total employment in Poland in 1985 (Lipton and Sachs 1990).

Public entities and energy intensity

Public entities in Poland that exceeded their budgets could expect to receive regular external assistance. Some discussion of the ways in which this can occur are in the section, *Environmental Effects of the Transition to a Market Economy: Challenges for the Future*, but the mechanism is not relevant here. What is important, however, is the consequences, namely, firms had no incentive either to minimize input use for a given technology, or to use more efficient technologies in the production process.[8] These points were empirically validated in a World Bank study that surveyed the likely responses of industrial consumers of energy in Poland, to, inter alia, an increase in energy prices. The results suggested that "in the short to medium term, these changes would have little impact on either the pattern of industrial fuel use or the general level of fuel efficiency" (World Bank 1991, p. 16). In retrospect, a perverse justification for low input prices in a "cost plus" pricing scenario was precisely this: increases in prices of key inputs, such as energy, would have been

---

[7]In addition to direct consumption of primary energy, final consumers also receive energy, mainly heat and electricity, from the transformation and energy sector.

---

[8]See the subsection, *General features of a socialist economy*, above.

passed on via higher output prices, causing inflation without diminishing energy intensity.[9]

In general, the Polish development process from the 1950s to the 1980s was dominated by extensive rather than intensive growth. In other words, increases in output were accompanied by increasing use of factors of production, particularly energy, and not by increasing productivity. The fact that extensive growth was the dominant form of output growth in Poland has been noted by several studies, such as Fallenbuchl (1977) and Kemme and Crane (1984). The latter use a Cobb-Douglas production function to estimate the relative contributions of capital, labor, and imported inputs to the rate of growth of industrial output in Poland from 1971 to 1981.[10] They find that "the rapid expansion of output in the 1970s was the result of extensive growth in factor inputs, especially capital services"[11] (Kemme and Crane 1984, p. 35).

In terms of specific examples of the absence of intensive growth, in the 1960s, only 4.2 percent of the coal extracted was mechani-

cally enriched, mainly for coal exports.[12] Technological improvements were particularly limited in activities that related to the environment: fluidized bed combustion of coal was not started until 1989, no flue gas desulfurization facility is operational to date, and only one hard coal mine is equipped to desalinate mining water.

An additional influence on productivity is worth noting in the case of public entities that are suppliers as well as consumers of energy, because of the revenue implications of low energy prices. Given the financial constraints imposed by low prices, energy suppliers tend to concentrate their limited resources on quantity throughput, rather than investing in maintenance and other measures that reduce costs and/or increase efficiency. Hence, producer price controls result in greater input use and reduced maintenance, further aggravating high energy intensity.[13] We provide illustrations here from the coal mining and energy conversion sectors.

Although the share of coal in primary energy consumption declined from 95 percent in 1960 to approximately 78 percent in 1991, it is still the dominant category.[14] Against this backdrop of "coal monoculture," the coal industry itself was characterized by declining labor productivity and growing raw material and energy intensity. The energy intensity of coal extraction (hard coal and lignite) increased by approximately 31 percent between 1978 and 1985; and the self-consumption of coal increased by about 20 percent over the same period (Bates, Gupta, and Fiedor 1994).

---

[9]Artificially low prices do matter, however, from an overall macroeconomic perspective, since they result in subsidies that create budgetary pressures. Thus, higher energy prices would have eased budgetary pressures and/or some of these revenues could have been used to alleviate environmental problems. Another area where low energy prices would matter is energy consumption by private entities, discussed in the subsection, *Private entities and energy intensity*, below.

[10]Quarterly data is used in the study, from the first quarter (Q1) of 1971 to mid-1981 (Q2). This period is also divided into two distinct subperiods: 1971Q1 to mid-1978 and mid-1978 to mid-1981. This division is made because, not only does the rate of growth of output fall in the later period, but output actually declines.

[11]Of the 2.9 percent rate of growth in industrial output between 1971 and 1978, about 1.6 percent was due to growth in services. Capital utilization in turn depends, inter alia, on total energy consumption. The residual that measures productivity (among other things), was consistently negative over the entire period of the study.

---

[12]This is a relatively simple and inexpensive method of coal purification that increases its calorific value.

[13]See Bates (1993) for a detailed discussion on the consequences of producer price controls.

[14]See Bates, Gupta, and Fiedor (1994), Table 5, for the structure of primary energy use. The share of coal in primary energy produced is greater than its share in primary energy used, due to exports of coal and imports of oil and natural gas.

Hard coal and lignite extraction, however, increased by less than 7 percent during 1978–85.[15] Thus, the coal industry was no exception to the hypothesis that soft budgets lead to increased use of inputs, including energy.

The financial impact of the decline in labor productivity was exacerbated by increasing wages. Between 1965 and 1989, wages in hard coal mining increased continuously in real terms, and at a faster rate than other sectors of the economy (Syzdlo 1990). Coupled with a policy of low coal prices, this implied a growing discrepancy between costs and retail prices.[16] Between 1970 and 1990, the ratio of costs to prices in the coal industry increased from 90 percent to 132 percent; while the cost of producing a ton of coal went up forty-three times between 1980 and 1989, the retail price only increased thirty times.[17] This implicit subsidy contributed to budgetary deficits. Although we would argue that an increase in coal prices would not have materially reduced coal consumption, it would have reduced the deficit; moreover, the excess revenues could have been available to finance environmental protection activities.

The energy conversion sector used a third of the primary energy produced in 1990. In this sector again, as in the coal sector, we notice inefficiency in production: own use, and transmission and distribution losses amounted to 25 percent in 1990. Further, between 1978 and 1985, the rate of increase in final energy production was about half of that for primary energy.[18]

Poland is one of the most intensive users of district heating in the world, and accounted for 27 percent of final energy consumed in 1990, including industrial uses (IEA 1992). In terms of specific examples of inefficiency in the district heating sector, there are significant water losses in many district heating systems in Poland. It is estimated that water losses are three to five times higher than those in Western Europe,[19] largely due to poor maintenance and corrosion (water is generally not demineralized or treated). Further, comparisons of heat sales with heat dispatches show theoretical heat losses of 10–45 percent, "a range that reflects the shortfall in metering equipment that would enable distributors to identify corroded and poorly insulated mains that leak heat and water" (World Bank 1993b, Vol. 5, p. 2).

Private entities and energy intensity

Since private entities in socialist economies face hard budget constraints, their behavior should be similar to that of private agents in market economies, except that they also face quantity constraints and fixed prices; goods are rationed and sold at fixed official prices, which are below market-clearing levels. Hence, a more rational energy use on the part of private consumers could have been induced by reducing price distortions. Retail energy prices, however, were consistently too low relative to costs. Further, during the 1980s, while retail prices for consumer goods increased by 30–70 times, retail energy prices increased only by about 9–10 times (Bates, Gupta, and Fiedor 1994).

In any case, in an important part of the retail market, namely district heating, there were (and still are) technical impediments to using pricing incentives: residential consumption of secondary energy (heat and hot water),

---

[15]Bates, Gupta, and Fiedor (1994), Tables 11(a) and 11(b).

[16]We refer to financial costs, as data on economic costs are not available.

[17]Bates, Gupta, and Fiedor (1994), Tables 12 and 13.

[18]Bates, Gupta, and Fiedor (1994), Table 9.

[19]The figure for Poland is 100–150 m^3 per terajoule (TJ) of heat produced, compared with only 20–50 m^3/TJ in Western Europe (World Bank 1993b, Vol. 5).

showed the features of a public good. Residential use of heat accounted for 10.6 percent of final energy and 11.5 percent of primary energy consumption in 1990.[20] Of the 7 million dwellings in urban areas, 70 percent are supplied with heat for central heating and 50 percent with hot water (IEA 1990). Nationally, 93 percent of the heat sent out by district heating enterprises (DHEs), is supplied to consumers via networks, with the rest supplied by local boilers feeding individual buildings. The heat distribution systems are constant volume, full flow (i.e., the same volume of water is pumped irrespective of the heat load). The flow temperature of the major heat sources is, however, adjusted according to weather conditions by the heat despatcher (World Bank 1993b, Vol. 5).

Charges for heat and hot water were (and still are) proportional to the floor area of, and the number of persons in an apartment, respectively. It is obvious that this lump sum pricing method did not encourage rational use of heat and hot water. Further, "the ability of consumers to control their heat consumption is at present very limited" and "individual control of heat consumption is generally limited to the use of manual radiator valves" (World Bank 1993b, Vol. 5, p. 33).[21] Finally, in addition to all these factors, apartments were poorly insulated (as discussed below). Hence, it was only for the residual portion of energy directly purchased by private entities, that price signals would have mattered. While these data are not available, an upper bound on them can be inferred from energy balance statistics: direct purchases of final energy by private entities in 1990 were at most 31.4 percent of total final energy consumed.[22]

The pattern of industrial development

The energy intensity of the Polish economy is not only due to the general resource intensity of a socialist economy, as outlined above, but is also related to the strategy of industrial development. According to Kharas (1991), the share of industry in Poland's GDP in 1989 was 51.7 percent, while the average for countries in similar income brackets and degree of urbanization was 39 percent.[23] Given the emphasis on rapid industrialization in general, and development of heavy industry in particular, it is not surprising that four sectors—energy, metallurgy, chemicals, and minerals—accounted for over half of total fixed capital stock in the entire industrial sector between 1960 and 1991. These sectors also dominated industrial output, contributing approximately 40 percent of the gross output over the same period.[24] They accounted for 70–80 percent of energy used by industry (Bates, Gupta, and Fiedor 1994, Table 17), and their energy intensity was higher than industry as a whole (Bates, Gupta, and Fiedor 1994, Table 18). As a result, they were the most polluting sectors in industry: their share in particulate and SO_2 emissions ranges from 80 to 94 percent (Tables 5-3 and 5-4, respectively).

While an industrialization strategy based on heavy industry is common to most centrally planned economies, in the case of Poland it

---

[20]To arrive at the share of residential heat in primary energy, an efficiency factor of 0.62 was used (personal communication from A. Umer, Polish Academy of Sciences).

[21]In contrast, in an experiment reported by Wilczynski (1990), when households were provided with measuring devices, hot water use declined by 50–60 percent, and power consumption for heating purposes was lowered by 18–25 percent.

[22]For difficulties in measuring private sector energy consumption, see IEA (1992), p. 380.

[23]Even the highly industrial middle income nations of East Asia had only a 43 percent industry share (Kharas 1991).

[24]Their share in net output, however, was 30 percent or less (Bates, Gupta, and Fiedor 1994, Tables 15 and 16, respectively). This implies a larger than average share in depreciation, or a more antiquated (and polluting) capital stock.

exacerbated the consequences of energy intensity. Other sectors also favored energy-intensive development, such as housing construction, where there was an emphasis on physical quantities, by way of mass production of apartment buildings. Not only were these apartments poorly insulated (and therefore consumed a lot of heat), but they also intensively used raw materials such as steel and cement, which in themselves were energy intensive. Construction of these buildings also entailed huge transportation costs, since large parts of them were prefabricated in what could be called apartment factories.

The political economy of energy intensity

In addition to the causes of energy intensity that emerge from this analytical framework, there were other factors at work that may be described under the rubric of political economy. They include the role of special interests (such as the Upper Silesian lobby and the coal and steel lobbies), ideological compulsions for energy security, and the lack of citizen pressure for a cleaner environment.

With respect to the influence of lobbies, plan allocations were often distorted by special interest groups in the energy-intensive sectors. Thus, during the 1966–70 Plan period, 40 percent of the investment that was in excess of plan outlays went to chemicals, hard coal and metallurgy (Bates, Gupta, and Fiedor 1994). In the 1970s, the concept of an "open plan" created numerous avenues of influence for the lobbies to impose new projects, even completely new directions of investment. For example, the efforts of the metallurgical lobby resulted in construction of the Centrum steel works, with a cost overrun of twenty times (Bates, Gupta, and Fiedor 1994). Similarly, the fact that the Upper Silesian lobby held key political positions in the 1970s also spurred the development of the hard coal industry during that period. While initially it may have been the coal monoculture itself which gave rise to the coal lobby, subsequently, this interest group became self-reinforcing.

We have argued that the "logic" of the system created a demand for energy that was constrained only by resource availability, but the ideology of energy security provided it with an ideological justification. Since energy security and national security are often viewed as synonymous, the former can be an emotive issue, even in market economies. It was thus imperative to ensure adequate supplies of energy for domestic needs which, as we have seen above, were insatiable.

Finally, the role of grassroots environmental groups in forcing environmental improvements is well documented in the West. Given the absence of democracy in Poland, however, as in other communist countries, this avenue did not exist at least until the 1980s. With respect to the decisionmaking process, as Wilczynski (1990) points out, "the centralization of governmental decisionmaking weakens local authorities and enterprises. In environmental matters this is very important because the problems of pollution and degradation are of a local nature" (p. 41).

Environmental policy in Poland

Environmental problems in Poland stem not only from high energy intensity, but also from the failure of environmental policy. In particular, in a centrally planned economy, the efficacy of market-based approaches is seriously reduced, given the lack of price responsiveness on the part of state-owned firms, and soft budgets. For example, while Poland implemented an apparently sophisticated system of pollution taxes—known as fines and fees—their basic rationale was questionable. Along these lines, Polish environmental experts like Zylicz (1993) have argued that "financial instruments were doomed to failure in an economy where all essential inputs were allocated administratively, and plant managers had little incentive to pay attention to price stimuli. As a result, instead of addressing the real issues, environmental policymakers were complaining that fees were too low, and poor environmental performance was linked to an inadequate level of these fees" (p. 7). Thus, the questionable rationale of the whole system of ecological fines and fees and other instruments of environmental protection in Poland has to be viewed in the context of a lack of property rights, as well as the contradictory role of the state, acting both as a producer and regulator of the environment.

One can, however, argue that if properly enforced and collected, fees and fines do at least generate revenue, which in turn can be used for environmental protection activities. Thus, fees and fines can be viewed as transfer payments, and this seems to have been their role in Poland. Even viewed in these limited terms, environmental policy in Poland cannot be judged to have been a success. For instance, the expenditure on environmental protection in most industrial sectors amounted to only 2–3 percent of production costs in 1986; at the same time fines collected from state-owned enterprises (SOEs) were less than 0.1 percent of the profits, partly due to poor enforcement (Bates, Gupta, and Fiedor 1994).

What is also notable about Polish environmental policy is the lax enforcement of the command-and-control (CAC) measures. For instance, by the end of the 1980s only a third of the plants emitting air pollutants had emission permits. The corresponding figure for plants discharging sewage was 50 percent (Bates, Gupta, and Fiedor 1994). Thus, for units without permits, the question of being in violation did not even arise. In addition, fines that were imposed were often rescinded, and the fine collection ratio (fines actually paid versus fines imposed) ranged around 40 percent.[25] To make matters worse, standards were frequently "liberalized," which undermined the entire basis of the system of fines and fees. In general, environmental inspection and audit capabilities were weak, and state and regional monitoring networks underdeveloped. Over-

all, investment outlays on environmental protection in Poland, up to 1990, ranged from 0.27 percent to 0.7 percent (Poland, Ministry of Environmental Protection, Natural Resources and Forestry 1992, and Gorka 1991). In 1991, however, this figure reached 1 percent, a level comparable to that for OECD countries, and corresponds to an actual expenditure of US$840 million (Poland, Ministry of Environmental Protection, Natural Resources and Forestry 1992).

Environmental Effects of the Transition to a Market Economy: Challenges for the Future

The section, *Environmental Effects of a Centrally Planned Economy: A Retrospective View*, argued that a central planning approach to resource allocation, relying extensively on physical planning targets, combined with soft-budget constraints, seriously damaged the environment in Poland. Those economywide policies resulted in the overuse of energy in general, and coal in particular, with no offsetting environmental policies.

However, profound changes in economic policy, which started to take place after 1988, are expected to lead to major improvements in the environmental situation in Poland, even without the implementation of specific environmental measures. Inter alia, these improvements will come through a further strengthening of the enterprise and banking sectors, and the setting of energy prices, which reflect economic costs. Not only will such changes result in the much-needed hardening of budget constraints and the consequent improvement in resource utilization, the privatization of large segments of the Polish economy will introduce more effective property rights, a precondition for medium- to long-term productivity gains.

---

[25]The fine collection ratio was 37 percent and 45 percent in 1985 and 1989, respectively (Bates, Gupta, and Fiedor 1994).

The economic transformation program

Poland made some progress in privatization following enactment of the Law on Joint Ventures, in December 1988, but the results were limited. A major step forward occurred in early 1990, when the government initiated its Economic Transformation Program (ETP), which was supported by two reform initiatives: in the enterprise sector, Poland embarked on an unprecedented privatization program, while, in banking, the reform program encompassed a number of policy measures which, inter alia, were intended to strengthen the governance and institutional capabilities of the nine newly-created state-owned commercial banks (SOCBs). A key component of the ETP was the program (announced in February 1991) to privatize about 50 percent of the 9,000 SOEs within a period of three years. A "multitrack" approach was adopted, although the two main routes have been "commercialization" and "liquidation." The former case is intended to be transitory: the SOE is converted to a joint stock (or limited liability) company, with a view to later sale or distribution of shares, either through "individual" or "mass" privatization. With "liquidation," assets are transferred to a new private company, through their contribution, sale or lease. The "mass" privatization component is an interesting feature of the ETP, designed to enable the public at large to participate, eventually, in the transfer of ownership from public to private hands.

From the beginning of the privatization efforts, rapid progress was made in the small business and retail sectors, although privatization has now been extended to other parts of the economy. By 1993, the share of private sector activity had reached one-third in industry and three-quarters in construction. The private sector also accounted for most of the growth in GDP during 1993. Productivity growth was much slower among SOEs, where the task of privatization was clearly never going to be easy. Even so, Poland had privatized over 2,000 SOEs by the end of 1993, 423

enterprises had been commercialized, and SOEs were showing better productivity performance under the influence of hard budget constraints. Nevertheless, at the end of 1993, Poland had succeeded in privatizing only one-quarter of its SOEs, rather than one-half, which had been the original goal. Nearly 6,000 enterprises remained in public hands, mainly in the industrial and construction sectors.[26]

The enterprise and bank restructuring program

While significant progress was made under the ETP, the pace of privatization was slowed in the wake of the recession, which followed its introduction, and the simultaneous collapse of trading arrangements, linked to the CMEA. Furthermore, the process of privatization proved to be much more complex and lengthy than initially expected. For example, the principle of voluntary enterprise transformation, embodied in the privatization process, meant that it could be retarded by recalcitrant workers' councils; and there was insufficient implementation capability in virtually all the responsible institutions. The severe financial difficulties of the SOEs, which did not service their debts, transmitted themselves to other sectors of the economy, through the buildup of debt-service arrears—in particular, through a deterioration in the quality of the banking system's loan portfolio, and fiscal problems faced by the government. As of September 1992, SOE loans represented the primary exposure of the SOCBs, and SOEs accounted for most of the roughly 2,000 enterprises, mainly in heavy industry, not servicing their debt. The government recognized that the future success of the ETP in achieving the objective of private sector-led growth, requires functioning financial intermediaries.

To address the range of problems faced by the enterprise and banking sectors, the govern-

---

[26]Information in this paragraph is based on World Bank (1994), Chapter 3.

ment, with the assistance of the World Bank, developed an Enterprise and Bank Restructuring Program (EBRP), to address the interrelated problems of the SOEs, which are not servicing their debts, and of the commercial banks. The EBRP contains additional measures designed to facilitate the restructuring of enterprises, using the nine SOCBs as key agents of change (through "conciliation" procedures). Given the fundamental role to be assumed by the banks, the EBRP also aims to stimulate their efficiency, including (ultimately) privatization. A crucial outcome of the EBRP will be further movement from soft to hard budgets, in both the enterprise and banking sectors. However, the government has identified four sectors in which it wishes to retain ownership of selected enterprises in the medium term, where privatization will be decided on a case-by-case basis, in the next three years. These are the energy, mining, steel and defense sectors, which include about 300 enterprises, accounting for about 20 percent of industrial output. Otherwise, all enterprises are eligible for privatization as rapidly as possible.

Despite these changes, however, it is obvious that SOEs will continue to be major players in the Polish economy, at least in the medium term. In this context, there is encouraging evidence from a recent survey of 75 large state-owned manufacturing enterprises (Pinto, Belka, and Krajewski 1993; Hume and Pinto 1993). Contrary to negative stereotypes of SOEs as resistant to change and carrying on in a business-as-usual manner, the survey shows that even without privatization SOEs are adjusting, restructuring, and increasing profitability in response to the ETP. Of particular relevance is the finding that "all firms managed to reduce the consumption of materials and energy per unit of sales" (Hume and Pinto 1993, p. 19). Specifically, the 31 best companies reduced energy and material consumption by 22 percent between 1991 and 1992, and the remaining ones by approximately 17 percent (Hume and Pinto 1993).

Energy sector restructuring

As stated in the preceding section, energy is one of the sectors where the government wishes to retain ownership in the medium term. Therefore, restructuring efforts have so far focused more on commercialization of SOEs and the creation of an institutional, legal, and economic framework that will facilitate competition and greater private sector participation in the longer term.[27]

In the coal sector, the monopolistic Hard Coal Corporation was abolished in 1990 and replaced by the State Hard Coal Agency, an advisory and planning body, which is also supervising the planned closure of unprofitable mines. Around ten independent and competing companies are envisaged to handle production activities, with six or more in wholesale distribution (Poland, Ministry of Industry and Trade 1992; World Bank 1993b, Vol. 1). Operating subsidies to coal mines were abolished on April 1, 1992, except for those mines being closed, although loss-making continues at a high level. Given the fact that lignite is sold almost exclusively to the electric power industry, lignite mines are to be vertically integrated with the mine-mouth power plants to which they are attached, through one or more holding companies.

Efforts to introduce competition to the electric power sector started with the dissolution (in 1990) of the Power and Lignite Corporation, which controlled 106 enterprises; and creation of the Polish Power Grid Company (PPGC), along with 34 autonomous generating and 33 distributing companies. While these companies are all public, their monopoly power is much less. The PPGC handles electricity transmission, and is moving toward a more stringent system of merit order dispatching, to minimize system costs.

---

[27]The description of energy restructuring in this section serves to show the direction of change, and is based on available published sources. The Polish government is continuously reviewing the situation, and the actual numbers are likely to change periodically.

Under a restructuring program, prepared with the assistance of the Bank, it is proposed to reduce the number of generating companies to (a) four to five companies based on hard coal, nine to ten combined heating and power enterprises, and one to two integrated power-lignite companies. There would be 12–15 distribution companies. The PPGC would purchase power competitively from alternative generation sources and resell to the distribution companies, which would also be permitted to buy from industrial generators and small combined heat and power plants (Gula 1992).

In oil and gas, less progress has been made in restructuring, although the aim is to create two independent exploration and production companies from the existing Polish Oil and Gas Company (PGNG). These two companies would compete with foreign enterprises in the access to new oil and gas deposits. A single transmission company would be formed for gas, selling to six independent regional distribution entities. The state would retain a controlling interest in the distribution of petroleum products and in refining, although a strong private sector participation would be encouraged (Poland, Ministry of Industry and Trade 1992). Finally, district heating has traditionally been decentralized, with about fifty independent heating companies supplying heat to large and small towns. The largest heating systems could be based on a transmission company purchasing from several different suppliers and selling to different local distribution companies. Of course, as systems decrease in size, integration of transmission and distribution is likely to occur, and in the smallest systems, a single integrated company may be justifiable for production, transmission, and distribution (Poland, Ministry of Industry and Trade 1992).

The results of restructuring in the energy sector have so far been limited, with only three large power plants and two large district heating enterprises commercialized. Among other obstacles, workers fear large-scale layoffs, social pressures are exerted by miners,

foreign investors are apprehensive about future uncertainty (including environmental policy), and municipalities are reluctant to assume ownership of heat supply sources, given existing unprofitable conditions.

Energy pricing reform

Aside from the restructuring of enterprises and banking, a central component of the ETP was energy pricing reform, which gained momentum in the early part of 1990. As in the case of privatization, less successful earlier attempts had been made in 1988 and 1989. The benefits of these earlier attempts to raise energy prices were largely eroded by inflation and exchange rate depreciation: despite the doubling of energy prices in 1988, and further increases in 1989 (in nominal terms), the average energy price in Poland was barely one-third that of Western Europe at the end of 1989, and lower than Bulgaria, Czechoslovakia, and Hungary (Hughes 1991, Figure 10). However, major reforms in energy prices took place from the beginning of 1990 (Bates, Gupta, and Fiedor 1994, Figures 3–6).

After eliminating uniform national coal pricing and the subsidies on coal transport, in 1990, coal prices (ex mine) rose from under US$6 per metric ton of coal equivalent (tce) (at the end of 1989) to US$37 per tce (in May 1991). Some erosion took place thereafter, but coal prices (ex mine) were still at US$33 per tce in January 1992, in line with export parity, allowing for local transport and other costs; further price increases brought coal to US$45 per metric ton a year later. In the gas sector, delivered prices to industry and residential consumers (in U.S. dollar equivalent), increased by factors of 3 and 46, respectively, from the end of 1989 to the beginning of 1992. They stood at US$0.12/m^3 and US$0.18/m^3, respectively, on February 1, 1993. Although still lower than Western

European levels,[28] they demonstrate that substantial progress in energy pricing reform had occurred over a thirty-seven-month period. Similar large price increases were implemented for electricity—by factors of 3.5 for industry and 12 for households, in U.S. dollar equivalent, from the end of 1989 to the beginning of 1992. In US$/kWh, they rose from roughly US$0.01 to US$0.04 for industry, and from US$0.005 to US$0.06 for residential consumers between December 1989 and February 1, 1993. Again, however, these were below the corresponding average Western European prices.[29]

Following a history of heavy subsidies, district heat prices for residential consumers were doubled in February 1991; increases, of 60 percent and 84 percent respectively, occurred in August 1991 and January 1992. Subsequent increases raised the price paid by residential consumers to US$5.66 per gigajoule (GJ) by July 1993, compared with US$0.51/GJ only three years earlier, cutting subsidies to 35 percent. Finally, the prices of liquid fuels have been raised to cover production costs, although the values (US$0.45 per liter for gasoline and US$0.32 per liter for diesel oil at the beginning of 1992) were very low by Western European standards, due to the relatively low tax component (Poland, Ministry of Industry and Trade 1992, p. 135).

The above comparisons between energy prices in Poland and in Western Europe are intended to be indicative, since cost differences can be expected between countries and between consumer categories, according to the particular supply and demand characteristics. Reliable data on the economic costs of energy supply in Poland are not easy to obtain, but information from Bates, Cofala, and Toman (1994) tends to confirm that there is room for further price increases.[30] Nevertheless, the achievements so far should not be underestimated: as a crude indication of the priority attached to reforms in energy pricing, it can be noted that the share of household expenditures on fuel and power increased from 1.7 percent in 1989 to 8 percent in the first half of 1992, while the food share fell from 45.8 percent to 39.1 percent, and the share of clothing and footwear fell from 16.9 percent to 8.1 percent over the same period (Bates, Gupta, and Fiedor 1994, p. 18). The index of aggregate expenditures more than doubled from 1990 to the first half of 1992, but the component of the index related to fuel, heat, and electricity went up nearly six times (Bates, Gupta, and Fiedor 1994, Table 26).

The impact of restructuring and energy pricing reform

While these profound changes in economic policy are already in train, and beneficial results discernible, the timing and speed of further change are matters of considerable uncertainty in Poland, as in the other economies in transition. The effects of decades of central planning will take years to attenuate. However, we have developed scenarios to obtain quantitative indications of the orders of magnitude of the impact of economic policy change on the environment (Bates, Cofala, and Toman 1994). By comparing the results of these scenarios, which we term the IBRD simulations, with other work, reasonable conclusions about likely changes in the future

---

[28]For example, natural gas prices for households in Poland were substantially below those in France, Ireland, Switzerland, and the United Kingdom in the first quarter of 1993. Polish industrial prices were also lower, except in the case of the United Kingdom, where they were comparable (IEA 1993, Part D, Tables 10 and 12).

[29]Polish electricity prices for industry and households were 50 percent or more below those in Denmark, Germany, Italy, Portugal, and Switzerland in the first quarter of 1993 (IEA 1993, Part D, Tables 8 and 9).

---

[30]Table A1.4 in Bates, Cofala, and Toman (1994), which calculates fuel prices to final energy consumers, on the assumption that prices fully cover economic costs from 1995 onwards, is the basis for this conclusion.

environmental situation can be drawn.

The IBRD simulations use projections of GDP and its breakdown by energy-using activity to find a time-path of final energy demands and a least-cost solution to satisfy those demands. The dynamic optimization part of the model is carried out using multiperiod linear programming (LP). The decision variables in the LP analysis include new plant investments and fuel choices (e.g., coals of different grades, as well as coal washing). More than seventy technologies and twenty-two primary energy types are covered in the framework, including energy imports and exports. Projections are carried out at five-year intervals from 1995 to 2015, inclusive. The LP objective function gives us the total cost of meeting final energy demands. A key assumption underlying the model is that energy prices in Poland fully reflect economic costs by 1995, which is plausible in view of the progress already made (see the subsection, *Energy pricing reform*).

The model's projections of GDP growth are in line with those recently prepared by the World Bank (World Bank 1993c). Following the drop that occurred during 1989–91, GDP is expected to continue growing in 1993 and 1994 to a level about 5 percent above the 1990 level by 1995; the growth rate reaches 4.5 percent per annum (p.a.) in the period 1996–2000, and tapers off to 4 percent p.a. after 2000. On that basis, GDP reattains the 1988 level by 1997 and doubles from the 1990 level soon after 2010. Higher living standards, along with market reforms, cause a steady reduction of the share of industry in GDP from 46 percent in 1990 to 40 percent by 2010, a ratio which is more in line with the developed countries of Western Europe. The shares of agriculture and construction also decline after 1990, but there are increases in the shares of transport and (especially) services (Bates, Gupta, and Fiedor 1994, Table 27), as would be expected in an economy in transition toward a market-oriented framework. Within the industrial component of

GDP, the production of the energy sector itself and that of certain heavy energy users, such as pig iron and steel, decline in absolute terms after 1990, while the production of most other energy-intensive intermediate products diminishes in relative terms (copper, aluminum, sulfur, ammonia, and cement). Freight and passenger transport, along with housing, naturally increases with population and economic growth (Bates, Gupta, and Fiedor 1994, Table 28). Furthermore, driven by higher energy prices and competition, energy consumption per unit of value added falls across all the productive sectors (industry, construction, agriculture, and transport). However, per capita energy consumption in the residential sector is expected to increase due to higher per capita needs, including an expansion in space heating (Bates, Gupta, and Fiedor 1994, Table 29).

These changes in the level and structure of GDP, and in economic activity and energy intensity at the sectoral level, are based upon a mixture of analysis and judgement, using the views of Polish sectoral experts, in combination with past experience, both in Poland and other countries. They result in the aggregate primary energy demands and energy intensities shown in Table 5-5. It is noticeable that the sharp drop in the share of hard coal and lignite—from a combined 76.9 percent in 1988 to 68.5 percent in 2000 and 63.8 percent in 2010—is offset mainly by increasing use of natural gas and oil. Although GDP in 2000 is 17 percent above the 1988 level, total primary energy consumption actually falls. Hence, energy intensity drops by nearly 20 percent. By 2010, energy intensity is only 63 percent of the 1988 figure. In line with the experience in OECD countries, electricity consumption increases more rapidly than energy consumption overall, so that the decrease in the intensity of electricity consumption is less than that of aggregate energy.

We have also calculated in Table 5-5 emissions of PM, SO_2, NO_x, and CO_2 that are implied by the above scenarios, on the assumption that no new environmental policies are put into place. However, we have allowed for some improvements in the transport sector, as new diesel vehicles are purchased, with emissions comparable to Western European standards. The decline in the total emissions of SO_2, NO_x, and (especially) PM are striking, in view of the increase in real income over the period. Only CO_2 emissions increase in total. However, emissions per unit of GDP fall in all cases, the most dramatic being those of PM, which are cut to below 60 percent of the 1988 level by 2000.

We compare the results obtained in the IBRD simulations first with those in the report produced recently by the Polish Ministry of Industry and Trade (MIT), using essentially the same methodology (Poland, Ministry of Industry and Trade 1992). While the latter are not regarded as official government forecasts, they observed, as closely as possible, official data and known government policies. The MIT report incorporates a High and a Low Scenario for GDP growth, reflecting annual growth rates of 4.2 percent and 2.3 percent, respectively. These growth rates imply levels of GDP in 2010 which are, respectively, 17 percent higher and 24 percent lower than the one we have used, thus providing a useful range about our estimate for comparison purposes. In the MIT Scenarios, economic restructuring and energy price increases cause improvements in energy efficiency, and the shares of industry, construction and agriculture in GDP decline to values which are comparable to ours, while those of transport and services also rise (Bates, Gupta, and Fiedor 1994, Table 32). Within the industrial sector, the MIT results again parallel ours, with falling or stationary shares for heavy energy users—such as iron and steel, chemicals, and nonferrous metals—as well as the energy sector itself. As in our scenarios, economic restructuring and energy price increases lead to declines in energy intensity for the economy as a whole, by about the same order of magnitude (Table 5-6); and energy consumption per

capita in the residential sector increases. While, in the High Scenario of the MIT report, the overall intensity of the economy also falls less with respect to electricity consumption than with respect to energy as a whole, electricity intensity of GDP rises in the Low Scenario, in contrast to our results (Table 5-6).

Of particular interest are the MIT results for primary energy demands and emissions, under the assumption of no new environmental controls (Table 5-6). The combined hard coal and lignite share of primary energy demand in 2010 is 62–63 percent, almost the same as our result. Emissions of PM (1.3 million metric tons), SO_2 (3.5–3.8 million metric tons), NO_x (1.3–1.6 million metric tons) and CO_2 (430–510 million metric tons) are all very close to the results obtained in Table 5-5.

Another set of simulations was conducted by the IBRD staff in the course of preparing an environmental action plan (EAP) for Central and Eastern Europe (EAP 1993). The results were submitted to the ministerial conference which took place in Switzerland, in April 1993. The EAP methodology, however, is quite different. Instead of a dynamic LP approach, the simulations are based on an input-output framework, using forty-eight-sector input-output tables for each country for various years. There are different input-output coefficients for new and old capital stock. The former are assumed to be the same as those prevailing in Western Europe in the mid-1980s and do not change. On the other hand, the coefficients for old capital stock change in response to increases in efficiency, and to changes in relative prices.

Five scenarios are examined in the study. Of these, the first three illustrate the impact of differences in the nature and speed of economic reform on the environment. The last two examine the impact of more stringent environmental policies (as compared with the Base Case). Only the first three EAP scenarios are discussed here, as both the IBRD and MIT simulations that we presented above, which assume no new environmental policies, are put into place. The three EAP scenarios are (a) the Base Case, which presupposes a reasonably comprehensive price and enterprise reform program; (b) Slow/Delayed Reform, which assumes that pricing and other market reforms are delayed until 1995/96; and (c) Accelerated Reform, where the "government presses ahead with radical economic reforms and strict enforcement of hard budget constraints for enterprises" (EAP 1993, Annex 5, p. 1). In practice, this implies different adjustment periods for the input-output coefficients associated with old capital stock. Thus, in the Base Case, improvements in efficiency and the adjustment of energy and other inputs per unit of output produced using old capital are phased over a period of ten years. Under the Slow and Accelerated Reform scenarios, this adjustment period is twenty years and five years, respectively, and the latter scenario assumes that 20 percent of the old capital stock is scrapped by 1995, as enterprises contract or shut down. In addition, under the Slow/Delayed Reform scenario, it is assumed that new investment has (input-output) coefficients based on typical Soviet technology rather than Western technology.

Like the IBRD simulations, the projections of GDP growth in the EAP scenarios follow current World Bank estimates up to 1995. Projections of primary energy demand, electricity consumption, and energy intensity for the three scenarios are shown in Table 5-7. Note the sharp drop in the share of coal in primary energy by 2010. This drop, however, occurs after 2000, unlike in the IBRD and MIT simulations. The other notable change is a marked increase in the share of natural gas in the demand for primary energy to approximately 30 percent by 2010. The substitution of (clean burning) natural gas for coal in the EAP scenarios, occurs against a backdrop of declining energy intensity of GDP.[31] It is not surpris

ing then that emissions of PM, SO_2, NO_x, and CO_2 (Table 5-7), are all much lower than in the MIT and IBRD simulations (as discussed below).

To conclude, all three simulations point to clear environmental gains from restructuring, combined with energy pricing reform, although we have not attempted to estimate the relative impact of each component. The robustness of the results is evident from the data in Tables 5-5, 5-6, and 5-7, in terms of the four major types of emissions (SO_2, NO_x, PM, and CO_2) across the simulations. The reductions in emissions are greatest for the EAP simulations for all pollutants.[32] Comparing across emissions, it is reassuring to note that the biggest drop occurs for particulates, which have the worst effect on health.[33] While the reductions are not as dramatic for the other pollutants, it should be kept in mind that GDP increases by 1.5 to 2 times over the same period, implying a significant decline in emissions per unit of GDP (see, for instance, the results for IBRD simulations in Table 5-5).

The impact of changes in environmental policy

In the subsection, *Environmental policy in Poland*, we argued that, while Poland had an elaborate system of pollution taxes on paper, its implementation left much to be desired. Further, we also stated that the efficacy of financial instruments itself was questionable,

---

Scenario).

[32]This is mainly due to a sharp increase in the share of natural gas in primary energy demand and a big decline in energy intensity in the EAP simulations. In fact, of all three simulations, the decrease in energy intensity is greatest for the Base Case in the EAP simulations. This, in turn, is due to the fact that 20 percent of the old capital stock is scrapped and replaced by new capital by 2000 (in the EAP Base Case).

[33]"Particulates in the air (soot, dust, metal dust) are thought to be the most serious type of pollution, both with regard to health impacts as well as economic costs" (World Bank 1992, p. iii).

---

[31]In fact, as discussed below, EAP energy intensity projections show a sharper drop, compared to the IBRD and MIT simulations (except under the Slow Reform

given the incentive structure that prevailed. In light of the ETP, however, and all that it implies for firm-level behavior, it is logical to expect greater responsiveness to these instruments in the future.

In May 1991, the Polish government issued the National Environmental Policy of Poland (NEPP) (Ministry of Environmental Protection, Natural Resources and Forestry 1990), indicating its environmental goals and priorities, and the direction that environmental policy would take in Poland. In particular, "the greatest possible advantage will be taken of market mechanisms" (NEPP 1990, p. 4) and the medium-term goal is to follow environmental policies that "enable Poland to move closer to European environmental standards and allow it to join the EEC" (NEPP 1990, p. 12). With regard to air quality, a noticeable reduction in the emissions of particulates and gases was identified as a short-term priority. Specific medium-term goals include, inter alia, a reduction of SO_2 emissions by 30 percent, NO_x emissions by 10 percent, and PM emissions by 50 percent (implying an increase in removal efficiency for large stationary sources from 92 percent to 96 percent) by the year 2000 (compared with 1980 levels). Thus, the goal is to reduce SO_2 emissions from 4.2 million metric tons per year (mt/year) to 2.9 mt/year, NO_x emissions from 1.5 mt/year to 1.3–1.4 mt/year (NEPP 1990, p. 13), and PM emissions from 2.82 mt/year to 1.41 mt/year.[34]

From Tables 5-5 and 5-6, it is clear that under the IBRD and MIT simulations, the medium-term goal for SO_2 emissions will not be met. While the IBRD, MIT (Low), and EAP simulations achieve the goal for NO_x emissions (Tables 5-5, 5-6, and 5-7), the assumptions in the IBRD and MIT simulations should be kept in mind. In both, though no new environmental policies are employed, it is

[34]Actual emissions of particulates in 1980 are not stated in NEPP, but they are shown as 2.82 mt/year in the MIT Report.

assumed that after 1995, new diesel engines in the transport sector will have 20 percent lower unit emissions of NO_x. For particulates, while there is a substantial decline in emissions in all three simulations, as in the case of SO_2 emissions, only the EAP simulations meet the NEPP target. The IBRD simulations come close, with PM emissions at approximately 1.46 mt in 2000 (Table 5-5), but the MIT simulations fall short, at 1.6 mt (Table 5-6).

It should also be emphasized that the simulation results with respect to emission levels are based on a number of assumptions, all of which may not come true. For instance, under the Base Case EAP scenario, 20 percent of the capital stock is replaced by the year 2000. It could be argued that this is too optimistic. Thus, in addition to restructuring and energy pricing reform, Poland will need to go further and deal with air pollution through a stronger environmental policy, if it is to achieve its medium- and long-term environmental goals.

In this context, the sharp increases in nominal and real levels of fees from 1990 to 1993 are steps in the right direction (Tables 5-8 and 5-9). According to Zylicz (1993), the current sulfur dioxide rate ($75/metric ton) is "higher than almost anywhere in the world" (p. 13). At the same time, however, he concedes that the SO_2 fee is still lower than the marginal cost of a 30 percent reduction, estimated at approximately $600 per metric ton. In light of the IBRD simulations, even larger increases in fees are necessary to attain plausible emissions objectives for Poland in the longer term (Table 5-9). The need for increases in NO_x charges (from US$75/metric ton to US$2,700/metric ton by 2010) is particularly great, due to the high unit cost of controlling NO_x. Although PM and SO_2 fees also might have to be subject to significant increases, by factors of 10–20 (to around US$700/metric ton by 2010). As a matter of interest, the calculated NO_x tax of over US$1,000/metric ton in 2000, translates into taxes of approximately US$0.056/liter on diesel fuel and US$0.025/liter on gasoline.

An indication of future developments in environmental policy is also provided in the government's February 1990 Ordinance on the Protection of Air Against Pollution, which contains plant-level performance standards for new and existing large stationary sources (expressed in emissions per unit fuel input). Existing stationary sources refer to plants started after the Ordinance and completed after 1994. New source standards are effective from 1995. Existing sources must meet weaker interim standards until 1998, after which the standards are tightened, but are still less stringent than the new source standards. Note that since these are plant-level standards, it may still be possible to treat the plant as a bubble and trade off intraplant emissions. Another important point to note is that the Ordinance does not specify how these standards are to be met. For instance, there is no stipulation that best available technology (BAT) is to be used. Thus, some flexibility for the polluters is already built into the regulations.

It is obvious that the 1990 regulations will further reduce emissions in addition to what will be achieved through enterprise and price reform. The IBRD simulations, discussed earlier, tried to quantify the impact of these regulations on emissions, using a CAC scenario.[35] CAC, however, as specified, also includes a number of regulations for the household and transport sectors which, while plausible, have not yet been incorporated in Polish environmental policy, namely, a ban on urban coal use by households and mandatory catalytic converters for all cars. These restrictions are supposed to be 50 percent effective by 2000 and fully operational by 2005. Further, CAC assumes an additional 30 percent reduction in heavy-duty diesel engine emissions, and a 75 percent decline in the sulfur content of diesel oil (from 0.6 percent to 0.15 percent) after 2000. The results for CAC are shown in Bates, Cofala, and Toman (1994), Tables A2.4 and A2.5, from which it will be noted that coal demand under CAC is about 4 percent lower than in the Base Case, while gas demand is about 8 percent higher. As expected, environmental standards make a switch toward lower-emitting fuel more attractive. Figures 5-2 and 5-3 bring together the salient information for emissions of SO_2, NO_x, PM, and CO_2. The actual data for 1988 and 1990 are also included, as well as the Base Case as a benchmark. Substitution away from coal causes a large drop in SO_2, NO_x, PM, and CO_2 emissions as compared with the Base Case.

The costs of these improvements, however, are high. The net present value of costs from 1990–2015, at a real discount rate of 12 percent, amounts to over US$12 billion, comprising increased cost of energy conversion and emission reduction, loss of producer surplus, the cost imposed on final energy demand in the household and transport sectors, and loss of consumer surplus from reduced final energy demand.[36] Of these costs, large point source controls and loss of producer surplus account for more than half, whereas transport controls contribute less than half of the total. The loss in consumer surplus and the cost of alterations in final energy demand by households are negligible. As Table 5-10 shows, however, unit costs of reducing emissions vary considerably between stationary and transport controls, and also across different options within the latter category. Thus, while low-NO_x diesel engines appear to be cost-effective methods for emission reduction, catalytic converters and diesel oil desulfurization are very expensive. It does not follow, however, that these transport controls should be avoided. To make that judgment, we need information on the benefits as well.

Despite the difficulties inherent in the IBRD simulations, one result emerges clearly:

---

[35]The scenario discussed earlier was the Base Case, where no new environmental policies are put into place.

[36]For details, see Bates, Cofala, and Toman (1994), Chapters 2 and 3.

given the magnitude of costs required to meet environmental objectives, and the substantial competing claims for limited resources in an economy in transition, such as Poland, there is a potentially important role for the application of economic instruments to air pollution control. Notably, the IBRD simulations estimate that replacing CAC regulations by a uniform emissions tax on all sources, which yields the same total emissions as CAC, could cut control costs by as much as one-half, although the result requires the extension of incentive-based policies to decentralized sources. Nevertheless, even with limited application of economic incentives to large stationary sources, the cost savings are not trivial.

Table 5-1: Energy Intensity of National Income for Selected Countries (national income estimated according to purchasing power parity)

Country	Energy intensity in kgoe/US$000 (1975 prices)			Average yearly decline (%)	
	1960	*1975*	*1986*	*1960–73*	*1973–86*
Poland	1,796	1,237	1,136	2.83	0.65
France	468	460	337	0.13	2.33
United Kingdom	745	557	490	2.21	0.97
Czechoslovakia	1,602	1,146	902	2.53	1.82
German Democratic Republic	2,019	1,495	1,055	2.29	2.64
Developed Western countries	540	513	418	0.40	1.57
CMEA countries	1,545	1,212	1,014	1.85	1.37

CMEA = Council of Mutual Economic Assistance.

kgoe = kilograms of oil equivalent.

Source: Bates, Gupta, and Fiedor (1994), Table 1.

Table 5-2: Energy Intensity Relative to OECD for Selected CEE Countries, 1988

	Energy use per unit of GNP; OECD = 1	
	Total	*Oil and gas*
Bulgaria	2.2	1.7
CSFR	1.9	1.0
Hungary	1.3	1.3
Poland	**1.9**	**0.6**
Romania	2.5	2.9
U.S.S.R.	2.7	3.1
CEE5	2.0	1.3
All CEE	2.5	2.6

CEE5 = Bulgaria, CSFR, Hungary, Poland, and Romania.
CSFR = Czech and Slovak Federal Republic.
Source: OECD (1990), Table 20, and OECD (1992).

Table 5-3: Poland: Composition of Estimated Particulate Emissions (percent)

	1975	*1980*	*1985*	*1989*	*1991*
Energy	41.9	50.2	53.6	53.3	55.2
Metallurgical	12.5	12.2	13.2	9.8	8.4
Chemical	11.4	10.7	11.6	11.4	9.3
Mineral	24.4	18.7	11.1	9.1	7.6
Subtotal	**90.2**	**91.8**	**89.5**	**83.6**	**80.5**
All industry	100.0	100.0	100.0	100.0	100.0

Source: Bates, Gupta, and Fiedor (1994), Table 20.

Table 5-4: Poland: Composition of Estimated SO_2 Emissions (percent)

	1975	*1980*	*1985*	*1989*	*1991*
Energy	69.5	72.5	76.8	74.0	78.1
Metallurgical	10.6	12.5	7.3	5.0	4.6
Chemical	9.5	6.9	6.2	5.2	4.9
Mineral	3.2	1.8	1.2	1.5	1.3
Subtotal	**92.8**	**93.7**	**91.5**	**85.7**	**88.9**
All industry	100.0	100.0	100.0	100.0	100.0

Source: Bates, Gupta, and Fiedor (1994), Table 21.

Table 5-5: IBRD Simulations: Scenarios for Energy Demand, Energy Intensities, and Emissions

	1988	1990	2000	2010
Primary energy demand (PJ)	5,387	4,223	5,071	5,848
Fuel shares (%)	65.9	61.1	58.4	55.1
– Hard coal	11.0	13.4	10.1	8.7
– Lignite	7.5	8.9	11.2	12.9
– Natural gas	13.7	15.3	17.3	18.8
– Oil	1.9	1.4	3.0	4.5
– Other				
Gross electricity consumption (TWh)	146	133	173	230
Energy intensity of GDP (1988=100)	100	89	81	63
Electricity intensity of GDP (1988=100)	100	102	100	92
SO_2 – total	3,827	2,832	3,192	3,575
– per unit of GDP ('000 metric tons per billion Zl)	5.587	4.666	4.000	3.027
NO_x – total	1,363	1,187	1,179	1,321
– per unit of GDP ('000 metric tons per billion Zl)	1.990	1.956	1.477	1.119
PM – total	2,145	1,468	1,463	1,211
– per unit of GDP ('000 metric tons per billion Zl)	3.131	2.419	1.833	1.025
CO_2 – total (million metric tons)	454	364	432	490
– per unit of GDP ('000 metric tons per billion Zl)	663	600	541	415

PJ = petajoule.

TWh = terawatt-hour.

Source: Bates, Cofala, and Toman (1994), Tables A2.1 and A2.3.

Table 5-6: MIT Scenarios for Energy Demand, Energy Intensities, and Emissions

	High		Low	
	2000	*2010*	*2000*	*2010*
Primary energy demand (PJ)	5,327	6,143	4,783	5,192
Fuel shares (%)				
– Hard coal	59.3	55.0	56.8	52.0
– Lignite	9.6	8.3	10.7	9.9
– Natural gas	12.0	13.7	11.0	13.1
– Oil	16.1	18.0	18.6	20.2
– Other	3.0	5.0	3.0	4.8
Gross electricity consumption (TWh)	186	246	161	203
Energy intensity of GDP (1988=100)	76	59	93	72
Electricity intensity of GDP (1988=100)	97	86	114	103
Emissions (thousands of tons)				
SO_2	3,460	3,800	3,290	3,510
NO_x	1,380	1,550	1,220	1,280
PM	1,630	1,290	1,600	1,310
CO_2 (millions of tons)	455	510	405	429

PJ = petajoule.

TWh = terawatt-hour.

Source: Poland (1992b).

Table 5-7: EAP Scenarios for Energy Demand, Energy Intensities, and Emissions

	Base case		Fast reform		Slow reform	
	2000	*2010*	*2000*	*2010*	*2000*	*2010*
Primary energy demand (PJ)	2,474	3,528	2,433	4,364	3,231	4,531
Fuel shares (%)						
– Coal	72.0	54.2	71.6	56.8	75.6	62.1
– Natural gas	13.9	32.1	14.0	28.7	11.8	26.7
– Oil	14.1	13.7	14.4	14.5	12.6	11.2
– Other	0.0	0.0	0.0	0.0	0.0	0.0
Electricity consumption (TWh)	99.2	177.5	97.6	223.6	127.9	215.5
Energy intensity of GDP (1988=100)	57.3	52.6	49.2	47.0	90.4	89.9
Emissions (thousands of metric tons)						
SO_2	1,381	1,469	1,352	1,880	1,838	2,022
NO_x	633	901	625	1,119	823	1,156
PM	821	574	813	858	1,121	891
CO_2 (millions of metric tons)	232	308	230	390	308	411

PJ = petajoule.
TWh = terawatt-hour.
Source: EAP (1993) and Gordon Hughes (1993).

Table 5-8: Poland: Increases in Nominal Emissions Fees (Zl/kg)

	1990	*1992*
SO_2	4.80	1,100
NO_x	4.80	1,100
CO_2	0.90	300
Aromatic hydrocarbons	48.00	3,000
Lead	960.00	500,000

Source: Bates, Gupta, and Fiedor (1994), Table 39.

Table 5-9: Poland: Increases in Real Emissions Fees—Actual and IBRD Simulations (US$/metric ton)

	End of 1990	April 1993	1995	2000	2010
SO_2	28	75	430	541	780
NO_x	28	75	542	1,029	2,716
PM	7	38	176	640	640

Source: Bates, Cofala, and Toman (1994), Table 5.4.

Table 5-10: Poland: Costs of Emission Control Measures for Large Stationary and Transport Sources

Measure	Pollutant reduced	Unit cost (US$/metric ton)
Car catalytic converters	NO_x	9,700
Low emission diesel engines	NO_x	810
Diesel oil desulfurization	SO_2	4,000
Selective catalytic reduction, new power plant	NO_x	1,800–2,000[a]
Desulfurization, new hard coal power plant	SO_2	510

a. Approximately 35 percent higher for a combined heat and power plant.
Source: Bates, Cofala, and Toman (1994), Table A2.12.

Figure 5-1: Poland: Energy Sector Balance

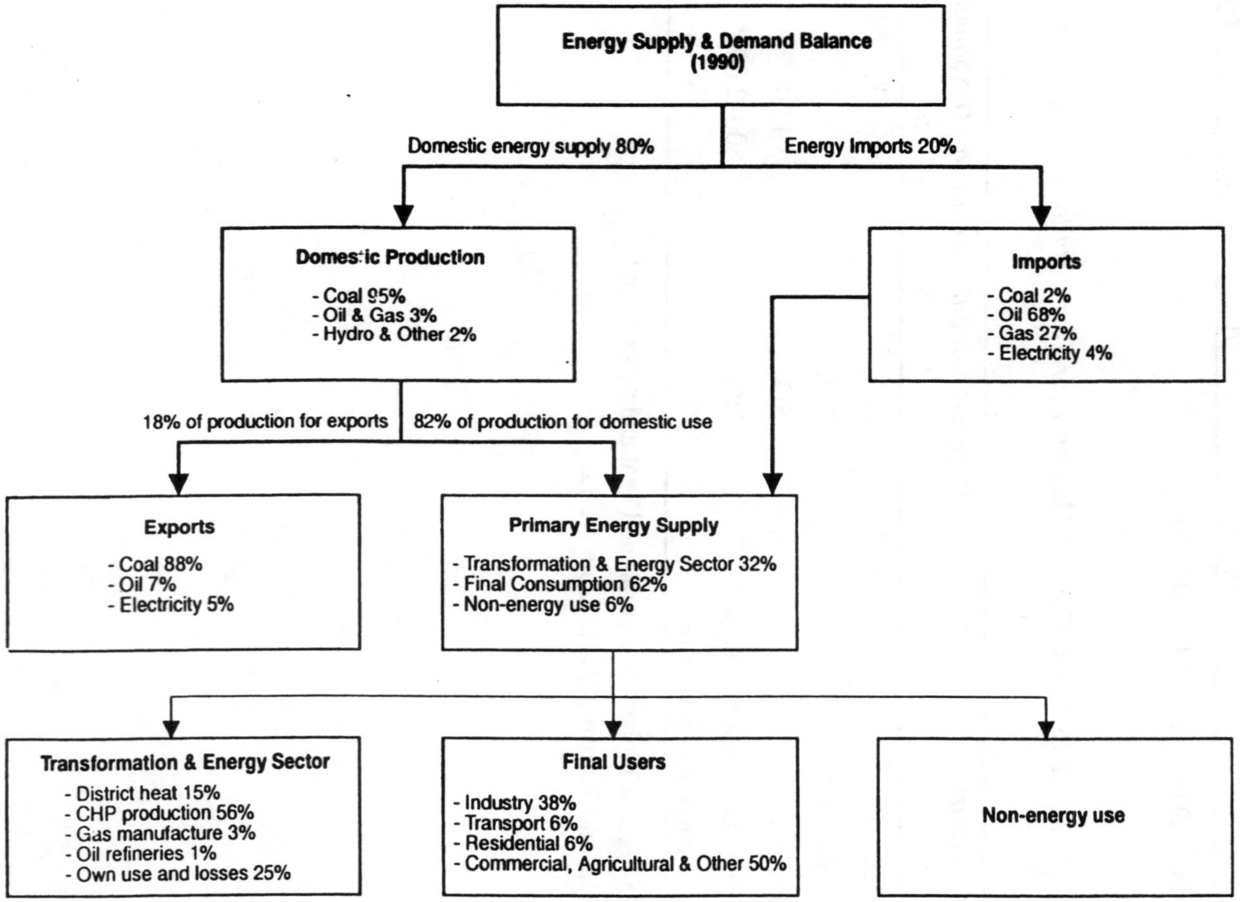

Energy Supply & Demand Balance (1990)

Energy Imports 20%

Domestic energy supply 80%

Imports
- Coal 2%
- Oil 68%
- Gas 27%
- Electricity 4%

Domestic Production
- Coal 95%
- Oil & Gas 3%
- Hydro & Other 2%

82% of production for domestic use

18% of production for exports

Primary Energy Supply
- Transformation & Energy Sector 32%
- Final Consumption 62%
- Non-energy use 6%

Exports
- Coal 88%
- Oil 7%
- Electricity 5%

Non-energy use

Final Users
- Industry 38%
- Transport 6%
- Residential 6%
- Commercial, Agricultural & Other 50%

Transformation & Energy Sector
- District heat 15%
- CHP production 56%
- Gas manufacture 3%
- Oil refineries 1%
- Own use and losses 25%

Source: World Bank (1993b).

Figure 5-2: Emissions under Base Case and CAC Scenarios (IBRD simulations)

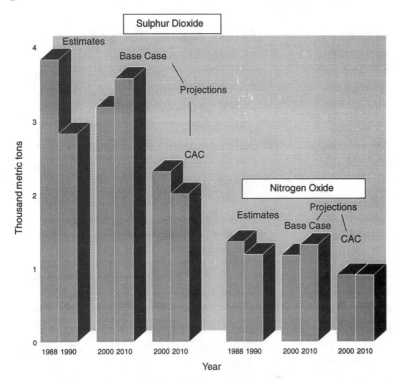

Source: Bates, Cofala, and Toman (1994).

Figure 5-3: Emissions under Base Case and CAC Scenarios (IBRD simulations)

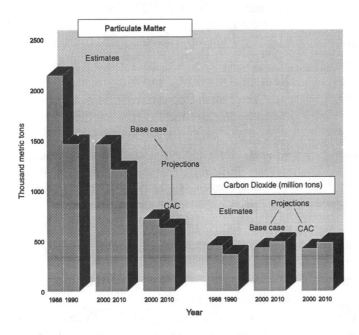

Source: Bates, Cofala, and Toman (1994).

Bibliography

Bates, Robin W. 1993. "The Impact of Economic Policy on Energy and the Environment in Developing Countries." *Annual Review of Energy and the Environment* 18:479–506.

Bates, Robin W., Janusz Cofala, and Michael Toman. 1994. *Alternative Policies for the Control of Air Pollution in Poland.* World Bank Environment Paper, Number 7.

Bates, Robin W., Shreekant Gupta, and Boguslaw Fiedor. 1994. "Economywide Policies and the Environment: A Case Study of Poland." World Bank, Environment Department, Working Paper No. 63.

Bates, Robin W., and Edwin A. Moore. 1992. "Commercial Energy Efficiency and the Environment." World Bank, Policy Research Department, WPS 972.

Bergson, Abram. 1987. "Comparative Productivity: U.S.S.R., Eastern Europe, and the West." *American Economic Review* 77(3):342–57.

British Petroleum Company p.l.c. 1992. *BP Statistical Review of World Energy.* London.

Environmental Action Programme for Central and Eastern Europe (EAP). 1993. Document submitted to the Ministerial Conference, Lucerne, Switzerland, April 28–30, 1993.

Fallenbuchl, Zbigniew. 1977. "The Polish Economy in the 1970s." In *East European Economies Post-Helsinki.* Comp. of Papers, Joint Economic Committee, U.S. Congress. Washington, D.C.: U.S. Government Printing Office.

Gomulka, Stanislaw, and Jacek Rostowski. 1988. "An International Comparison of Material Intensity." *Journal of Comparative Economics* 12:475–501.

Gorka, Kazimierz. 1991. "Changes in the Environmental Protection Policy of Poland." In Kazimierz Gorka (ed.), *Environmental and Economic Aspects of the Industrial Development in Poland: Selected Papers.* Krakow: The Krakow Academy of Sciences.

Gula, A. 1992. "Energy Policy in Poland: a Focus on Institutional Changes and Energy Efficiency." *Revue de l'énergie* 444 (December).

Hughes, Gordon A. 1990. "Energy Policy and the Environment in Poland." *European Economy* 43 (March):151–67.

———. 1991. "The Energy Sector and Problems of Energy Policy in Eastern Europe." *Oxford Review of Economic Policy* 7(2):77–98.

———. 1993. Personal communication at the World Bank.

Hume, Ian M., and Brian Pinto. 1993. "Prejudice and Fact in Poland's Industrial Transformation." *Finance and Development* (June).

International Energy Agency (IEA). 1990. "Energy Policies: Poland. 1990 Survey." Paris: OECD.

———. 1992. "Energy Statistics and Balances of Non-OECD Countries." Paris: OECD.

———. 1993. "Energy Prices and Taxes, First Quarter 1993." Paris: OECD.

Kemme, David M., and Keith Crane. 1984. "The Polish Economic Collapse: Contributing Factors and Economic Costs." *Journal of Comparative Economics* 8:25–40.

Kharas, Homi J. 1991. "Restructuring Socialist Industry: Poland's Experience in 1990." World Bank Discussion Paper No. 142.

Kornai, Janos. 1980. *Economics of Shortage.* Two volumes. Amsterdam: North-Holland.

———. 1986. "The Soft Budget Constraint." *Kyklos* 39(1):3–30.

———. 1992. *The Socialist System: The Political Economy of Communism.* Princeton, N.J.: Princeton University Press.

Lipton, D., and J. Sachs. 1990. "Privatization in Eastern Europe: The Case of Poland."

Brookings Papers on Economic Activity 2:293–341.

Marrese, Michael, and Janet L. Mitchell. 1984. "Kornai's Resource-Constrained Economy: A Survey and an Appraisal." *Journal of Comparative Economics* 8:74–84.

Milanovic, Branko. 1989. *Liberalization and Entrepreneurship. Dynamics of Reform in Socialism and Capitalism.* Armonk and London: Sharpe.

Ministry of Environmental Protection, Natural Resources and Forestry. 1990. "National Environmental Policy of Poland (NEPP)." November.

Moroney, John R. 1990. "Energy Consumption, Capital and Real Output: A Comparison of Market and Planned Economies." *Journal of Comparative Economics* 14:199–220.

Nowicki, Maciej. 1993. *Environment in Poland: Issues and Solutions.* Dordrecht, the Netherlands; Boston and London: Kluwer.

Organisation for Economic Co-operation and Development (OECD). 1990. *OECD Economic Outlook* 48 (December). Paris: OECD.

———. 1992. *Reforming the Economies of Central and Eastern Europe.* Paris: OECD.

Pinto, Brian, Marek Belka, and Stefan Krajewski. 1993. "Transforming State Enterprises in Poland: Microeconomic Evidence on Adjustment." World Bank, Policy Research Working Paper Series No. 1101.

Poland, Ministry of Environmental Protection, Natural Resources and Forestry. 1992. *Poland's Environmental Investment Expenditures in 1991 and Their Trends Since 1988.* Unpublished.

Poland, Ministry of Industry and Trade. 1992. *Energy Policy of Poland and the Draft Programme to the Year 2010.* Warsaw, November.

Slama, Jiri. 1986. "An International Comparison of Sulphur Dioxide Emissions." *Jour-*nal of Comparative Economics 10:277–92.

Syzdlo, S. 1990. "The Average Wage Level in Coal Mining and its Consequences for the National Economy." In *Rachunek Ekonomiczny w Gospodarce Surowcami Mineralnymi.* Krakow: Polish Academy of Sciences, pp. 270–82.

Umer, A. 1993. Personal communication. Polish Academy of Sciences.

United Nations Environment Programme (UNEP). 1992. *Saving Our Planet: Challenges and Hopes.* Nairobi.

U.S. Energy Information Administration (EIA). 1990. *Annual Prospects for World Coal Trade 1990.* DOE/EIA-0363(90). Washington D.C.: U.S. Government Printing Office.

Wilczynski, Piotr. 1990. "Environmental Management in Centrally Planned Non-Market Economies of Eastern Europe." World Bank, Environment Department, Working Paper No. 35.

World Bank. 1991. "Poland: Energy Market Development." Report No. 8224–POL.

———. 1992. "Poland: Environmental Strategy." Report No. 9808–POL.

———. 1993a. "Poland—Cogeneration Privatization Project." Staff Appraisal Report No. 11353–POL (Annex 2–3), March 1.

———. 1993b. "Poland: Energy Sector Restructuring Program." Five volumes. Report No. 153/93, Industry and Energy Department, Energy Sector Management Assistance Program (ESMAP).

———. 1993c. "The Report and Recommendation of the President of the International Bank for Reconstruction and Development to the Executive Directors on a Proposed Enterprise and Financial Sector Adjustment Loan in an Amount Equivalent to US$450 million to the Republic of Poland." Report No. P-5940-POL, April 8.

———. 1994. *Poland: Policies for Growth with Equity.* A World Bank Country Study.

World Resources Institute (WRI). 1992. *World Resources, 1992–93*. New York: Oxford University Press.

Zylicz, Tomasz. 1993. "Environmental Taxes in Poland." Paper presented at the Workshop on Taxation and Environment in European Economies in Transition, OECD Environment Directorate, CCEET/ENV/DAFFE (92)243.

6

Energy Sector Policy and the Environment: A Case Study of Sri Lanka

Peter Meier, Mohan Munasinghe, and Tilak Siyambalapitiya

THE ENVIRONMENTAL IMPACTS of specific energy investments are fairly well recognized, and environmental impact assessments of energy projects in developing countries have become a routine and integral part of the Bank's policies to promote sustainable development. But much less well understood are the linkages between broader sectoral policies and the environment. For example, the environmental consequences of energy sector pricing reforms that have become a quite common component of structural adjustment lending remain largely unexplored. Similarly, effective procedures for incorporating environmental concerns into energy and electricity sector planning are not well established beyond some routinely affirmed general principles about the importance of economic efficiency, and the presumption that the environmental impacts of an economically efficient energy sector will be less than one characterized by subsidized prices and technological inefficiency (such as inordinately high transmission and distribution (T&D) losses, poor heat rates of thermal electric generation plants, etc).

The authors acknowledge the many contributions from their colleagues in Sri Lanka, especially D. C. Wijeratne and K. Nanthakumar. Others who provided valuable review and comments of earlier versions of this study included Kenneth King and Wilfrido Cruz.

The impact of direct environmental constraints on sectoral policy are equally poorly understood, except perhaps in the general sense that if energy costs fully reflect the environmental damages of energy production, optimal resource allocation is ensured. For example, very little work has been done to analyze alternative policy options for achieving greenhouse gas emission reductions in developing countries, again beyond routinely stated assertions of the importance of efficient resource utilization, and that renewable energy and natural gas should replace coal. Indeed, such studies of this subject as have appeared are based on highly aggregated macro models that offer little guidance on the specific measures to be undertaken at the sectoral level.

In this chapter we analyze and quantify representative examples of both types of linkages using Sri Lanka as a case study. First, as an example of a sectorwide policy with potentially broad environmental consequences, we examine electricity price reform. Second, as an example of a direct environmental constraint with broad energy sector and economywide consequences, we analyze options for greenhouse gas emission reductions to meet possible targets externally mandated by the World Climate Convention.

Electricity pricing reform

The economic rationale for efficient pricing of electricity is well established, and has been documented in many studies.[1] Reforms to eliminate subsidies, and to raise tariffs in order to improve the financial health of electric utilities, have been proposed and implemented in numerous instances.[2] Indeed, cove

nants between the Bank and its borrowers that provide for tariff increases to generate sufficient revenue to meet self-financing targets or rate of return on equity have become an increasingly frequent part of Bank power sector loans.

Many methodological problems arise in evaluating the environmental consequences of such sectoral policies. Although the environmental benefits of an efficient pricing policy are perhaps intuitive, in practice the relationships are quite complex, and the magnitude of the impacts will be dependent upon a variety of specific assumptions. If higher prices, based say on established long run marginal cost (LRMC) pricing principles, served simply to depress demand (relative to subsidized prices), then merit order dispatch would be expected to result in reduced use of older, less efficient thermal plants, and therefore pollutant emissions from thermal plants would certainly be lower. Lower demand, however, will also affect the least cost expansion path, such that the addition of more efficient units is delayed. This may result in older units being dispatched more than would otherwise be the case, resulting in an increase in emissions. The extent to which the latter effect is in fact offset by a lower generation requirement is an empirical one, and can only be answered by looking at a specific case.

Part of the problem in estimating the benefits of pricing policy in an actual case is also analytical. Financial models of the electric power sector have long been used in project appraisal work, and it is standard practice to use such models, typically Lotus 123™ spreadsheets, to examine the financial impacts of alternative tariffs and financial covenants. In the typical case, one examines (either by trial and error, or by an appropriate iterative computation) what the tariff must be to meet

---

[1]For a recent review, see, for example, Munasinghe 1990.

[2]A recent review of such lending found that electricity tariff reform was an extremely common component of adjustment policy packages—see, e.g., Warford et al. 1992. Between FY88 and FY92, tariff reforms were part of structural adjustment lending in Bangladesh, Laos, Papua New Guinea, Guyana,

Honduras, Panama, Venezuela, Bulgaria, Czechoslovakia, Egypt, Hungary, Poland, Rumania, Benin, Burundi, Ivory Coast, Rwanda, Senegal, and Zimbabwe.

some specific target for the rate of return on equity or on fixed revalued assets, or for the percentage of self-financing of the future investment program. These estimates then become part of the financial covenants that are entered into as a condition for lending by an external donor.

Unfortunately almost all the standard financial models take the technical data as exogenous inputs derived from other, more detailed engineering models. For example, the fuel bill in the income statement is taken from a production costing model, the debt service assumptions are taken from the capacity expansion model, and so forth. It thus becomes extremely difficult to assess the feedbacks that arise from changes in the tariff, because the detailed models that provide the technical inputs are not directly linked (and in many utilities they are run by different departments with little or no attempt to ensure mutual consistency).

Greenhouse gas emissions

With the agreement on the World Climate Convention having been signed by over one hundred countries at the recent earth summit in Rio de Janeiro, the practical problems of how the obligations to reduce greenhouse gas (GHG) emissions can be met in the most cost-effective manner requires urgent attention, particularly in developing countries that have limited resources. Simply put, there exists a wide range of potential policy options, ranging from direct technology substitution (e.g., replacing coal-burning power plants with wind generating plants) to indirect pricing and taxation policies (such as the imposition of carbon taxes on fuels, or the imposition of emissions charges). How this wide range of options is to be evaluated on a consistent basis, and how the many tradeoffs are to be assessed in a systemic manner, is still subject to considerable question.

Although the number of GHG mitigation cost studies continues to grow, most studies continue to focus on the United States[3] and other Organisation for Economic Co-operation and Development (OECD) countries. Modeling studies fall into two general categories: "top-down" equilibrium models (with varying degrees of disaggregation),[4] and "bottom up" models, typically simulation models with much engineering detail.

The main focus of much of this modeling effort is to assess the potential economic impact of GHG emissions reduction options, particularly in relation to the commitments made by many developed countries to stabilize GHG emissions at their 1990 levels. Hourcade et al. (1995) provide a comprehensive review of this literature in the forthcoming Report of the Intergovernmental Panel on Climate Change (IPCC). They conclude that top down model generally indicate larger economic impacts than bottom-up models, and that in OECD countries the annual cost of stabilizing emissions at their 1990 levels would typically exceed 1–2 percent of gross domestic product (GDP).[5] They also note that whatever lost-cost

---

[3]Manne and Richels (1990), for the case of the United States, Goto and Sawa (1993), for the case of Japan, or Proost and Regemorter (1992), for the case of Belgium, typify the genre: time scales that run in some cases to the year 2100, new technologies whose earliest introduction at a significant level is 2010 and beyond, and highly aggregated sectoral descriptions of the economy. For example, in the case of Global 2100, a variant of the earlier ETA-MACRO model, the system has three sectors: goods, electric energy, and delivered nonelectric energy. The production function for goods is a hierarchical system with a constant elasticity combination of Cobb-Douglas value added and energy inputs. (See also Hogan, 1990, for a succinct review.)

[4]For a systematic review of top-down studies in the United States, see EMF (1993). Well-known models of this type include Global 2100 (Manne and Richels 1990) and the GREEN model (OECD 1993).

[5]The results broadly tend to show that the losses to GDP growth resulting from a fairly wide range of carbon emission restriction scenarios are rather small: as noted by Hogan (1990), the Manne-Richels calculations suggest that stabilizing CO_2 emissions at 80 percent of the 1990 level would account for about 5 percent of the total GDP through the next century.

emission reduction options may exist for developing countries, they are likely to be insufficient to offset increasing emissions from economic growth.

In what appears to be the first such analysis of GHG emissions for a developing country, Blitzer et al. (1993) apply a general equilibrium model to Egypt—with six nonenergy sectors, and four energy sectors—crude oil, natural gas, petroleum products, and electricity. GDP losses—ranging from 4.5 percent for a 20 percent reduction in annual carbon emissions to 22 percent for a 40 percent reduction over the base case—are much higher than those estimated for the developed countries. Yet even with these higher GDP impacts, there is still a significant increase in actual CO_2 emissions. Moreover, these results are for a country for which the assumed backstop technologies—natural gas-powered transport and nuclear power—are feasible options. Sri Lanka, like many low-income countries, has no natural gas resources of its own, and nuclear power is not an option for the foreseeable future.

Indeed, there is no chance whatsoever that a country like Sri Lanka could stabilize its CO_2 emissions at the present level, or even at twice the present level. Given the low existing level of per capita commercial energy use, future demand growth to support economic development needs will be high. Therefore, even if electricity demand growth could be entirely accommodated by renewable energy (which, in light of projected electricity demand growth of 7 percent to 9 percent per year, requires heroic assumptions about the feasibility of building large hydro plants), the anticipated growth in transportation sector fuel consumption, even under highly optimistic expectations about mass transit and fuel efficient vehicles, precludes stabilization of CO_2 emissions in the near future.

A somewhat different approach has been taken by Burgess (1990), Larsen (1993), and Anderson and Williams (1993). Addressing merely the impact of eliminating price subsidies, these studies estimate the level of reduction in GHG emissions by application of assumed price elasticities to the difference between the subsidized and unsubsidized price. Burgess (1990) uses the difference between actual average cost of electricity and the estimated long-run marginal cost (LRMC), applies an assumed long-run price elasticity of -1, and estimates the reduction in GHG emissions for eleven countries, including the United States, China, India, and some small developing countries, such as Tanzania and Peru. Not surprisingly, the bulk of the total carbon emission savings of 124 million tons per year (mt/y) come from coal fuel savings, of which India accounts for 11.9 mt/y, China 26.6 mt/y, and the United States 85.4 mt/y. Larsen (1993) does the same analysis, but from the perspective of fuel prices, applies estimated own- and cross-price elasticities for the different fossil fuels to the difference between an appropriately adjusted border price and the domestic subsidized fuel price, and, more significantly, includes the countries of the former Soviet Union (FSU) and Eastern Europe. In this analysis, the former (FSU) (917 mt/y) and Poland (105.2 mt/y) dominate the results; indeed, the combined estimated impact in India (54 mt/y), and China (45.4 mt/y) together is less than that for Poland. Anderson and Williams (1993), using a simple demand model and an assumed -0.5 value for the price elasticity of demand, estimate that total subsidies due to unrealistic electricity tariffs in developing countries amount to more than US$100 billion, and that improvements in price and managerial efficiency would reduce pollution in developing countries by up to 40 percent.

Such studies certainly provide some estimates of the efficacy of pricing instruments, but tell us little about the actual impacts, and therefore also the barriers, likely to be encountered if indeed the policy reforms were to be implemented. Clearly, as relative fuel prices change, hydro-electricity may become more attractive for electricity generation, which has its own set of significant environmental impacts. Moreover, while shifts from coal to natural gas may well be desirable not just from the perspective of CO_2 emissions, but also from the perspective of reducing SO_2, NO_x and trace metals, that is small comfort for countries such as Sri Lanka that have no natural gas resources of their own. In any event, countries for which imported fossil fuel is the least cost fuel for baseload thermal electricity generation (as is again the case for Sri Lanka) have no fossil fuel price subsidies to eliminate.

In fact the most widespread approach to exploring policy options for GHG emissions reductions in developing countries is the bottom-up approach largely focused on technology options (see, e.g., Van Dang (1993) for Thailand; TERI (1992) for India or Moreira et al. (1992) for Brazil)[6] While these provide useful guidance, none compare technology interventions with pricing and tax policy options, and most are based on rather broad scenario exercises rather than the sort of least-cost planning models that are actually used for electricity planning.

Yet any consistent assessment of policy options for GHG emissions reduction—even if limited to bottom-up examinations of technology interventions—requires a comprehensive representation of the technical, environmental, economic, and financial characteristics of the energy system.[7] This is a major

challenge, insofar as most energy models presently available tend to focus on only part of the problem. Most attempts at providing an "environmental impact assessment" capability to energy models are little more than add-on modules to calculate residuals (Markandya 1990). In the case of GHG emissions, that such models are limited to residuals is perhaps not very serious, but certainly there is very little reason to believe that the actual impacts of other pollutants, such as SO_2 and particulates, are linearly related to emissions levels. More serious from our perspective, however, is the fact that such models are of limited use to assess price and tax policies on a consistent basis, since they generally lack integration with financial models, and energy demands tend to be defined exogenously.

Several additional methodological problems relate to the workings of the Global Environment Facility (GEF). This is the funding mechanism, on an interim basis, to provide for financial resources needed by developing countries to meet the "full incremental costs incurred" in complying with their obligations under the Convention on Global Climate Change.

(a)　If the GEF is to fund the "incremental costs" of GHG reduction measures, this presupposes that a baseline can be unambiguously defined, against which such incremental costs be defined. One obvious approach here is to define the baseline as the "least cost" solution to expansion of the energy system. As is now fairly well recognized in the case of electric sector expansion, however, the concept of "least cost" is extremely fragile (Crousillat 1989; Meier 1990). Such a solution may be valid only for a very narrow band of input assumptions, and if these assumptions prove to be different, then an investment program predicated upon the "least cost" plan may ultimately be distinctly nonoptimal. In short, any deterministic definition of

---

[6]For a review of the country studies being undertaken by the United Nations Environment Program (UNEP), see, e.g., UNEP (1992). A more recent status report on country studies is to be found in Fuglestvedt et al. (1994).

[7]Particularly in the case of electric sector technologies, the proposition that technologies can be evaluated in isolation from the systems context is extremely tenuous: the impacts of different technologies cannot be linearly superimposed because of the interactions that occur through the system load curve. For example, the impact of load management and transmission and distribution (T&D) loss reduction when implemented together is demonstrably less than the sum of the impacts of each evaluated alone.

"incremental cost" will run into a range of practical operational difficulties.

(b)   Equally difficult is the treatment of "joint products." Options that reduce GHG emissions may also provide significant changes in other pollutants whose impacts are of a quite different scale. For example, the substitution of renewable energy technologies for coal will reduce not just CO_2 emissions, (a global benefit), but also SO_2 and particulate emissions that bring a reduction in local environmental damages. On the other hand, the increased use of renewable energy technologies (such as hydroelectric generation), which also reduce CO_2 emissions, may also impose new and different local environmental costs (such as loss of biodiversity associated with reservoir inundation).[8]

Estimates of the importance of joint benefits and costs vary widely (in part because valuing the costs and benefits of other environmental impacts may be subject to similar difficulties of valuation and scientific uncertainty as for GHG emissions), but most lie in the range of US$1 to US$10 of additional benefits for every dollar of benefit from GHG emissions reduction. A recent Norwegian study (Alfsen, Brendemoen, and Glomsrod 1992) indicated that when the joint products of carbon reduction were taken into account (such as reduction in environmental damages to forests and lakes, health damages, reduced traffic congestion, road damage), such benefits go a long way toward compensating the economic loss measured as a reduction in GDP.

Again the growing literature on the benefits of GHG emissions control is thoroughly reviewed in the forthcoming IPCC report by Pearce et al. (1995).

Approach

In this chapter we address these various analytical and methodological issues by the application of the ENVIROPLAN model, an integrated energy sector model (see Figure 6-1). At its core is a fairly conventional financial representation of the electric utility and the refinery—with the usual income statement, sources and uses of funds, and balance sheet. The model allows the user to specify one or more balance sheet ratios as the criterion for setting the level of the tariff—such as return on equity or assets, self-financing ratio, and so on. The financial model is then linked to technical representation of the energy sector, with demand and supply modules for each major subsector—in the case of the electric sector, for example, including merit order dispatching and capacity expansion, and driven by an econometrically specified demand model (that in turn takes prices from the current tariff in the financial statements). The model is closed by passing the investment requirements for capacity expansion back to the financial module. Thus, adjustments in the capacity expansion plan, say in response to lower demands caused by higher prices, feed back automatically into the asset and liability accounts in the financial statements. We thus achieve a completely consistent set of prices, demands, technical sector configuration, investment, and financial representations of the major sector institutions that permits simulation of a wide range of policy options.

A multiattribute environmental analysis is integrated into the model. While in this chapter, the focus is on CO_2 emissions and air quality and related health impacts, elsewhere (Meier and Munasinghe 1994), using the same methodology and model, we develop tradeoff curves for a much wider range of environmental attributes (including biodiversity and acid

---

[8]These methodological problems have been recognized by GEF, which has initiated a research program to find an operational approach for measuring and agreeing upon full incremental costs within the context of the Climate Change Convention: the so-called PRINCE study (Program for Measuring Incremental Costs for the Environment). For a full discussion, see, e.g., King (1993a) and King (1993b).

rain indicators). The model is described in detail in Meier (1995).[9]

The main limitation of the analysis reported herein is that common to all partial equilibrium models, the results do not take into account any macroeconomic impacts and feedbacks. In a second stage of our work, currently under way, this limitation is being addressed, in which the energy sector model is being linked to a general equilibrium model of the Sri Lanka macroeconomy.

The Sri Lanka electric sector

The present installed capacity in Sri Lanka is 1,225 megawatts, of which 1,115 megawatts is hydro, the balance combustion turbines (108 megawatts), diesel (64 megawatts), and an oil-fired 44 megawatt steam plant. Generation for 1992 was 3,377 gigawatt-hours, with a T&D loss rate of 18.8 percent (of generation). The rate of demand growth over the next decade is expected to be about 7–9 percent per year. Assuming no fresh discoveries of oil or natural gas, the conventional wisdom is that for the next twenty years the generation options for Sri Lanka are quite limited. While substantial hydropower resources could be developed, the remaining sites are limited in size, and have substantially higher costs than alternative options (see Table 6-1). The least cost system expansion studies conducted annually by the Ceylon Electricity Board (CEB) show that the least cost plan is to begin building coal-fired baseload stations using imported Australian coal by the end of the decade.

The larger hydro plants, such as the high dam variant of the Kukule project, involve substantial resettlement and removal of forest area, and are likely to be fiercely opposed by environmentalists. As a matter of practicality, expansion of conventional hydro will be limited to smaller run-of-river schemes, such as Broadlands, and the run-of-river variant of the Kukule project. Yet even some run-of-river schemes will likely encounter fierce opposition: the proposed Talawakelle run-of-river plant, part of a proposed hydro development scheme on the Upper Kotmale, would cut off river flow from the St. Clair's waterfall, a well-known scenic attraction.

Nuclear power is not likely to be a feasible option for Sri Lanka for some time, even aside from the environmental issues. Present indications are that even under very high rates of demand growth, it would be at least 2030 before the system is of a sufficient size to accommodate 500–600 megawatts nuclear unit.

There are also substantial environmental concerns associated with the introduction of coal-fired power stations in Sri Lanka. The environmental impact assessment prepared for a proposed coal-burning station at Trincomalee, in the Northeast, revealed a range of important issues ranging from impacts to the aquatic ecosystems of Trincomalee Bay caused by the discharge of thermal effluents, to air pollution concerns caused by particulate and sulfur oxide emissions.

In short, expansion of the power system to meet future electricity needs of the country will have significant environmental implications. Even if appropriate mitigation measures are taken at the project level, sectorwide policies must also take account of environmental implications in order to assure sustainable development.

HG reduction issues for Sri Lanka

Carbon emissions in Sri Lanka, both in absolute terms, as well as in per capita terms, are presently still quite low, a reflection of the dominance of hydro in the electric sector, and low energy intensity of the industrial sector.[10]

---

[9] The electric sector version of ENVIROPLAN is currently being used by a number of other utilities for integrated resource planning (IRP), including BCHydro in Canada and Andhra Pradesh in India.

[10] 1993 emissions of carbon at some 6 metric tons per capita in the United States, 2 tons per capita in

However, beyond the year 2000, CO_2 emissions will rise very sharply as the electric sector generation mix moves toward fossil fuel, as indicated on Figure 6-2. GHG emissions are expected to triple over the next fifteen years in the absence of any focused policies to reduce GHG emissions. This has important consequences for the negotiating posture of Sri Lanka in the event that a consensus emerges for tradable CO_2 emission rights. Clearly, it will be in the interests of small developing countries whose present electric systems are hydro dominated to argue that the initial allocation of emission rights be based on population, or income, rather than on present fossil fuel consumption.

The future course of GHG emissions in Sri Lanka itself will be largely determined by policy and investment choices in three main areas. First is the generation mix in the electric sector—clearly, the extent to which coal (and other imported fossil fuels) are used as a major fuel, and how much of the remaining hydro potential can in fact be exploited, will have a major impact on CO_2 emissions. Second is the traditional fuels sector—biomass still accounts for two thirds of energy consumption in Sri Lanka—and any shift from biomass to petroleum-based fuels will have a major impact on CO_2 emissions.[11] Third is the rapidly growing transportation sector, which accounts for about half of the petroleum product consumption.

The impacts of global warming that might be experienced by Sri Lanka are quite uncertain. Some researchers expect an intensification of the monsoon in tropical latitudes, which, in Sri Lanka, would adversely affect soil erosion and stability in the hill country watersheds where deforestation rates already represent a threat to the sedimentation rates experienced by hydro and irrigation reservoirs. Unlike many other countries in Southeast Asia, the tectonic conditions in Sri Lanka are relatively stable, with little significant seismic activity of the type that has produced significant surface depressions of coastal areas in the Philippines.[12] Nor are the major cities presently threatened by major subsidence problems caused by excessive exploitation of groundwater. Nevertheless, extensive areas of the coast, especially in the south and southwest, are already threatened by coastal erosion (that can, at least in part, be attributed to large-scale mining of coral reefs), and there are extensive areas of highly populated coastal areas that would be severely affected by sea level rises of 1-3 meters. One of the immediate consequences of sea level rise is likely to be contamination of the limestone aquifers that are important sources of groundwater in the north.[13]

Europe, and between 0.1 and 0.5 tons per capita in most developing countries of Asia. We estimate per capita emissions in Sri Lanka at less than 0.1 ton per capita. Estimates of carbon emissions per unit of GNP, expressed in kilograms per million U.S. dollars, are about 1.3 for China, 0.7 for India, and 0.25 for the United States. We estimate the corresponding figure for Sri Lanka at about 0.15 (see, e.g., Banuri et al. (1995); Baron and Hills (1990)).

[11]The main causes of deforestation are land clearing for agricultural and commercial timber operations, rather than fuelwood demand per se. Indeed, a substantial fraction of the biomass energy consumption is made up of coconut husks, rubber wood (old trees that are replaced by replanting), and other agricultural wastes. However, if deforestation continues at its historical rate, the supply of fuelwood may become seriously constrained in the future.

[12]An earthquake on the east coast of Luzon in July 1990, for example, caused a 2.5 meter fall in large areas of the coast, requiring large scale evacuation of coastal villages.

[13]For a good review of the likely impacts of global warming in the South Asian countries, see, e.g., Pachauri (1991). It would seem that the impacts of sea level rise, however serious for Sri Lanka, will not have the cataclysmic consequences that seem likely for the Maldives and the East Coast of Bangladesh.

The options

Wind energy

Although there are a number of renewable energy technologies that may be considered for Sri Lanka, the technology with the largest potential impact on the operations of the CEB is wind energy. Utility scale solar thermal plants are still extremely expensive, while the use of photovoltaics probably has greatest potential in remote rural areas that do not have grid access (Wijeratne 1994b). The wind feasibility assessment recently completed for the southern lowlands of Sri Lanka estimated the ultimate potential at about 300 megawatts. In this study we assume that six 50 megawatt wind farms will be built in this area during the period 1998 to 2006 (CEB 1992c). The most important finding of the monitoring program conducted at the site concerns the hourly variations, with a peak during the afternoon hours. There are also very strong seasonal variations. During the summer monsoon period, monthly outputs for a 50 megawatt facility are estimated at about 10 gigawatt-hours per month, falling to a low of about 2.5 gigawatt-hours per month in March and November. Consequently, wind plants will do little to reduce installed capacity requirements, but will serve primarily to displace thermal power and reduce expected deficits in dry years.

T&D loss reduction

As can be seen from Figure 6-3, the progress in reducing losses to the present 12 percent target set by CEB has been much slower than anticipated. As recently as 1989, it was projected that the 12 percent target would be attained by 1993, yet by 1992 that target had been delayed to 1996, and by 1993 to 2012! In the 1994 study, the target year for achievement of 12 percent was advanced again to 2004 (which is the assumption used in our reference case). Given the lack of progress over the past few years (in 1989 and 1991 losses actually increased), there is some ques-

tion as to whether even this target can be attained.[14] We define three policy cases for analysis: in the first (indicated on the figure by "T&D(+)"), we bring losses to the CEB target by 2001; in the second (indicated by "T&D(++)"), we bring down losses further to 10 percent overall by 2010; and in the third, a there is a delay in achieving the 12 percent target to 2010 ("T&D(-)").

It might be noted that LECO, the privatized distribution company, appears as if it will meet its 8 percent loss target by 1996. However, since LECO buys its power from CEB at 33 kV, 8 percent would not be a reasonable target for the system as a whole, which also needs to include losses in the high-tension transmission system.

Demand-side management (DSM)

A systematic assessment of DSM options has yet to be conducted in Sri Lanka. Indeed, comprehensive DSM assessments have been conducted for only a very few developing countries to date. Nevertheless, there are indications that there exist some significant opportunities for the introduction of energy-efficient, end-use technologies in Sri Lanka. Both the World Bank power system efficiency study of Sri Lanka (World Bank 1983) and the electricity Masterplan (GTZ 1989) made some preliminary estimates of the potential for load management and energy conservation by the systematic replacement of incandescent lights by fluorescent lights.[15]

---

[14]In fact, actual loss rates are likely to be somewhat higher, since CEB treats HT sales to the Lanka Electricity Company (LECO), a privatized (although still government-owned) distribution company established in 1984, as a consumer. Since LECO has losses of its own (and some of the municipal systems that were absorbed by LECO had loss rates exceeding 30 percent prior to rehabilitation), total losses in the system are at least 2–3 percent higher than CEB's estimate based on its generation and sales.

[15]The World Bank study also examined the possibility of replacing self-ballasting mercury vapor and incandescent lamps used for street lighting by high-pressure sodium vapor bulbs.

In this study, we examine two specific technologies to improve the efficiency of electricity utilization: increased penetration of compact fluorescent lighting (in the domestic and commercial sectors),[16] and the introduction of energy-efficient refrigerators.[17] The former is largely a load management measure, with very large megawatt savings during the evening peak, but relatively modest energy savings, while the latter is largely just an energy-saving measure, with little impact on the peak. Sri Lanka has a very pronounced evening peak that coincides with the hours immediately after sundown, indicative of the importance of the lighting load.[18]

---

[16]For a review of the European experience, see, e.g., Mills (1991). The average cost of conserved energy of these programs is reported at about 2.1 cents per kilowatt-hour (c/kWh), including 0.3 c/kWh for indirect administrative, promotional, and evaluation costs: this is significantly below the cost of new electric power plants. An analysis for Pakistan (Miller, Geller, and de Almeida 1992) concludes that even if the government offered a 100 percent subsidy—i.e., literally gives them away—it would save US$10 per bulb in avoided power plant construction costs.

[17]Improving the energy efficiency of refrigerators appears as a top-ranked option in many assessments of demand side management measures in developing countries. For example, this measure emerging as the best among 23 options, along with improvements to compressors and insulation of Thai refrigerators, are estimated to reduce unit electrical use from 400 kWh to below 200 kWh per year (Florida Solar Energy Center 1991). Indeed, an analysis of efficiency improvements in major residential appliances in the United States (Schipper and Hawk 1991) indicates that refrigerators and freezers have shown the best improvements in efficiency since 1972, improving 70–90 percent, whereas efficiency improvements of other major devices have been much more modest (air conditioners 33 percent, space heaters 10–25 percent).

[18]It must, however, be stressed that there is little empirical data on the composition of the hour-by-hour loads by end-use device. However, peak air conditioning loads almost certainly occur during the daylight hours (since the bulk of air conditioning is installed in offices and hotels rather than private residences). Consequently, the assumption that a significant share of the evening peak is attributable to residential lighting seems reasonable (Wijeratne 1993).

Mini-hydro

The electricity Masterplan identified a series of potential mini-hydro sites. In this option, we assume that the four with the lowest specific generation cost will be implemented in the 1998–2002 time frame, to provide a total additional hydro capacity of 30 megawatts.

Clean coal technology

Conventional pulverized coal plants have been part of CEB's expansion plans since the mid-1980s. Since the new clean coal technologies not only provide substantial improvements in emissions, but also gains in efficiency, we have examined the impact of using combined cycle-pressurized fluidized bed combustion as an alternative, under two assumptions about capital costs.[19]

No coal

A "no coal" option has been evaluated by the CEB in its annual generation planning studies for some time—although the rationale had less to do with GHG emissions than with the extent of public opposition to large thermal plants located in the coastal zone. In this option, we assume that coal base-load units would be replaced by steam cycle, residual oil-fueled plants at the same locations. Resid-

---

[19]For a recent review of technology developments, and their application to developing countries, see, e.g., Tavoulareas and Charpentier (1995). The capital cost estimates are based on EPRI (1993). The optimistic estimate of pressurized fluidized bed combustion (PFBC) is taken at the Electric Power Research Institute (EPRI) values: the average cost of PFBC plants analyzed in that report is US$1176 per kW (in December 1992 dollars, excluding interest during construction), which is only US$50 per kW more than conventional coal plants without flue gas desulfurization (FGD). The pessimistic estimate is taken as US$350 per kW higher. With a high proportion of the total fuel cost accounted for by transportation (from Australia or South Africa), the efficiency gain provides an important offset to the higher installed capital cost.

ual oil is assumed to be imported from Singapore spot markets, using the 1993 World bank oil price forecast.[20]

We examine several oil price cases. Burning high-sulfur fuel oil—about 3.5 percent by weight is the specification on Singapore spot markets—without sulfur removal may be problematic: when corrected for calorific value, this would be equivalent to about 2 percent sulfur coal (in contrast to the 0.6 percent sulfur coal that is planned in Sri Lanka). The differential between 0.3 percent low-sulfur fuel oil and high-sulfur fuel oil in Far Eastern markets is quite varied. Over the past five years, the difference has ranged from US$3.70 per barrel (bbl) in 1989 to as little as US$1 per bbl in 1994. We also examine a high world oil price case (in which the price rises to US$30 per bbl by 2004, as opposed to US$21.5 in the base case).

Maximum hydro

Maximum reduction of GHGs is achieved by maximum use of hydro plants. Because of the high costs, this again has to be forced into the solution. In this scenario, all the remaining major hydro plants in Sri Lanka are assumed to be built by 2011.[21]

Transportation sector measure—vehicle inspection and maintenance programs: Over the past decade, motor vehicle traffic in Sri Lanka has risen very fast. Particularly in the Colombo metropolitan area, problems of traffic congestion, and of related environmen-

tal concerns such as lead and particulate emissions, have begun to emerge. Urban air quality is a priority issue in the National Environmental Action Plan (Ministry of Environment 1991), and the Metropolitan Environmental Improvement Program has recently issued an action plan for Colombo in which the transportation sector is a major target (Metropolitan Environmental Improvement Programme 1992). Combustion of gasoline and auto-diesel is presently also the largest source of carbon emissions in Sri Lanka, and even if large-scale generation of electricity from coal commences in the late 1990s, the transportation sector will continue to represent a major source of total national GHG emissions.

In a related study, we examined the entire set of urban air quality improvement measures being proposed by the Colombo Action Plan that range from reduction of the proportion of two-stroke motorcycles (which have higher emissions than four-stroke motorcycles) and a lowering of the lead content in gasoline, to the introduction of vehicle inspection and maintenance programs (VIM), particularly for diesel vehicles. All these measures are justified on the basis of local urban air quality concerns, but a number of them prove to have significant GHG reduction impacts as well. We include in this analysis the transportation sector measure that has the most significant GHG impact, namely VIM.

Electricity pricing reform

As noted in the introduction, the rationale for and importance of economically efficient pricing is well established and has been documented in many studies. Historically, Sri Lanka has followed the same cyclical pattern observed in many other developing countries—in which long periods during which the government has been reluctant to raise tariffs results in a gradual deterioration of the financial condition of the utility, in turn followed by sharp increases necessary to ward off a crisis. Thus, for example, between 1972 and

---

[20]For example, in 2000, according to these projections, the delivered cost of residual fuel oil, c.i.f. Sri Lanka, is US$13.90 per gigacalorie (based on US$150 per ton marker crude price, US$135 per ton for residual oil c.i.f. Sri Lanka), as opposed to US$7.58 per gigacalorie (US$50.5 per ton) for imported Australian coal.

[21]Including the high dam version of the Kukule project (at 144 megawatts, rather than the 70 megawatt variant that is currently under consideration), both plants in the Upper Kotmale scheme (rather than just the lower run-of-river project at Talawakelle), and the Uma Oya multipurpose scheme.

1978, there were no changes in the tariff—resulting in a gradual decline in real electricity price level. This was followed by a series of very sharp rate increases in the period 1978–80 (see Figure 6-4). Prices drifted downward again in the early 1980s, with a correction in 1988. Yet again they drifted downwards until 1992, when a further series of significant tariff increases occurred.

In addition to the expected and obvious impact upon the financial condition of the utility, the failure to maintain a consistent pricing policy has a number of possible environmental impacts as well. When tariffs are substantially below long-run marginal cost (LRMC), it becomes difficult to raise the resources necessary to expand and upgrade the T&D system, resulting in turn in high loss rates characteristic of overstressed systems. This is compounded by wasteful consumption—and hence also higher levels of generation—where price levels are significantly below their economic level. The result is that the environmental impacts associated with electricity generation are higher than they would be in an efficient system. With the new projects becoming increasingly controversial—hydro projects because of the impacts associated with inundation, and fossil-fueled projects because of impacts associated with air pollution, solid waste disposal and thermal effluents—eliminating those environmental impacts associated with inefficiency becomes increasingly important.

Electricity prices in Sri Lanka have historically been at levels substantially below LRMC.[22] In 1992 a series of tariff increases raised the average price to Rs 2.6 per kWh; however, even this price level is below the latest estimate of the CEB (Table 6-2).[23]

It thus comes as no surprise that the financial performance has been below target levels

of return on assets (or equity) as well—although prior to 1984, when the fuel adjustment clause was invoked,[24] financial performance was subject to sharp deterioration during periods of drought as a consequence of heavy use of thermal plants dependent upon imported fuels. Thus, the drought year 1983 resulted in heavy financial losses. Nevertheless, since 1983 the real price has drifted downward, as has the return on equity (from a post-drought peak of 4 percent in 1985 to less than 1 percent in 1991. These returns are substantially below normal target levels of 5–10 percent.

The price elasticity of demand

Is electricity demand in Sri Lanka in fact price elastic? Some load forecasting models used by the CEB do not in fact include a price variable.[25] And, simple econometric models do not show any statistically significant evidence of demand elasticity (Meier et al. 1993). Indeed, in order to derive a satisfactory econometric model, it becomes necessary to first examine the underlying structure of electricity demand. Over the past two decades, demand growth has averaged 7 percent per year. Real GDP growth experienced a sharp upturn in 1978 with the liberalization of the economy started by the incoming Jayawardena administration, but civil disturbances in the late 1980s caused a decline in both economic growth and in the growth rate of electricity demand (which was negative in 1989).

Perhaps the most important underlying trend, however, has been the fall in kWh per customer account. For the industrial sector, this is a sharp and consistent trend, indicative of long-term structural adjustments in the industrial sector, with many small medium- to

---

[22]The first rigorous estimates of LRMC for Sri Lanka, made in 1982, are by Munasinghe—see Chapter 9—of Munasinghe and Schramm (1983).

[23]Ceylon Electricity Board (1992a).

[24]In fact, a fuel adjustment clause was introduced into the tariff in 1978, but was not implemented until October 1980 due to difficulties in calculation and assessment. For a discussion of electricity pricing in the 1970s, see World Bank (1982).

[25]See, e.g., CEB 1992b.

small-sized light manufacturing enterprises taking the place of large state-owned facilities as the dominant consumers.

The trend is observed also in the household sector, with a consistent decrease from the peak consumption of 1.2 megawatt-hours (MWh) per account per year in 1983 to 0.9 MWh per account per year in 1991. For commercial accounts, there is no discernible trend in 1987–88, but then there is a sudden fall in the period 1988 to 1991. This corresponds precisely with the onset of significant civil disturbances, during which shopping hours were dramatically curtailed in the evening. It remains to be seen (once the 1992 data are compiled) whether shopping habits and store hours have returned to previous patterns now that normal conditions prevail in most of the country. One might note that these declines in consumption per connection are not obviously related to price: since in the period 1988–91, real prices decreased.

A further significant distortion of the aggregate data has occurred as a result of the gradual takeover of local municipalities by the CEB and by the Lanka Electricity Company (LECO), a private sector distribution company established in 1983 to take over some of the more egregiously run municipal authorities on the perimeter of Colombo, some of which had loss rates of over 40 percent at time of takeover![26] The significant progress made by LECO in reducing losses in its system is another factor in decreasing consumption per consumer (since, all other things being equal, its wholesale purchases from CEB will be less the lower the T&D loss rate is).[27]

In sum, it is inevitable that the combination of special circumstances that has prevailed since the mid-1980s will make econometric analysis more difficult. Structural changes in manufacturing, takeover of municipal systems, civil disturbances, and severe droughts in 1983 and 1987 that resulted in significant curtailments all combine to make this an unusual period[28]

Pricing scenarios

To examine the impacts of alternative pricing policies, we define a series of pricing scenarios. A first case, obviously, is what might be termed "business as usual," in which we set the tariff in such a way as to maintain the historical average of 3 percent return on equity. This has a rather small chance of realization, for it generates insufficient cash to also maintain satisfactory self-financing ratios.

Consequently, we define a second "base case" tariff policy based upon a postulated covenant that requires an 8 percent rate of return on equity. This reflects typical World Bank practice for power sector lending and, as is evident from Figure 6-5, implies a substantially higher rate of return than has been achieved at any time over the past twenty years.

An iterative adjustment algorithm is used in the model to identify the average tariff level required in each year to maintain the required balance sheet ratio. Because of the lumpiness of capital investment, the year-to-year level of the tariff may show considerable variation, which would not only be hard to implement,

---

[26]However, the shares are still held by the government.

[27]In 1990, the overall loss rate in the LECO service area was 14 percent. Mahara, taken over in June 1985, with a loss rate of 48 percent, was brought down to 13 percent by 1989; Welisara, taken over in December 1987 with a loss rate of 41 percent, had losses of 11 percent by 1989; and Kolonnawa, taken over in November 1985 with a 50 percent loss rate, was down to 21 percent by 1989. This substantial improvement in performance was attained by a combination of system

rehabilitation (mostly with Asian Development Bank assistance), in which the distribution system in some areas was almost completely rebuilt, and an aggressive policy of disconnection for nonpayment of bills.

[28]As soon as the model is properly specified, with due recognition of the impact of structural changes in customer demand, statistically significant price elasticities can be identified. Estimated values lie in the range of -0.07 to -0.5: only for the industrial sector was the estimated value (of -0.07) not statistically significant.

but likely send confusing signals to consumers as well. The assumption here is that an appropriate smoothing process would be applied at the stage of policy implementation.

A further option is to base the tariff on the LRMC. When the LRMC at each voltage level is weighted by the fraction of demand delivered at that level, an "average" LRMC of Rs 5.29 per kWh results, implying that the incremental marginal cost of transmission and distribution is Rs 3.68 per kWh.[29]

ENVIROPLAN calculates average incremental costs (AICs), which is also a measure used by the CEB generation planning branch to compare system expansion alternatives in its annual generation plan.[30] The AIC of generation proves to be a good proxy for LRMC at the generation bus. Our base case values of generation AIC lie in the range of Rs 2.15–2.38 per kWh (depending upon fuel price and capital cost assumptions), very close to the rigorously estimated LRMC of Rs 2.21 per kWh (all in 1992 rupees). To obtain the total estimated LRMC to the consumer, used in turn as the level of the average tariff in the financial statements and the demand forecasting equation,[31] we add Rs 3.68 per kWh (i.e., that component of LRMC attributable to T&D) to the generation AIC.

With the current tariff on the order of Rs 2.6 per kWh, and the AIC in the range of Rs 6 per kWh, such an LRMC-based tariff would require a phase-in period. We assume a five-year period, such that the 1994 tariff be at least at 20 percent of the LRMC, the 1995 at 40 percent, and so on, with the tariff at the full level of the LRMC by 1998.

Table 6-3 shows the impact of these different pricing policy scenarios on some key indicators. Even to meet all the existing covenants, the tariff needs to be raised to over Rs 4 per kWh. In fact, of the three covenants now in place, it is the current ratio that proves to be binding for most of the next decade (see Figure 6-5).

Results

Figure 6-6 displays a plot of system cost[32] vs. GHG emissions. Each point represents a perturbation of the base case with a technology option (open circle) or a pricing option

---

[29]That is, generation Rs 2.21/kWh + T&D = Rs 3.68/kWh = Rs 5.29/kWh overall.

[30]The exact definition used by CEB is the present value of total system costs (capital and operating costs of new facilities plus operating costs of existing facilities) over the next 15 years divided by the present value of generation requirements over the same period less the present value of generation from existing hydro. This is a good approximation of the AIC since in the average hydro year, the current energy demand is almost exactly met by the existing hydro plants.

[31]Ideally, the LRMC at the consumer level would also be endogenously calculated by the model: this becomes important primarily for the assessment of the cost-effectiveness of T&D system rehabilitation. Obviously, if the target level of losses moves from 12 to 10 percent, the incremental LRMC for T&D would also decline. For the moment, this effect is not considered in our model.

[32]System cost is defined as the present value of all future electric system costs using a 10 percent discount rate (the rate used by the Government of Sri Lanka). GHG emissions are also discounted at the same rate. The question of the choice of discount rate has of course been fiercely debated by both economists and environmentalists (see, e.g., Markandya and Pearce, 1988), and a review of this literature goes well beyond the scope of this study. The consensus view on this is that the opportunity cost of capital, with discount rates in the 6–12 percent range, is appropriate for environmental cost-benefit analyses (see also the forthcoming report of the Inter Governmental Panel on Climate Change (IPCC), Working Group III, which deals with this question at some length). With respect to the discounting of GHG emissions, elsewhere (Meier, Munasinghe and Siyambalapitiya 1993) we show on an empirical basis how the tradeoff curves, and the resulting policy conclusions, differ as a function of the discounting of GHG emissions. The conclusions are (a) that the results are much more sensitive to the discount rate used for financial flows than for GHG emissions and (b) that because discounting of GHG emissions tends to give more weight to emissions in the near future than those in the distant future, the rationale for short-term policy interventions is more easily demonstrated.

(solid circle). The abbreviations used for each option are indicated on Table 6-4.

The base case used here—identified as point "B" in the figures—is based on CEB's official generation expansion plan, which is derived on the basis of the WASP model that determines the optimal expansion sequence to meet the official load forecast under a given reliability criterion (namely, a loss-of-load probability of about three days per year). The principal conclusion of recent CEB studies is that the first 150 megawatt coal-fired unit is required by 2004, with diesels and combustion turbines, and two run-of-river hydro schemes being built in the earlier years.

The options fall into four types, corresponding to the four quadrants defined by the base case. The most desirable options naturally fall into quadrant III, where both costs *and* GHG emissions decrease—options described as "win-win," or "no regrets." Compact fluorescent lighting (CFL), T&D loss reduction to the 10 percent target, and oil steam-electric (OS) under present oil price projections are seen to fall in this quadrant.

On the other hand, options in quadrant I are those for which both costs and GHG increase—the "lose-lose" options. Business-as-usual pricing (3 percent return on equity) and delays in achieving the 12 percent T&D loss target fall into this quadrant. The options in quadrant II lower system costs, but increase GHG emissions, while in quadrant IV, system costs increase, and GHG emissions decrease. In other words, these are the quadrants for which tradeoffs between the cost and GHG emissions objectives must be made.

Options that are mutually exclusive are indicated by the dotted lines. Note that the use of oil-steam cycle plants falls in the "win-win" quadrant for the current oil price projection, but moves to the tradeoff quadrant under the high oil price scenario. Note also that the use of low-sulfur oil (LSOS(-),LSOS(+)), increases costs over using high-sulfur oil (OS), but GHG emissions decrease. There is a further decrease in GHG emissions in the high

world oil price case. This is a price effect: as the tariff goes up, demand is depressed, in turn lowering emissions.

That DSM options appear in the "win-win" quadrant may come as no surprise, and raises the obvious question why they are not included in the base case, i.e., in the official plan. Market imperfections, high transaction costs, vested interests, unavailability of finance, lack of information are often cited as reasons: the fact that many DSM programs that lower total resource costs, but result in increased rates, would be another explanation.[33] In fact, in the case of Sri Lanka, while both DSM measures lower total resource costs, energy-efficient refrigerators (EERs) increase rates very slightly, and CFL lowers rates significantly. In 1994, the Ceylon Electricity Board created a DSM unit, included an analysis of DSM options in its generation plan, and is now attempting to get World Bank assistance to begin an active DSM program.

However, it is also evident that the impact of all of these technology interventions is a great deal less than the impact of efficient pricing. Of course, it could be argued that the actual environmental impact of the pricing effect is largely premised on the assumed price elasticity of demand, which is admittedly subject to some uncertainty. However, this uncertainty is arguably less than the uncertainty associated with the cost assumptions for many of the technology options. This empirical analysis of Sri Lanka indicates that the effect of efficient pricing, relative to the historical case, reduces GHG emissions (of the electric sector) by some 28 percent , which is somewhat lower than the general estimate of

---

[33]While the U.S. literature on the appropriate criteria for selecting DSM programs is large and contentious—see, e.g., Joskow and Marron (1992); Hirst (1992); Hobbs (1991)—the question of rate impacts receives only passing mention in most DSM studies for developing countries. In the Philippines Assessment, for example, rate impacts are simply dismissed as "modest," and no specific calculations are presented on whether proposed measures might pass a rate impact measure test (see USAID 1994, pp. 2–15).

40 percent suggested by Anderson and Williams (1993) noted above.

An optimal portfolio may be constructed by combining the various options in such a way as to provide a progressive decrease in GHG emissions (Figure 6-7). (See Annex 6-B for a discussion of dominance of options and trade-off curves.) We have modified the axes for this plot. The x-axis now includes transportation sector emissions, and the y-axis includes an adjustment (dE) for the savings associated with the vehicle inspection and maintenance program (namely, the avoided cost of fuel saved by better fuel efficiency, less the VIM program cost).

We begin with the base case and add the cost-effective measures one by one. This could be done in a variety of different ways—here we select probable ease of implementation as the order. Thus, among the "win-win" options, implementing further T&D loss reductions is seen as the easiest, and pricing reform as the most difficult.

This can be redrawn as on Figure 6-8: we show cumulative GHG emissions avoided over the planning period considered, in order of the cost (benefit) per ton. For Sri Lanka, it is evident that among options requiring a cost tradeoff, mini-hydros have the least impact (less than US$2 per ton of CO_2 avoided), while wind plants are seen to be the most expensive, at US$93 per ton. The replacement of coal by oil plants (for the current oil price projection) is only US$4 per ton.

Extensive sensitivity analyses were also undertaken to test the robustness of the conclusions about the effectiveness of pricing reform, both in terms of additional environmental attributes (such as biodiversity), as well as in terms of input assumptions. In fact, the conclusions are remarkably robust with respect to a range of uncertainties. For example, sensitivity analysis results indicate the benefits of pricing policy reform over wide ranges of assumptions about world energy

prices[34] and construction delays.[35] Similar sensitivity analyses were also conducted to test the impact on economic growth, income and price elasticities. Indeed, the main conclusion can be stated quite unequivocally: while the magnitude of the environmental benefit may be debatable because of uncertainties concerning the price elasticity effect, at worst (i.e., in the case of no price effect), one can be certain that there is no *negative* effect

Conclusions

The following are the main conclusions that can be drawn from our discussion:

(a)   Setting electricity prices to reflect the LRMC has a significant and unambiguously beneficial impact on the environment (both in-country and global). The expected benefits predicted on theoreti-

---

[34]Our base case uses, as does the 1992 generation planning study of the CEB, the 1992 World Bank world crude oil price projection, which calls for a gradual increase (in 1992 dollars) from US$16 per bbl in 1992 to US$21.4 per bbl (f.o.b. Singapore) by 2000, and constant thereafter. In our low case ("-wop"), we assume that after an initial increase, the price falls, to US$15.30 per bbl by 2010. In our "oil shock" scenario, the real price of crude oil rises sharply to US$38 per bbl in 1999, and US$40 per bbl in 2000; then it parallels the trajectory of the 1980s with a slow drift downwards and a sudden collapse in 1985 (2005), followed by a gradual increase back to US$20 per bbl by 2010. Clearly, history is not likely to repeat itself exactly, but such an oil shock scenario is probably a lot more likely than gradual changes.

[35]In the litigation delay scenario, we assume that four years into construction, there is a two-year delay, applicable only to large hydro and coal plants. The rationale is that such plants are the ones most likely to incur delays: smaller run-of-river plants are assumed less likely to incur delays, not just because engineering geological uncertainties tend to be less, but primarily because they largely avoid the problems associated with resettlement of inundated villages. For example, the run-of-river variant of the 70 megawatt Kukule hydro project requires resettlement of some 27 families, while the 270 megawatt Upper Kotmale scheme requires resettlement of some 1,900 families (Japan International Cooperation Agency 1987).

cal and intuitive grounds are in fact confirmed by the specific case examined. For example, the difference between an AIC-based tariff and one based merely on achievement of a financial covenant to assure a 10 percent rate of return is a 28 percent reduction of power sector GHG emissions over the planning horizon, and a 23 percent reduction in the health effects related to the exposure of human populations to the incremental ambient concentration of air pollutants.

(b) Pricing policy has a more general impact than physical approaches to demand-side management. DSM programs are difficult to implement, and limited in scope. Moreover, even though the results of this study appear to suggest that DSM programs may be cost-effective, these conclusions are based on very limited actual data on load shapes.

(c) While some measures to reduce GHG emissions imply a significant increase in other local environmental impacts, these measures also tend to be very expensive, and therefore unlikely to be implemented. The maximum hydro-no coal scenario, which brings very large GHG emissions reductions, would have a high impact on biodiversity and resettlement requirements (because some of the larger hydro projects, such as upper reservoir of the Upper Kotmale project, involve reservoirs of significant size). However, among those measures that are more modest in cost—or even those, like certain DSM measures that will *reduce* costs—there is a coincidence of global and local impact reduction.

(d) A number of transportation sector measures, advocated on grounds of ameliorating local air quality impacts, or general improvements in the fuel efficiency of the sector, prove to have significant

GHG emissions reduction benefits as well. The introduction of vehicle inspection and maintenance programs would bring significant reductions in both particulate and GHG emissions. Most of the other road transport sector measures advocated by the Clean Air 2000 program for air quality improvement in the Colombo Metropolitan area have a more limited impact on GHG emissions.

(e) The use of flue gas desulfurization (FGD) systems for SO_2 control emerges as a particularly poor option. Indeed, the results emphasize the importance of making decisions about FGD systems at the planning rather than at the project level. If indeed FGD systems are to be required at coal plants, it may be that coal plants ought not to be built at all. At least in the case of Sri Lanka, a policy that would require FGD systems results in the least cost system moving to diesels and hydro plants. In any event, new clean coal technologies, such as pressurized fluidized bed combustion (PFBC) reduce not only SO_2 emissions, but particulates, and NO_x and CO_2 emissions (per kWh generated) as well. And finally, when one examines impacts (such as the value of the health index), rather than just emissions (such as SO_2 emissions), it becomes obvious that fitting FGD systems to remotely located coal plants with high stacks brings little reduction in impacts in comparison to measures taken at older urban fossil plants (with typically short stacks) that burn high-sulfur residual oil in close proximity to population centers.

(f) Perhaps the most significant finding relates to the potential replacement of coal plants by steam-cycle oil fired plants. To date, these have not been considered by CEB. The decision to focus on coal plants to meet baseload requirements goes back to the early 1980s, some years before the collapse of world oil prices in 1986. This analysis suggests that significant GHG emissions reductions are possible by this option, and at present levels of oil prices, may even provide economic benefits as well. It is of course true—as also shown by this analysis—that if oil prices return to the US$30 per bbl level, costs would increase; the coal strategy undoubtedly lowers exposure to this price risk.[36]

---

[36]To be sure, if other coal-using utilities in the region were to change to residual fuel oil as a GHG emissions reduction measure, there may be an upward pressure on fuel oil prices. However, most of these other countries would be much more likely to switch to natural gas. Moreover, Sri Lanka is perhaps unique in that both coal and oil are imported, and therefore the differential between them is much narrower than in countries such as Indonesia, where the economics of mine-mouth coal-fired plants makes it very unlikely that a shift to oil for GHG emissions reduction purposes would be likely.

However, if the increase in price is seen purely as a GHG emissions reduction measure, then the relevant comparison is against other GHG emissions reduction options that have obtained GEF support, such as wind plants, which are certainly more expensive.

(g)   In conclusion, the emphasis given to efficient pricing in both project loans and adjustment lending is therefore justified not only on grounds of economic efficiency, but also on grounds of minimizing the environmental damages of economic development. This report clearly and explicitly demonstrates that efficient pricing makes a significant contribution to environmentally sustainable development.

Table 6-1: Specific Generation Costs

Project/plant	Capacity, MW	Specific costs, U.S. cents/kWh
Remaining hydro projects		
Upper Kotmale	150	4.69
Kukule (run-of-river)	70	5.40
Ging Ganga	49	5.30
Belihul Oya	17	6.26
Broadlands	40	7.52
Moragolla	27	7.90
Uma Oya	150	8.12
Thermal		
Coal (70%PF)[150 MW]	150	6.1
Coal(70%PF)[300 MW]	300	5.00
Diesel (70%PF)	10	5.51
Combustion turbine (20%PF)	22	11.00

Source: CEB Report on Long Term Generation Expansion Planning Studies, 1993–2007, October 1992.

Table 6-2: CEB Estimates of the LRMC

	LRMC Rs/kWh	Losses, as % of generation	Fraction of total demand (%)
Generation	2.21	1.9	
HT transmission		3.9	
HV	2.63		
Grid substation		1.8	
HV2	2.75		0.94
Transmission		4.8	
MV3	4.23		11.56
Substation		1.3	
MV2	5.28		48.75
Distribution		3.5	
LV	5.7		38.75

Table 6-3: The Impact of Pricing Policy

	3% return	Meet all covenants	AIC
PV(capital investment), US$m	1,214	1,159	963
Levelized tariff, Rs/kWh	2.82	3.46	5.17
Impacts in year 2005			
Fuel imports, US$m	73	64	51
Installed capacity, MW	2,170	2,130	2,050
CO_2 emissions, mt/year	4.07	3.63	3.03
Demand, gwh	7,638	7,197	6,624
Tariff, Rs/kWh	3.1	4.2	6.2

Table 6-4: Summary of Options Examined

Option	Comments	Symbol
Technology options		
Wind energy	305 MW total	**wind**
Mini-hydro		**minihy**
DSM: energy efficient refrigerators		**EER**
DSM: compact fluorescents		**CFL**
T&D loss reduction	12% T&D loss target by 2001 (rather than 2004 in reference case)	**T&D(+)**
	10% T&D losses by 2005	**T&D(++)**
	12% T&D loss target delayed to 2010	**T&D(-)**
Max hydro	Builds both reservoirs in the Upper Kotmale project; all hydro project listed on Table 6-1 are built by 2008. Coal plants replaced by diesels.	**maxHy(D)**
	As above, but using steam-cycle oil plants	**maxHy(oil)**
Clean coal technology	Pressurized fluidized bed combustion-combined cycle units; assumed for all coal units after 2000:	**PFBC**
	With pessimistic capital cost assumptions (US$350/kW increase in capital cost, vs. US$175/kW in the less pessimistic case).	**PFBC(-)**
	Flue gas desulfurization systems forced onto reference case coal plants	****FGD**
	Coal plants must be fitted wth FGD; model free to chose least cost expansion path	**FGD**
No coal	Model free to choose least-cost combination of oil-steam and hydro. Oil plants assumed to use high-sulfur oil.	**OS**
	As no coal, but using low-sulfur oil, low price differential to high-sulfur oil (US$0.5/bbl)	**LSOS(-)**
	As no coal, but using low-sulfur fuel oil, high price differential to high-sulfur oil (US$3.50/bbl)	**LSOS(+)**
	As no coal, but with high world oil price (US$30/bbl by 2004)	**OS(highWoP)**
Transportation sector	Vehicle inspection and maintenance programs	**V/M**
Pricing policy options		
Historical		**RoE=3%**
Financial		**R**
LRMC/AIC		**AIC**

Figure 6-1: The Model

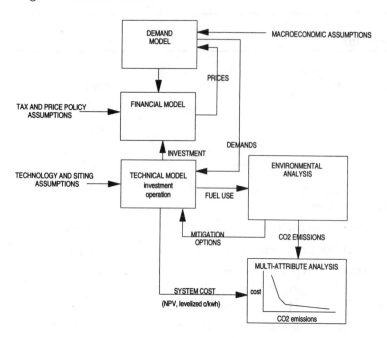

Source: Meier and Munasinghe (1994), p. 162.

Figure 6-2: Expected Trends for CO_2 Emissions in Sri Lanka

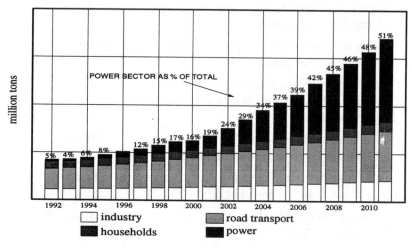

Source: Meier and Munasinghe (1994), p. 162.

Assumptions

Ceylon Electricity Board (CEB) base case load forecast for electricity (about 8 percent growth per annum (p.a.)) and the Official Generation Plan (that has a first 150 megawatts coal-fired unit on line in 2001). Household, industry, and road transport emissions are based on a Petroleum Product forecast of the Ceylon Petroleum Corporation. The household sector includes only liquified petroleum gas and kerosene consumption; net contribution to GHGs from fuelwood combustion assumed to be zero.

Figure 6-3: T&D Loss Predictions (technical plus nontechnical, as a percentage of generation)

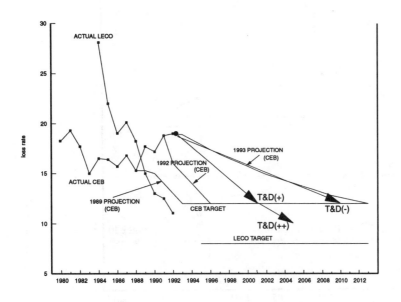

Figure 6-4: The Real Price of Electricity

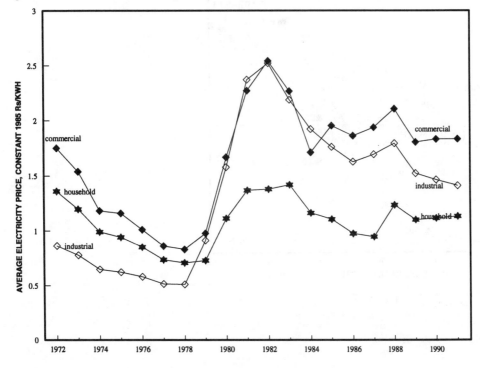

Sources: Munasinghe (1990) and CEB (1992a).

Figure 6-5: Balance Sheet Ratios

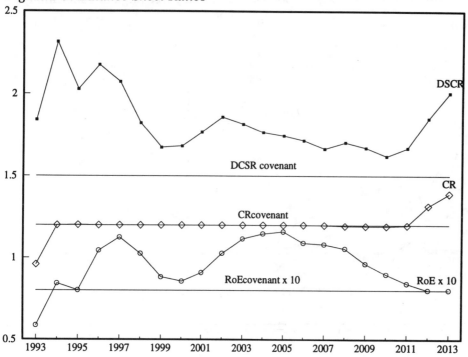

Figure 6-6: System Cost versus GHG Emissions

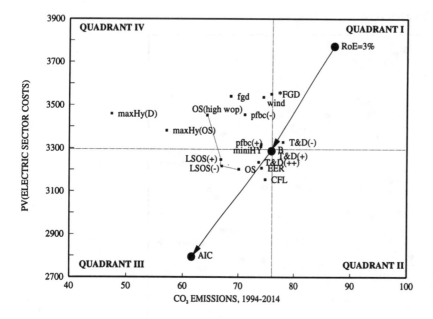

Figure 6-7: The Optimum Portfolio for GHG Reduction

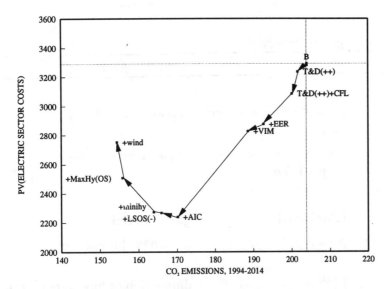

Source: Meier, Munasinghe, and Siyambalapitiya (1993).

Figure 6-8: The Cost Curve for GHG Emission Reductions

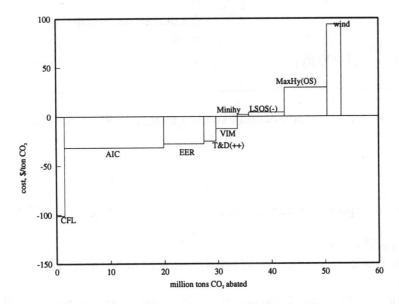

Source: Meier, Munasinghe, and Siyambalapitiya (1993).

Annex 6-A: Attributes

List of attributes in the Sri Lanka energy sector model

Attribute	Units	Impact/objective
Nonenvironmental		
System cost	present value of system costs	economic efficiency
Tariff	levelized average rate, Rs per kWh	impact on consumers
Environmental		
Emissions of carbon dioxide	[1000 tons]	global warming.
Population exposure to air pollutants (1)	person-μg/m^3/yr	human health impacts
Biodiversity index (2)	[ ].$^{(2)}$	diminution of biodiversity; impact on habitat of endemic species.
Increase in surface temperature > 1°C	[ha]	ecosystem impacts from thermal plumes.
Employment		discounted incremental employment
Emissions of acid rain precursors (SO$_2$ and NO$_x$)	[1,000 t/y]	potential for acid rain damages

(1) The health impact index that reflected the population exposure to these pollutants. This was defined as

$$X = C_j P_j$$

where X is the cumulative population exposure to the incremental ambient concentration attributable to the power plant.

P_j is the population in the j-th grid square.
C_j is the incremental average annual concentration in the j-th square, attributable to the emissions from the source in question.
The C_j were calculated using a simple Gaussian plume model run for some given number of wind direction and wind speed combinations. The total concentration in square j is then simply the sum of the individual plume contributions:

$$C_j = c_{jk}$$

where C_{jk} is the incremental contribution in square j attributable to the k-th plume.

(2) The biodiversity index was developed to quantify the relative biodiversity value of habitat lost. The index value was based on the relative probability of finding an endemic species in each of Sri

Lanka's major terrestrial habitat types. Thus 1 hectare of lowland wet evergreen forest was assigned a value of 1; a comparable hectare of monocultures (rice paddies, tea plantations) was assigned a value of 0.001, with other habitats assigned intermediate values. While such scales do involve subjective judgment, the scale was developed by the eminent ecologist K. Arudpragasam, professor of ecology at the University of Colombo and former chairman of the Central Environment Authority of Sri Lanka. For further details, see Meier and Munasinghe 1994, Chapter 8.

Annex 6-B: The Concept of Dominance and Tradeoff Curves

On Figure 6B-1, we illustrate the concept of dominance and the tradeoff curve.[37] Consider the option "MaxHy(D)," in which are built all hydro plants indicated on Table 6-1 (in the main text), and in which coal plants are replaced by diesels. This is better (lower) in both GHG emissions and cost than all of the options in the hatched quadrant—namely, wind, FGD, *FGD, and RoE=3%. These options are said to be "dominated" by MaxHy(D). The tradeoff curve is then defined as the set of nondominated options (or "noninferior" set).

Note that among a set of mutually exclusive options, only one member of such a set can be on each tradeoff curve. In the case of the oil-steam options, the curve as drawn assumes that the relevant scenario is under present oil prices, and a low differential for low-sulfur oil (LSOS(-)); under high world oil prices, the curve would shift to the north, and include EER, a lower T&D loss rate target, and none of the oil-steam cycle options would lie on the tradeoff curve. In other words, each scenario (of exogenous assumptions) will have its own tradeoff curve.

We distinguish here between two flue gas desulfurization FGD options: the one indicated by "**FGD" forces FGD onto the reference case coal plants, while in the solution indicated as "FGD," the model is free to build whatever it likes—but if coal plants are selected, they must be fitted with FGD. Inspection of the solution shows that if FGD systems are required, and the model is free to build the least cost sequence (i.e., case "FGD"), then the first coal plant is delayed from 2004 in the reference case to 2007, and the Broadlands and Uma Oya hydro plants are built in 2004 (plants that are not built in the reference case).

Therefore, GHG emissions decrease relative to the base case. Note also that pressurized fluidized bed combustion (PFBC), under both the optimistic "PFBC(+)" and pessimistic "PFBC(-)" capital cost assumptions, dominate the case in which FGD is forced on conventional coal plants ("*FGD").

This analysis shows very clearly the desirability of making decisions about whether or not FGD systems are to be required on a systemwide basis, at the planning stage, rather than on a case-by-case basis at the project level, at the stage of the project environmental assessment. The usual analysis of FGD systems that is often provided in project-level environmental impact statements, in which the only options that are considered are with and without an FGD system, is thus very likely to lead to poor decisions.

On Figure 6B-2, we examine the tradeoff curve for a local environmental impact. Rather than just use local air emissions as the attribute, we define a health impact index, in which a Gaussian dispersion air quality model was applied to prospective power plant locations, and the resulting increments in ambient air quality for fine particulates and NO_x was overlaid with population distribution. Although we do not go one step further and apply mortality or morbidity functions, the use of population weighted ambient air quality changes is distinctly preferable to the use of just emissions as a measure of actual impact.[38]

This figure illustrates the importance of siting assumptions. In the case "MaxHy(D)," coal plants are assumed replaced by diesels,

---

[37]For a full discussion of the concepts of dominance, noninferior sets, and other ideas of multiattribute decision analysis as applied to energy-environmental analysis, see, e.g., Meier and Munasinghe (1994), Chapter 6.

[38]For example, the set of qualitative "air impact" ratings applied in a siting study for Sri Lanka performed in the mid-1980s suggested that the difference between the best-ranked and the worst-ranked score for this attribute was about 1:1.6. Yet the quantitative calculations using changes in this health index showed variations greater than one order of magnitude for the same set of sites. See Annex 6-A for further details on the health impact index calculation.

sited mainly in urban areas, whereas in "MaxHy(OS)," the coal plants are assumed replaced by steam-cycle oil plants at similar remote locations (namely Trincomalee in the northeast). Thus the MaxHy(D) case falls in the "lose-lose" quadrant for health effects. However, when the diesels are moved to locations identical to the coal plants, their health impacts also fall, indicated by the arrow on the figure.

Figure 6B–1: Definition of Dominance and the Trade-Off Curve

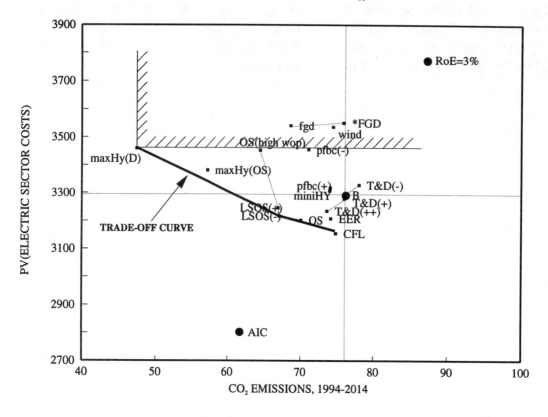

Figure 6B–2: Local Health Impacts

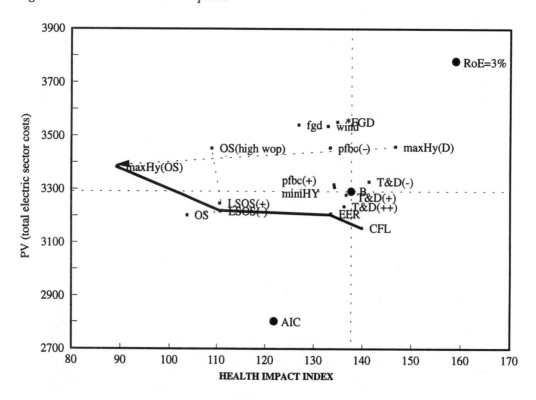

Bibliography

Alfsen, K. H., A. Brendemoen, and S. Glomsrod. 1992. "Benefits of Climate Policies: Some Tentative Calculations." Discussion Paper, Central Bureau of Statistics, Oslo.

Anderson, D., and R. H. Williams. 1993. "The Cost-Effectiveness of GEF Projects." Global Environment Facility, Working Paper No. 6, Washington, D.C.

Banuri, T., et al. 1995. "Equity and Social Considerations. Intergovernmental Panel on Climate Change." Working Group III, Chapter 3.

Baron, W., and P. Hills. 1990. "Greenhouse Gas Emissions; Issues and Possible Responses in Six Large Lower Income Asian Nations." Working Paper No. 45, Center for Urban Planning and Environmental Management, University of Hong Kong.

Bernstein, M. 1992). "Costs and Greenhouse Gas emissions of Energy Supply and Use." Environment Department, Working Paper 1993-40, World Bank, Washington, D.C.

Blitzer, C., R. Eckhaus, S. Lahiri, and A. Meeraus. 1993. "Growth and Welfare Losses from Carbon Emissions Restrictions: A General Equilibrium Analysis of Egypt." *The Energy Journal* 14(1):57–81.

Buhring, W., et al. 1991. *ENPEP: An Integrated Approach for Modeling National Energy Systems.* Argonne National Laboratory, Environmental Assessment and Information Sciences Division.

Burgess, J. 1990. "The contribution of efficient energy pricing to reducing carbon dioxide emissions." *Energy Policy* (June): 449–55.

Busch, B., P. DuPont, and S. Chirarattananon. 1993. "Energy Efficient Lighting in Thai Commercial Buildings." *Energy* 18(2):197–210.

Ceylon Electricity Board (CEB). 1992a. "Long Run Marginal Costing, 1992." Load Forecasting and Tariffs Section, Colombo, Sri Lanka.

———. 1992b. "Power and Demand Forecast 1992–2012." Load Forecasting and Tariffs Section, Colombo, Sri Lanka.

———. 1992c. "Wind Energy Resources Assessment: Southern Lowlands of Sri Lanka." Colombo, Sri Lanka.

Coppel, J. 1991. *An Analysis of Energy Policy Measures and Their Impact on CO_2 Emissions.* Proceedings, ESCAP Conference on Greenhouse Research, Bangkok, pp. 263–86.

Crousillat, E. 1989. *Incorporating Risk and Uncertainty in Power System Planning.* Energy series paper no. 17, Industry and Energy Department, World Bank, Washington, D.C.

Electric Power Research Institute (EPRI). 1993. *Proceedings of the SO_2 Control Symposium (Section 5A). Boston, Mass., August 24–27.*

Energy Modeling Forum (EMF). 1993. Reducing Global Carbon Emissions—Costs and Policy Options. EMF-12, Stanford University, Stanford.

Florida Solar Energy Center. 1991. *Residential Demand Side Management for Thailand.* Report to IIEC.

Fuglestvedt, J., et al. 1994. A Review of Country Case Studies on Climate Change. Global Environment Facility, Working Paper No. 7, Washington, D.C.

Gesellschaft für Technische Zusammenarbeit (German Technical Assistance Agency, GTZ). 1989. Electricity Masterplan. Colombo, Sri Lanka.

Global Environment Facility. 1992. "Economic Costs of Carbon Dioxide Reduction Strategies." Working Paper series Number III, Washington, D.C.

Goto, N., and T. Sawa. 1993. "An Analysis of the Macro-Economic Costs of Various CO_2 Emission Control Policies in Japan." *Energy Journal* 14(1):83–110.

Hirst, E. 1992. "Price and Cost Impacts of Utility DSM Programs." *Energy Journal* 13(4):75–90.

Hobbs, B. F. 1991. "The 'Most Value' Test: Economic Evaluation of Electricity Demand-Side Management Considering Customer Value." *Energy Journal* 12(2): 67–91.

Hogan, W. 1990. "Comments on Manne and Richels: CO_2 Emission Limits: An Economic Cost Analysis for the USA." *Energy Journal* 11(2):75–85.

Hourcade, J. C. et al. 1995. "A Review of Mitigation Cost Studies. Intergovernmental Panel on Climate Change." Working Group III Report, Chapter 9.

International Institute for Energy Conservation. 1993. "Thailand: Promotion of Energy Efficiency: Pre-investment Appraisal." Report to the USEPA, Global Climate Change Division, Bangkok, Thailand.

Japan International Cooperation Agency. 1987. "Feasibility Study on Upper Kotmale Hydro-electric Power Development Project." August.

Jones, B., and E. Wheeler (eds.). 1992. *Greenhouse Research Initiatives in the ESCAP Region.* Proceedings of a Conference, Bangkok, August 1991, ESCAP, Bangkok.

Joskow, P. L., and D. Marron. 1992. "What Does a Negawatt Really Cost? Evidence from Utility Conservation Programs." *Energy Journal* 13(4):41–74.

King, K. 1993a. "The Incremental Costs of Global Environmental Benefits, Global Environment Facility, Working Paper No. 5, Washington, D.C.

————. 1993b. "Issues to be Addressed by the Program for Measuring Incremental Costs for the Environment." Global Environment Facility, Working Paper No. 8, Washington, D.C.

Larsen, B. 1993. *World Fossil Fuel Subsidies and Global Carbon Emissions in a Model with Inter-Fuel Substitution.* World Bank, Washington, D.C.

Manne, A., and R. Richels. 1990. "CO_2 Emission Limits: An Economic Cost Analysis for the USA." *Energy Journal* 11(2): 51–74.

Markandya, A. 1990. "Environmental Costs and Power System Planning." *Utilities Policy* 1:13–27.

Markandya, A., and Pearce, D. 1988. *Environmental Considerations and the Choice of the Discount Rate in Developing Countries.* Environment Department Working paper No. 3. World bank, Washington, D.C.

Meier, P. 1990. "Power Sector Innovation in Developing Countries: Implementing Investment Planning under Capital and Environmental Constraints." *Annual Review of Energy* 15:277–306.

Meier, P., (1995). *ENVIROPLAN: A Multi-Attribute Decision-Analysis Model for Power Sector Planning.* IDEA, Inc., Washington, D.C.

Meier, P., and M. Munasinghe. 1994. *Incorporating Environmental Concerns into Power Sector Decision-Making: A Case Study of Sri Lanka.* Environment Department, World Bank, Washington D.C.

Meier, P., M. Munasinghe, and T. Siyambalapitiya. 1993. *Energy Sector Policy and the Environment: A Case Study of Sri Lanka.* Environment Department, World Bank, Washington, D.C.

Metropolitan Environmental Improvement Programme. 1992. *Clean Air 2000: An Action Plan for Air Quality Management in the Colombo Metropolitan Area.* Colombo.

Miller, P., H. Geller, and A. deAlmeida. 1992. "An Example of Energy Savings in LDCs: Improving Electrical Equipment in Pakistan." *Energy* 17(10):969–82.

Mills, E. 1991. "Evaluation of European Lighting Programs: Utilities Finance Energy Efficiency." *Energy Policy* (April): 266–78.

Ministry of Environment. 1991. *National Environmental Action Plan.* Colombo.

Ministry of Environment and Parliamentary Affairs. 1990. *National Environmental Action Plan.* Colombo, Sri Lanka.

Mintzer, I., and D. Von Hippel. 1993. *Greenhouse Gas Assessment Methodology.* Report to the Global Environment Facility, World Bank, Washington, D.C.

Moreira, J. R., et al. 1992. "UNEP Greenhouse Gas Abatement Costing Studies." Brazil Country Study.

Munasinghe, M. 1990. *Electric Power Economics.* London, U.K.: Butterworths.

Munasinghe, M., and G. Schramm. 1983. *Energy Economics, Demand Management, and Conservation Policy.* New York: Van Nostrand Reinhold.

Nordhaus, W. D. 1991. AThe Cost of Slowing Climate Change: A Survey." *Energy Journal* 12(1):37–65.

Ogawa, Y., and H. Awata. 1991. *Simulation Study of Greenhouse Gas Emissions due to Future Energy Consumption.* Proceedings, ESCAP Conference of Greenhouse Research, Bangkok, August 1991, p. 234–62.

OKO Institute. 1989. *Umweltanalyse von Energie Systemen: Gesamt Emissions Modell Integrierter Systeme (GEMIS).* Ministry of Economy and Technology, Hessen, Darmstadt, Germany.

Organisation for Economic Co-operation and Development (OECD). 1993. The Costs of Cutting Carbon Emissions: Results from Global Models. Paris.

Pachauri, R. K. 1991. *Global Warming: Impacts and Implications for South Asia.* Tata Energy Research Institute, New Delhi.

Pearce, D. 1990. The Role of Carbon Taxes in Adjusting to Global Warming. *Economic Journal.*

Pearce, D. W., et al. 1995. The Social Costs of Climate Change: Greenhouse Damage and the Benefits of Control. Intergovernmental Panel on Climate Change, Working Group III Report, Chapter 6.

Proost, S., and D. Van Regemorter. 1992. "Economic Effects of a Carbon Tax: With a General Equilibrium Illustration for Belgium." *Energy Policy* 136–49.

Schipper, L., and D. Hawk. 1991. "More Efficient Household Electricity Use: An International Perspective." *Energy Policy* (April):244–55.

Tata Energy Research Institute (TERI). 1992. UNEP Greenhouse Gas Abatement Costing Studies: India Country Study, Phase I. New Delhi, India.

Tavoulareas, E. S., and J.-P. Charpentier. 1995. "Clean Coal Technologies for Developing Countries." World Bank Technical Paper No. 286, Energy Series, World Bank, Washington, D.C.

United Nations Environment Programme (UNEP). 1992. UNEP Greenhouse Gas Abatement Costing Studies, Phase I Report, Riso National Laboratory, Denmark.

U.S. Agency for International Development (USAID). 1994. "Demand-Side Management Action Plan for the Philippines." Office of Energy, Environment and Technology, Washington, D.C.

Van Dang, G. 1993. "UNEP Greenhouse Gas Abatement Costing Studies: The Case of Thailand." Asian Institute of Technology, Bangkok, Thailand.

Warford, J., A. Schwab, W. Cruz, and S. Hansen. 1992. *The Evolution of Environmental Concerns in Adjustment Lending: A Review.* Washington, D.C.: World Bank, November.

Wijeratne, D. C. 1993. Potential for Efficient Lighting in Sri Lanka: An Economic Analysis. Transactions of the Institution of Engineers, Sri Lanka, Colombo.

Wijeratne, D. C. 1994a. Domestic refrigerators: Energy Consumption and the Potential for Conservation. Paper presented at the Annual Meeting, Sri Lanka Energy Managers Association, Colombo.

Wijeratne, D. C. 1994b. Sri Lanka: Renewable Projects and Programs. Ceylon Electricity Board, Colombo.

World Bank. 1982. "Sri Lanka, Issues and Options in the Energy Sector." Report 3794–CE. World Bank, Washington, D.C.
———. 1983. *Sri Lanka Power System Loss Reduction Study.* UNDP-World Bank Energy Sector Management Program, Report 007/83, Washington, D.C.

Yamagi, Y. et al. 1993. "A Study on Economic Measures for CO_2 Reduction in Japan." *Energy Policy* 21(2):123–31.

7

Tunisia: Livestock Policies and Environmental Impacts During Economic Adjustment

Zeinab Partow and Stephen D. Mink

TUNISIA'S CONCERN WITH INCREASING the country's self-sufficiency in livestock products and with the affordability of these products for its citizens has resulted in a web of pricing and subsidy interventions in the livestock sector. The environmental consequences of these measures, namely the degradation of Tunisia's rangelands, however, have rarely been a central consideration.

While a variety of subsidies has promoted the intensification of livestock production in parts of Tunisia, in other regions government subsidies and policies have encouraged the maintenance of the national herd at levels beyond the carrying capacity of the country's rangelands. Particularly during dry years, subsidized feed imports have provided a substitute for reduced grazing supplies, and have succeeded in averting the large declines in animal numbers often associated with droughts. This failure of livestock numbers to respond to diminished feed availability in natural pastures, however, has contributed to significant environmental degradation of the Tunisian range.

The continuing deterioration of Tunisia's rangelands has direct effects on livestock production, and longer-term, indirect implications for the entire agriculture sector. While important efforts at pasture improvement and reforestation are under way, the positive impacts of these and other measures are often undermined by subsidy and pricing policies that fail to consider or respond to environmental signals.

This chapter investigates the effect of subsidies and pricing policies on the livestock sector, evaluates the impact of these policies on the condition of Tunisia's rangelands, and considers the likely consequences of recent changes in these policies as part of the economic adjustment program that began in 1986.

The Context of Adjustment Policies

The macroeconomic context

In the early 1980s, Tunisia began to face growing macroeconomic imbalances. By 1985, with oil reserves and revenues declining, slow growth of other exports, and worsening indicators of the external debt burden, it was becoming clear that current account deficits could no longer be financed.

Stabilization policies were initiated in 1986. Reformers in government recognized the need for greater efficiency in investment and a greater role for the private sector in accomplishing this. They did not want to stop at short-term, macroeconomic stabilization, but rather aimed to get rid of the old dirigiste policies, to orient the economy outward, and to increase the role of market mechanisms. These reformers' objectives took a major step forward in 1987 when the regime of President Bourguiba was removed in a managed transition to a new government, under the leadership of President Ben Ali.

Despite the best intentions of the new government, adjustment policies were implemented with halting progress over the next five years. Severe droughts in 1988 and 1989 caused delays in initiating reforms that had high social costs initially. Just emerging from these economic blows, Tunisia was then hit by the consequences of the Gulf War during 1990–91, most immediately by a sharp drop in tourism, one of the principal foreign exchange earners of the economy.

Nonetheless, important elements of structural adjustment have been accomplished, and there have been improvements in macroeconomic indicators. Reform efforts have focused on (a) privatization and restructuring of state-owned enterprises; (b) liberalization of domestic price and imports; (c) rationalization of the structure of import tariffs, followed by a reduction in quantitative import restrictions; (d) removal of most credit and interest rate controls; and (e) tax reforms, including introduction of a value added tax in 1988 and revised direct tax in 1990.

The agricultural context

The agricultural sector is important in the overall economy, and has undergone substantial changes since 1987 because of adjustment policy reforms. Tunisian agriculture remains predominantly rainfed and prone to production risks linked to climate. Only 5 percent of cropped land is irrigated, although this land accounts for a much higher share of sector value added. The sector, excluding agro-industry, employs nearly one out of every three workers in the labor force, generates 13–15 percent of gross domestic product (GDP) and contributes about 11 percent to export earnings, although these indicators are undergoing structural decline.

Several objectives have motivated the adjustment process in the agricultural sector. First, adjustment has been concerned with the agricultural trade gap, particularly for cereals, meat, milk, and sugar, and is trying to increase the country's production of these staples. Second, it is oriented toward improving rural incomes, as a means of reducing migration to towns and cities, where unemployment is a problem at 15 percent. Buffering domestic production and incomes from the short-run consequences of drought is of particular concern, and various responses have been tried, including subsidies for irrigation infrastructure and water. Finally, maintaining affordable prices for a variety of food staples for consumers has been an objective, and has been pursued through food subsidies financed from the *Caisse de Compensation General* (CGC).

Pursuing these objectives, while undertaking fundamental structural adjustments in the agricultural sector, has required a delicate balancing act. Elements of the reform policy include (a) producer price realignment (mostly upward), followed by adjustments to international prices; (b) reduction in credit subsidies; (c) reforms of parastatals involved in cereals, olive oils, fisheries, and livestock; and (d) reduction of subsidies for inputs, including fertilizer, animal feed, and irrigation water. The latter reforms were meant to encourage private participation in marketing fertilizer and feed inputs, and to reduce the burden of their subsidization on the government budget through the CGC (see Table 7-1).

Significant liberalization of the sector has already occurred, with additional reforms being implemented with strong government commitment. Cereal producer prices have been raised and linked to world prices, input subsidies have been lowered, and restrictions on private sector involvement in internal marketing of cereals, exports of olive oil, and imports of beef and powdered milk were relaxed. Despite considerable progress, the agricultural sector still faces significant constraints.

These constraints are evident from the recent performance of the sector. Growth averaged 4.2 percent annually in real terms in the first half of the 1980s, then slowed to only 1.5 percent in the latter half because of three drought years, before recovering with a record cereals crop in 1991. Domestic production has not kept pace with rapidly growing demand, resulting from population and income growth, and reinforced by high consumer price subsidies on many staple foods. While exports of agricultural commodities have rapidly expanded (12.6 percent average for 1987–90), they have been outstripped by increasing imports (18.8 percent).

Livestock has traditionally played an important role within the agricultural sector, and continues to account for almost 30 percent of sectoral value added. Decades ago, nomads would move their herds over long distances from Central and Southern Tunisia to the North in a transhumant pattern that took advantage of seasonal pasture in the South and post-harvest crop stubble in the North. But intensification of agriculture has broken this cycle, and herds are less mobile today and more dependent on locally available feed resources. Sheep and goats continue to be an important part of the national herd, particularly where conditions are more difficult, while intensively run dairy and poultry operations have gained in importance over the past twenty years.

Environmental Trends

Livestock raising and its related input and marketing activities have a number of potential impacts on the environment. This chapter focuses primarily on one of these—range and grazing land degradation—rather than on potential problems such as pollution from intensive production systems and from slaughterhouses. Range and grazing land degradation is influenced by a broader array of the reforms under reconsideration by policymakers; it also poses a larger environmental problem because of its links to erosion and siltation of hydrological infrastructure.

Bioclimatic zones

Nearly twenty percent of Tunisia's total land area of 16.2 million hectares is rangeland, much of it severely overgrazed. Less than a third of the country's area is cultivable. An additional 6 percent of the land mass is classified as forests and woodland, primarily in the North and Northwest, and is commonly used for livestock grazing. The remaining land area is desert or other noncultivable land.

Tunisia's landmass can also be described according to five geographic regions defined by climatic characteristics. These are the humid, subhumid, semiarid, arid, and desert zones. Alternatively, the first three of these are often grouped as the North; the arid zone coincides roughly with the Center; and the desert zone with the South (see Figure 7-1).

The humid zone in the northwest tip of Tunisia enjoys an average annual rainfall often in excess of 1,000 millimeters per year. This area supports intensive cereal cultivation and diminishing areas of natural cork oak woodland. The continuous felling of the cork oak and Aleppo pine woodland, now covering less than 250,000 hectares, parallels an increase in degraded area of *maquis* or underbrush. Bordering the humid zone to the east is the subhumid zone, with average rainfall between 600 and 800 millimeters per year. It is a region dominated by cereal cultivation, with only relatively small pockets of rangeland remaining on steeply sloping land prone to erosion. Many unpalatable species of thistle and gorse are often present and indicate derelict or overgrazed land. To the south are the large semiarid and arid regions of the Central steppes where the majority of Tunisia's range resources are located, and where rainfall is limited to 300–600 millimeters per year and

100–300 millimeters per year, respectively. Average vegetation falls dramatically, and there is evidence of heavy overgrazing of rangelands. Vegetative cover is estimated to average 15 percent but drops to less than 8 percent over large areas. This zone becomes increasingly arid as one moves to the south and east and merges at about the 150 millimeters isohyet into the Sahara, a region characterized by very low rainfall (less than 100 millimeters per year) and extremes of temperature and wind (Kennedy 1989, p. 120).

Land degradation

Only piecemeal data exist on the severity and evolution of land degradation in Tunisia.[1] Nevertheless, various studies on the condition of Tunisia's rangelands, in addition to existing environmental data, indicate that Tunisian rangelands suffer from significant environmental deterioration. Unfortunately, this information is inadequate to determine the immediate environmental impacts of recent policy changes, but speculative conclusions will be suggested below. Future analysis will benefit by a rangeland inventory and analytic capacity currently being developed by the Ministry of Agriculture.

Estimates made in 1980 indicated that approximately 1.2 million hectares were seriously affected by erosion in North and Central Tunisia—representing 25 percent of land resources in those regions.[2] Another study estimates 23,000 hectares of productive land are removed from agricultural use each

---

[1]The term land degradation is used here to refer to a process of vegetation depletion which ultimately results in soil erosion, loss of nutrients, and decreased yields. In parts of Tunisia where desertification is a threat, degradation is also linked to wind erosion resulting from the reduction of the perennial plant cover below a critical threshold (Le Houerou 1990, pp. 100–104).

[2]World Bank 1989b, p. 12. Unfortunately, the study did not distinguish between arable and nonarable lands.

year due to a number of factors, primarily water and wind erosion, which affect 10,000 and 8,000 hectares, respectively.[3]

Most natural rangelands are in a state of continuous and advanced degradation as a result of overexploitation and poor management, often encouraged by inappropriate policies, and exacerbated by periodic droughts. Tunisia's rangelands are largely located in the arid and desert bioclimatic zones corresponding with the Center and South (Table 7-2). Here, wind erosion is a major problem. While reliable data on losses in soil fertility are difficult to find, it is estimated that 5.5 of the 10.6 million hectares south of Sfax are moderately or severely affected by desertification. Permanent loss is estimated to average about 8,000 hectares per year (World Bank 1989a, p. 40; Hamza and Bennour 1990, p. 79). Soil removal at a rate of over 1 millimeter per month has been measured on cultivated sandy steppes of Southern Tunisia (Le Houerou 1986, p. 112).

The direct causes of rangeland degradation in semiarid and arid zones of Tunisia are tree and shrub cutting for fuelwood, the overgrazing of rangelands, and the extension of rainfed cultivation onto traditional rangelands. Traditional grazing lands in the Center and South are also being lost to mechanized cultivation of cereals (particularly barley) during the wet years, as well as to tree crops (olives and almonds), only to be left denuded and unprotected from erosive winds during drier years. Over the past two decades, an estimated 500,000 hectares of land in semiarid and hilly areas have been brought into production, mainly for cereals (World Bank 1982, p. 27). Land policy has also encouraged the conversion of grazing land to crops through a policy to extend land ownership rights to those who invest in the land—i.e. clear and cultivate it—rather than to those who use it for tradi-

tional grazing (World Bank 1989a, p. 40).

In Northern Tunisia, land degradation is largely the consequence of water erosion. Gully erosion is common in the Tell, where the rate of soil loss has been measured at 1,020 tons per square kilometer per year (United States National Committee for Man and the Biosphere 1981, p. 23). Both physical and human factors account for the high levels of erosion. On the one hand, the land is steepest where the rainfall is highest; on the other, forest clearing, overgrazing, fuelwood collection, and cultivation of even the steepest slopes expose the soil to wind and rain. The limited rainfall often arrives in heavy showers between the months of October and April—50 percent of the rainfall occurs between the months of December and February—resulting in significant water erosion.

Carrying capacity

Rangelands in Central and Southern Tunisia have thus been subjected to multiple pressures that have tended to reduce their carrying capacity. Land conversion has shifted what are often the most fertile rangelands, in the highest rainfall zones, into crop lands, reducing both the quality and the quantity of the grazing resources available to ever-increasing numbers of livestock. The extension of farming into marginal lands has in turn contributed to soil erosion as permanent cover is lost and as the use of machinery to work the land increases. Carrying capacity has been further reduced by the gradual transformation of transhumant systems to sedentary livestock raising over the past decades, in effect reducing the range's restorative capacity.

Carrying capacity estimates are notoriously controversial, and difficult to specify for Tunisia. Ideally, carrying capacity estimates for different livestock management systems in the Tunisian context could be compared over time. Unfortunately, such estimates do not exist. Some analysts have extended rules of thumb applied in North American range management to the Tunisian rangelands, suggest-

---

[3]World Bank 1989a, pp. 38–39. An additional 1,000 hectares is lost to flooding, and 4,000 hectares of agricultural land is diverted to urban use each year.

ing a stocking rate of 1 livestock unit[4] per inch of rainfall per square mile per year. Converted into metric units and assuming average annual precipitation in the extensive pasture areas of Southern Tunisia to be 100 millimeters per year, this rule would allocate four livestock units to 2.63 square kilometers per year. Stocking rates in Tunisia were estimated in 1981 to be three to eight times greater than this ideal rate (United States National Committee for Man and the Biosphere 1981, p. 20). There are, of course, serious problems with extending this standard to Tunisia, particularly given the low levels of milk production and liveweight characteristic of Tunisian livestock. Nevertheless the orders of magnitude indicate that stocking rates did exceed carrying capacities over a decade ago. Given the growth of the national herd over the past ten years, the situation is likely to have worsened.

As land degradation progresses, the reduction in the consumable production of rangelands is quite dramatic. Rangelands in fair condition, with a plant cover of 25 percent, are capable of producing 820 kilograms of consumable plant material annually; overgrazed rangelands only produce about 490 kilograms; and lands where wind erosion has blown away most of the top soil, with plant cover only about 4 percent, produce under 300 kilograms. (Le Houerou 1986, p. 123). Such a process has resulted in more livestock grazing on poorer resources—both in terms of quality and quantity—in Central and Southern Tunisia, affecting not only the regenerative capacity of the range, but also the productivity of livestock.

Alongside the reduction in carrying capacity of rangelands has been a trend of increasingly intensive livestock production in the North of the country. This intensification has been largely based on the consumption of feed concentrates, forage crops, and agricultural by-products. The use of both irrigation and fertilizers on forage crops has increased, and a more intensive agriculture, supplying more by-products, is being practiced, aided by growing mechanization. Thus, two competing trends characterize the livestock sector: (a) the reduction of the carrying capacity of the rangelands of Central and Southern Tunisia on the one hand, and (b) the intensification of livestock production in the North, based on cultivated crops and concentrates on the other.

The Livestock-Feed Balance

In this section, we turn to a more detailed discussion of the livestock sector, and to the role of government policies within it. The balance between feed availability and livestock numbers is a central factor affecting environmental conditions in Tunisia's rangelands. This section will outline the trends in the number of animals making up the national herd, followed by a discussion of feed resources.

Growth of the national herd

Eighty years ago the national herd consisted of the equivalent of 360,600 livestock units, nearly half of which were cattle, a third were sheep, and under a fifth were goats. By 1991 the national herd had grown nearly sixfold to over 2 million livestock units: sheep increased to 59 percent of the total livestock units; cattle and goats decreased to 29 percent and 12 percent, respectively.[5]

Growth of the national herd has remained steady over the past twenty years, albeit fluctuating from year to year with changes in rainfall and feed availability (see Figure 7-2).

---

[4]A livestock unit is here defined in bovine units and is equal to one head of cattle or five adult sheep or goats, with or without young.

[5]In terms of heads of livestock, the 1911 national herd composition was 171,000 cattle, 123,200 sheep and 66,400 goats, while the corresponding 1991 figures were 631,000, 1258,000 and 262,600. Camels are also important in the South, although their numbers have not fluctuated dramatically over the past twenty years, remaining steady at about 180,000 units.

These generalizations, however, mask the striking differences between the growth trends of sheep, goats, and cattle.

The ovine (sheep) herd has exhibited a more cyclical growth pattern than the bovine herd, due both to a more rapid turnover of animals and the herd's heavier dependence on natural pastures and thus on rainfall conditions. Particularly large declines in animal numbers take place when two or more dry years occur in succession, such as what happened in the late 1960s when numbers fell by nearly 25 percent, and in the late 1970s when numbers fell by nearly a third. This at least was true until the 1988–89 drought. During this latest drought, the ovine herd suffered less than 3 percent decline in total population, due in some measure to the subsidized provision of barley feed to small herders in drought-stricken areas.

In the 1920s to 1950s, the caprine (goat) herd was much larger than it is today. At what may have been a peak in 1944, the herd numbered 2.25 million. This fell to less than 400,000 heads in 1969, but has since been steadily increasing to the current level of over 1.3 million. As is the case with the ovine herd, goat numbers have in the past fluctuated with the rains and the availability of pasture. Two or more years of consecutive dry weather have resulted in declines of 25–30 percent. In the most recent droughts of 1988–89, however, goat numbers actually increased by 30,000 head (2.5 percent), reflecting the impact of subsidized barley provided as part of a drought-relief program.

Cattle numbers grew rapidly and continuously from the mid-1960s until 1978 due to dairy promotion policies, but the herd size then fell precipitously during the drought of 1978–79. The cattle herd has not rebounded from that tremendous decline in numbers and has shown only modest growth over the 1980s. While the decline in numbers coincided with the droughts that struck the country in those two years, this is not a convincing explanation for the fall in cattle numbers,

since throughout the 1960s and 1970s, numbers had not shown any fluctuation with rainfall. Another explanation is the liberalization of mutton and goat meat prices in 1979 and the subsequent decline in the profitability of beef production, a topic which will be dealt with later in this chapter.

Livestock distribution by geographic zone and holding size

Nearly one-half of the national herd (in livestock units), is located in the Central and Southern regions of Tunisia. Livestock production in these regions is more heavily dependent on natural pastures, and therefore on rainfall conditions, than in the North.

Sheep are concentrated (46.9 percent) in the Center of the country, although there is a significant number in the North (39 percent). Sheep numbers in both areas are increasing, in contrast to the South where only 14.1 percent of the nearly 6.3 million sheep are located (see Figure 7-3).

The largest portion of the Tunisian goat herd is located in the arid Southern region of the country (41.6 percent), although the numbers in that region have not increased as significantly over the past ten years as they have in the North or the Center (see Figure 7-4). A third of the caprine herd is located in the North, and in this region numbers have increased steadily over the past decade. The Center accounts for 23 percent of the country's caprine herd, and here also, numbers have increased in recent years.

It is noteworthy that sheep and goat numbers in the South have shown only small increases and even declines over the past decade. The dependence of livestock on the natural range is greatest in the South, and the lack of increase in numbers suggests increasing degradation in this region, as well as to growing intensification of livestock production in other parts of the country.

The vast majority of the country's cattle herd is located in Northern Tunisia (81.5 percent). The Center is second with 17.5

percent, and last is the arid South with only 1 percent of the bovine herd. Total cattle numbers have been stable over the past decade and show no variation with rainfall, a reflection of the dairy herd's heavy dependence on concentrate feeds and cultivated forage crops.

Cattle ownership is concentrated in the smallest and largest farm size categories. Nearly half of all cattle are held in farms smaller than 10 hectares in size, while a quarter are held in farms of over 50 hectares. Small farms typically have fewer options in providing feed to their animals from on-farm resources, and are more dependent on pasturing their herd, partly on common property resources. Fewer sheep and goats are held in the smallest farms (25 percent and 35 percent in farms under 10 hectares, respectively). The sheep and goat herds are concentrated in the middle and larger farms over 20 hectares in size.

Feed sources

Five broad categories of feed resources are used in Tunisia: (a) pastures, both forested and nonforested; (b) agricultural by-products, such as straw, stubble, hay, and silage; (c) fallow; (d) forages and forage shrubs; and (e) feed concentrates. With the obvious exception of feed concentrates, the composition of the various feed sources, their biomass, and productivity vary enormously in response to varying degrees of social and environmental stress (Kennedy 1989, p. 120). The contributions to livestock feed requirements of the different resources for 1986, a dry year, were 30 percent for agricultural by-products, 25 percent for feed concentrates, 23 percent for forage, 12 percent for pasture and 10 percent of fallow lands (FAO 1988, Vol. I).

In broad terms, the strategy for improving availability and quality of feed resources has followed several paths. In the North, intensification of fodder production is possible. This has involved greater use of fertilizer and irrigation. Also, permanent pasture is being established in some forested areas in connec-

tion with forest regeneration projects on state land. The latter requires closing the areas to the traditional grazing use by neighboring communities.

In the drier regions of the South, socially oriented interventions have made available subsidized supplements of barley feed during drought. The policy goal was to protect the incomes of small herders. As an indirect consequence of agricultural intensification, fallow is declining, but crop residues have become more available. Also, in some areas of Central and Southern Tunisia, a policy is being pursued to privatize collective grazing land. Some of this land have shifted to grain production, thus further reducing the area available for pasturing herds.

The role of the various feed resources differs from zone to zone: (a) feed concentrates are relatively more important in the humid zone where much of the dairy cattle are located; (b) forage is also more important in the humid and subhumid zones; (c) pasture provides a major part of livestock feed in the arid and desert zones; and (d) hay, straw, stubble, and other agricultural by-products appear to be important in all but the arid and desert zones (FAO 1988, Vol. I, p. v).

Overall coverage of feed requirements

Two distinct trends characterize feed availability in Tunisia. Feed resources destined for intensive livestock production, forage and barley, appear to be increasing, with the growth in barley offsetting declines in concentrate feed production. However, for extensive livestock production, feed resources in the Center and South have not been able to keep pace with the requirements of the growing animal population. The best pasture land is increasingly being converted to marginal cereal cultivation, with the remaining pastures being degraded and overstocked, and weedy fallows previously used for grazing are being reduced by agricultural intensification.

These two divergent trends are illustrated in Figure 7-5. Central and Southern Tunisia (the arid and desert zones, respectively) cannot normally meet the feed requirements of their livestock, with the shortfall being on the order of 25–30 percent. Feed requirements are covered only in years with above-normal rainfall. The situation in the North is quite different, with only the humid zone falling below its feed requirements, while the subhumid and semiarid zones manage to cover their requirements even in dry years.

In the humid zone much of the shortfall can be met by the use of feed concentrates, particularly in the case of cattle. The same is not true for sheep and goats in the desert and arid zones, resulting in overgrazing and reduced livestock productivity (FAO 1988, Vol. II, p. 97).

Feed concentrates

Over the past three decades cattle, especially dairy cattle, have relied quite heavily on feed concentrates. Yet during the last ten years, small ruminant production has also become more dependent on concentrate feeds produced from partly imported barley, maize, and soya cake. This increased dependence is due to the expansion of cultivation in the South and Center which has reduced natural range resources, and to crop intensification in the North, which reduced the weedy fallow that had been an important source of grazing. In addition, as sheep have been increasingly integrated in the farming systems in the North, seasonal migrations from south to north for fallow and stubble grazing have declined in importance. The reduction of natural sources of grazing has resulted in recourse to transport of concentrates and hay from north to south. Consequently, sheep production has become more costly, but as a result of the liberalization of mutton and lamb prices in 1979, the increased use of concentrates, hay, and straw to supplement range grazing is still quite profitable (World Bank 1991a, p. 30).

Over the last fifteen years the use of concentrated feed, previously limited to less than 10 percent of the total requirements of small ruminants, has increased to 30 percent in normal years and to over 50 percent in drought years (World Bank 1991c, p. 12). As an illustration of the growing importance of feed concentrates for the ovine herd, a study (Ministry of Agriculture 1991, pp. 92–93) carried out in 1990 in Menzel Habib (governorate of Gabes in the arid region) reports that farmers owning small ruminants relied to a great extent on hay and concentrates to feed their herds, which averaged between twenty and fifty animals. Barley and agricultural by-products were also used, although pasture land did not seem to play an important role in animal rations.

The production of concentrate feeds grew dramatically between 1977 and 1981, from 100,000 tons to over 300,000 tons, but declined dramatically back to the initial level in 1982, subsequent to removal of subsidies. Production in more recent years has remained stable (apart from growth of the poultry feed sector). Of total production, concentrated feed for sheep increased rapidly in the 1980s relative to bovine use, whose production declined by over 50 percent.[6] This reflected the greater profitability of sheep and goat production relative to beef following liberalization of sheep and goat markets. (Dairy and beef prices continued to be controlled.)

Forage

Total area devoted to forage crops has increased by only 8 percent during 1977–91, but production has increased more due to increased use of irrigation and fertilizers. For example, fertilizer use grew by about 40 percent over the period. However, rainfed production remains predominant. On rainfed land, cereals and annual legumes sown in mixtures are common, or alternatively, barley

---

[6]Bovine feed concentrate production grew from 48 to 168 tons between 1976 and 1980, but subsequently fell to 71 tons in 1986. Ovine feed production in the same three years was 2, 25, and 89 tons (Chouchen and Alaya 1989, p. 130).

is grown for grazing early in its life cycle prior to maturation to a grain harvest. The composition of forage output has shifted some from perennial to annual species over this period. Perennial forages such as sulla and lucerne declined in area from about 108,000 hectares to 95,000 hectares, while annuals increased from 167,000 hectares to 203,000 hectares, or 18 percent. Production of annual forage crops increased by about 30 percent to 1.4 million tons over the period between 1985 and 1991, although the dependence of forage production on rainfall was evident in 1988 when production fell by nearly 50 percent due to severe drought conditions.

Only about 12–15 percent forage area is currently irrigated, but because of higher yields, this area accounts for about 35 percent of total forage production. The area in irrigated forage crops increased from 8,200 hectares in 1973 to 26,000 hectares in 1989 (World Bank 1988b; Ministry of Agriculture 1989, p. 16). Irrigated forage is largely fed green on a cut-and-carry system to stall-fed dairy cattle, although silage is becoming more common. The overall increase in forage production, in fact, has probably benefited the bovine herd rather than sheep and goats, and has contributed to the significant increases in milk production despite a stable cattle population.

Barley

Barley in its various forms—green barley, grain, straw, and in feed concentrates—is perhaps the single most important feed source for Tunisian cattle. Production of barley has become increasingly variable with rainfall. Since the mid-1980s, during humid years production almost doubled the previous output levels of good years. Yet production in recent dry years (1986, 1988, and 1989) differed little from past dry years. This performance reflects that much of the increase in production has resulted from an expansion into marginal zones previously used for livestock pasture. This makes a significant portion of

the barley harvest extremely dependent on rainfall conditions, with the magnitude of fluctuations in production between wet and dry years increasing since 1984. The environmental implications of this expansion have been noted above.[7] Barley price incentives do not seem to account for the large variability of year-to-year production, although this topic will be addressed more fully below.

Fallows

Fallows in Tunisia are typically unmanaged, with the land simply used for grazing of any natural growth. Total fallow area available for grazing has declined with the jump in farm mechanization through the mid-1980s that resulted in an increase in the practice of clean cultivated fallow, and the consequent decline in stubble and fallow grazing. It is uncertain whether this reduction in feed availability from fallow has been offset by the increase in the area under cultivated forages. Such may be case for cattle in the North, but is less likely in the case of sheep and goats in Central and Southern Tunisia for which forage feed sources are rarely used. Thus agricultural intensification and the consequent loss of stubble and fallow grazing land is likely to affect most seriously the small ruminants in the degraded pastoral areas ("Tunisia, Review of Prospects for Agricultural Diversification," p. 12).

Pastures

Grazing land provides the majority of livestock feed in the arid and desert zones. In addition to their increasing degradation, the productivity of the rangelands is heavily influenced by the amount of rainfall they

---

[7]Barley imports often partially fill the gaps resulting from reduced harvests during the dry years. The contribution of these imports to the fulfillment of feed requirements is largely reflected in the figures for feed concentrate production, since it is likely that much of the imported barley is used as input into these concentrates.

receive. The degree of variation in yields between a humid year (1985) and a dry one (1986) from pasture is on the order of 642 million forage units versus 293 million forage units, respectively, a variation of more than 220 percent (FAO 1988, Vol. II, p. 95).

Summary

Livestock numbers have been increasing in Tunisia over the past twenty or thirty years. The increases, however, reflect expansion of sheep and goat herds to a far greater extent than cattle stocks. In fact, cattle numbers are significantly lower today than they were in the mid-1970s. This suggests that the small ruminants have greater significance in terms of environmental pressures on degraded range-lands.

The impact of sheep and goat numbers on the environment is intensified by their heavy concentration in the Central and Southern regions of Tunisia, respectively, where most of the country's rangelands are located. Cattle, on the other hand, are almost exclusively found in the humid and subhumid North, where only a small portion of Tunisia's pasture resources remains. Moreover, the bovine herd is largely dependent on feed concentrates and forage crops, and thus puts relatively little pressure on rangelands. Although the dependence of sheep on feed concentrates is on the rise, particularly in Central Tunisia, grazing still provides the major portion of ovine and caprine feed requirements, especially in the South.

It can therefore be concluded that environmental degradation caused by the excessive growth of the livestock herd through overgrazing is primarily due to increasing numbers of small ruminants, particularly sheep, in Central regions of Tunisia, and only secondarily due to cattle production systems.

Livestock Policy and Natural Resource Use

Since the 1970s, Tunisia has used occasionally inconsistent price controls and subsidies directed both at the final product, meat, as well as at inputs such as feed and fertilizers, to achieve economic and social objectives. These have included the subsidies for importing red meat and milk products, production subsidies to encourage continued investment; maintenance of consumer prices at socially and politically acceptable levels, and income protection for livestock owners through subsidies for animal losses during drought years. This section analyzes the impact that government policies have had on the environment through their impact on livestock numbers and on animal feed production.

Meat prices and subsidies

Most price and subsidy policies that directly affect the livestock sector are managed through the *Caisse Generale de Compensation* (CGC), including consumer price ceilings and subsidies on inputs for feed production (including fertilizer, feed concentrate ingredients, and barley).

Beef was subject to production and consumption ceiling prices from 1970 until 1982, when producer prices were liberalized. Consumer prices continued to be fixed for meat sold through butchers subcontracting with the state-run Ellouhoum, which retained a monopoly on beef imports until 1990. While a significant portion of beef is processed by private slaughterhouses and butchers, the importance of Ellouhoum in beef marketing and distribution has meant that its policies have exerted significant downward pressure on beef prices in the market as a whole (AIRD 1989, pp. 119–20).

Mutton and goat meat were also subject to price controls until 1979, when prices were liberalized at all stages (AIRD 1989, p. 126). Even under the price controls, producer prices for mutton increased in real terms (see Figure

7-6), and this trend has continued since price liberalization at 1 percent annually in real terms (AIRD, pp. 131–32). Marketing of sheep and goat meat is free of price or market controls and generally is handled by the private sector (Tunisia: Review of the Prospects for Agricultural Diversification, pp. 88–89).

Thus, sheep and goat producers faced better price incentives than beef producers over the 1979–90 period. While mutton and goat meat prices increased by nearly 30 percent between 1970 and 1986, beef prices actually declined in real terms during that period (Figure 7-6). The combination of output price controls on beef and the support measures provided by the state in the form of input subsidies (to be addressed below) has resulted in the stagnation of local production and the consequent growth of beef imports. Allowing markets to function with less intervention has contributed to the growth of the ovine and caprine herds which experienced virtually uninterrupted growth in numbers since 1979.

Tunisian trade policies have influenced domestic price incentives for both beef and mutton production. Tunisia is self-sufficient in sheep and goat meat; reported mutton and lamb imports and officially reported exports are small. Tunisian mutton production appears to be somewhat protected from imports: while international mutton prices fell by over 30 percent over 1980–86, Tunisian prices rose over the same period. Such policies tend to exacerbate the degradation of range resources by raising financial returns to rangeland producers and raising animal numbers on the range.

Significant cross-border exports to Libya are thought to take place in some years, although no estimates exist of this illicit activity, which the Tunisian authorities try to regulate, and which the Libyan authorities periodically attempt to ban. Libya does import large numbers of live goats and sheep annually, and although the Tunisian share of this trade is generally small, it can be significant in absolute numbers for Tunisia. For example,

reports indicate that in 1988 some 50,000 Tunisian sheep were exported to Libya (AIRD 1989, p. 119). However, it is difficult to draw any firm conclusions regarding the effect of Libyan demand on the size of the Tunisian herd.

The impact of imports on beef prices has been perhaps more significant. To meet domestic demand which is augmented by subsidized meat prices, beef is bought on the international market—largely from the European Community—at artificially low prices and sold to butchers associated with Ellouhoum, at a fixed price (2.1 dinars per kilogram in 1987). By contrast, local meat is bought at a higher price than imported beef (2.3 dinars per kilogram in 1987) and sold at the same price as imported meat. The profits made by Ellouhoum from the sale of imported meat are meant to cross-subsidize local meat production, although the actual effect was the stagnation of domestic beef production due to low international prices that were passed through to domestic prices (Ministry of Agriculture and FAO 1987, p. 16).

Pricing policy for beef was reformed in 1990 as part of the structural adjustment program. The reforms consisted of liberalizing retail prices for beef and allowing private imports of refrigerated meat, while applying a variable levy sufficient to provide domestic producers with price protection of 15 percent. With these reforms in place, price incentives for domestic production have improved, and there appears to be increased interest in investing in cattle fattening and dairy operations.

These recent reforms in meat pricing have to some extent been facilitated by changes in meat consumption patterns (see Table 7-4). While total meat consumption per capita has increased by about 40 percent in the past 15 years, this is almost entirely due to an increase in consumption of poultry, which is now the largest source of meat in the average diet. Declines in ovine meat consumption can be linked to its increase in price relative to poultry meat, while the stagnation of beef consumption reflects the supply constraints related to inadequate production price incentives.

Input pricing and subsidies

Government price policy for meat was accompanied by the introduction of subsidies for inputs into livestock production. This was done to contain the growth of production costs, to protect producers' incomes, to encourage continued investment, and to maintain consumer prices at acceptable levels. Livestock feed and fertilizer subsidies are the major form of subsidy intervention by the CGC that affect the sector.

Subsidies for livestock feed date from 1965 when livestock producers were provided with subsidized feed concentrates to reduce the impact of climatic variability on the livestock herd and to increase the herd's productivity. (AIRD 1989, p. 128) This practice continued to play a central role in Tunisia's drought emergency assistance to livestock producers, although as can be seen from Table 7-1, while feed subsidies are higher during drought years, a significant subsidy has been in effect in nondrought years as well. For maize, subsidies were removed in 1992, as is expected to be done for soya meal in 1993. Barley continues to receive a subsidy.

Feed concentrate subsidies have had a considerable effect on the numbers of small ruminants. Subsidized concentrates constitute a growing share—30 percent—of total feed requirements of the ovine herd during normal rainfall years, a share comparable to that for the bovine herd. These subsidies, in conjunction with the liberalization of mutton and goat meat prices have contributed significantly to the profitability of mutton production and thus the rise in ovine numbers. In addition, feed subsidies and additional, free emergency feed supplies during the recent 1988–89 drought have maintained the size of the sheep flock when in previous droughts, a decline was evident. Thus the subsidies have encouraged both a trend increase in livestock numbers,

and also maintained herd size during periods of reduced carrying capacity of the natural range resources.

In addition to feed concentrates, sheep producers use significant amounts of barley grain as feed, particularly during the dry season. The strong demand for barley—further encouraged by strong demand for subsidized concentrates where barley is a major input—has meant that producer prices for the cereal have enjoyed about a one-third increase in real terms during 1970–90. The favorable producer prices and growing demand have led to the expansion of barley cultivation to more marginal lands in Central and Southern Tunisia previously used for grazing, resulting both in erosion due to cultivation and in increased pressure on the remaining rangelands.

Although it has been argued that feed subsidies have contributed to stagnation of forage crop production and thus discouraged the integration of livestock and farming systems, this claim is contestable. While the area in forage crops has indeed grown only slightly, forage production has increased due to increased use of irrigation and fertilizers. Although the removal of feed subsidies could further encourage forage production, there is really no hard evidence to support this. Furthermore, concentrate feed is increasingly used for the ovine herd, while forage is largely directed to dairy cattle; therefore the effect of concentrate feed prices on forage production may not be substantial. A more important disincentive to more rapid increases in forage production may be the low prices of beef and dairy products.

The growth in forage production has been encouraged by government subsidies on irrigation water and fertilizer that are available for forage and other crop production. The quantity of fertilizer use on forage crops increased by approximately 60 percent between 1981 and 1986, and the use of fertilizer on forage crops as a proportion of total fertilizer use has also been on the rise. Subsidies on fertilizer use for all crops increased significantly between the early 1970s and the mid-1980s, although they have declined as a percentage of total CGC expenditures. Use of ammonium nitrate on forage crops doubled between 1980 and 1986, while use of superphosphates rose by nearly 50 percent. Subsidies to fertilizer used on forage as a percentage of total subsidies to fertilizers increased from 11.6 percent in 1981 to 17.7 percent in 1986.

However, reduction of fertilizer subsidies was an objective of the structural adjustment program, and by 1992 subsidies had been removed on superphosphates and ammonium nitrate, with remaining subsidies on other fertilizers expected to be removed in 1993. Similar reductions in irrigation water subsidies have occurred over the past several years, as the authorities have targeted a 9 percent real increase in water charges annually, until costs of operations and maintenance are covered.

Fertilizer and irrigation subsidies have been successful in encouraging the production of forage crops by making their production more profitable. It has been estimated that these subsidies reduced production costs of green forage, silage, and straw by 40 percent, 26 percent, and 34 percent, respectively (Khaldi and Chaffai 1987, p. 5). Increases in cultivated forage signal a growing intensification of livestock production. However, since the bulk of forage production is used as feed for dairy cattle, the potential positive impacts of intensification are probably not realized. As has been argued above, dairy cattle do not currently pose the major environmental threat to Tunisia's grazing lands; the crucial problem concerns sheep, and available data do not indicate any significant increase in forage consumption by the ovine herd.

Fertilizer and irrigation subsidies have other environmental impacts. On the positive side, the inclusion of forages in the cereal production cycle is often recommended as it favors reconstitution of soil quality. Unlike barley, forage cultivation is not being ex-

tended into fragile marginal lands; production takes place largely in the humid and subhumid North. Nevertheless, in an arid country like Tunisia where water is extremely scarce, a more thorough analysis of the true costs of water subsidies is urgently needed.

Policy interventions and the 1988–89 droughts

Severe droughts were experienced by Tunisia in 1988 and again in 1989. Barely half the usual average annual rainfall occurred in 1988, and 1989 was only a marginal improvement, creating the largest deficit in rainfall experienced in the previous thirty years. In previous years, two consecutive years of drought typically induced a decline in sheep and goat numbers of over 30 percent, but little decline was experienced in 1988–89. Herd size only fell by 3 percent for sheep, while goat numbers actually increased.

This remarkable shift in herders' response to drought was largely the result of the government's drought emergency program and its price and subsidy policies. Barley production in 1988 fell to less than one fifth of average production over the previous five years, and only recovered slightly in 1989 to 200,000 tons, remaining well below the country's feed requirements. To ensure the availability of feed resources to sheep and goats, the government imported 680,000 tons of barley in 1988 alone. Barley and bran were then provided to herders at sharply subsidized prices, and, as an emergency grant, small livestock holders with fewer than 10 head of sheep or goats received a free ration of 200 grams of barley per head of cattle during the drought period (AIRD 1989, p. 130). In addition, fodder shrub reserves, established in previous years on public land, were opened for grazing, thereby buffering the drought's impact.

As a result of these measures, mutton and lamb production remained fairly stable between 1987 and 1991 at about 35,000 tons (World Bank 1991a, p. 30). Mutton production also continued to be favored by its relative profitability over beef due to government price controls on the latter. Paradoxically, it appears that not only were losses minimized, but that some livestock owners even reaped a net profit from the barley subsidies (AIRD 1989, p. 130).

The combined cost of the emergency interventions to the government was evaluated at 45.3 million Tunisian dinars in 1988 and 41 million in 1989. Nearly 90 percent of this was for feed subsidies. Explicit agricultural subsidies during the two years increased to around double their 1987 level in real terms. In particular, explicit production subsidies for feed increased by 117 and 180 percent in 1988 and 1989, respectively (World Bank 1991a, p. 6).

While the sheep and goat population was spared significant losses, Tunisia's grazing lands were affected not only by the severe drought, but also the lack of adjustment of the herd size to reduced carrying capacity. Monitoring is not yet providing continuous information on range productivity, but selective studies have shown that one dry year can reduce the productivity of the range by 60 percent (FAO 1988, Vol. II), and two consecutive dry years result in an even more severe decline. Furthermore, rangeland vegetation does not recover immediately, but rather requires several years of average to good precipitation to attain normal productivity (Le Houerou 1986). The combination of the reduction in rangeland productivity and the continued high numbers of sheep and goats during drought years has exacerbated pressures on an already degraded and shrinking range.

Conclusions

Environmentally, livestock sector policies have had different impacts on the North, Center, and South regions of Tunisia. Subsidies for feed, irrigation, and fertilizers have promoted intensification of livestock production in the North and its integration with cropping activities. This has occurred to a lesser extent in the Central part of the country,

where sheep herds have increased without commensurate increase in feed production. Rangeland appears to be degrading, exacerbated by stabilization of herd sizes in drought years through the subsidized distribution of barley feed imports, and more generally through the mild protection of domestic mutton production. Following liberalization of mutton prices in the late 1970s it became profitable to increase the use of feed concentrates for sheep production, but this has not been sufficient to alleviate the pressure on Tunisia's Central rangelands. In addition, government policy encouraged the conversion of marginal lands from pastures into cereals, mainly barley. Not only did this encourage land degradation through the removal of permanent cover, it also shifted some of the best pasture lands to marginal cereal production, further shrinking the rangeland resources available to a growing livestock herd.

Thus, while subsidies may have a beneficial effect when implemented in the North and perhaps in certain parts of Central Tunisia, their impact on rangelands in much of Central and Southern Tunisia has been negative. The inability of policies to distinguish between Tunisia's bioclimatic zones has thus contributed to the severe degradation of the country's range resources.

The government's intent in Central and Southern Tunisia has been to protect herders from major losses and from wide income fluctuations, and it has accomplished this in the short term. However, no durable solution has been found to alleviating herd pressure that is slowly degrading the capacity of rangeland to sustain herds and livestock income. In addition, subsidies on feed concentrates have reduced the incentives for forage production.

Sweeping policy changes introduced gradually since the launching of structural adjustment reforms in 1986 will ultimately have an important impact on how livestock activities affect rangeland. These policy changes were primarily driven by budget constraints and market-oriented strategies, with environmental consequences rarely taken into account. The interaction of these policies makes it difficult, in any case, to predict the magnitude of their impact on the various feed sources, and their introduction is still too recent for clear trends to be identifiable. It is probable that strengthening producer prices for beef will encourage growth in the cattle herd, after years of stagnation. This growth will be concentrated initially in the North where feed resources are more abundant, but a critical issue will be whether the derived demand generated by cattle herd growth will maintain fodder and barley production in the face of reduced subsidies on fodder crop inputs, such as irrigation water and fertilizer. In Central Tunisia, the financial returns to sheep herding are likely to decline with subsidies being eliminated on feed concentrates, and some shift to beef production can be expected. The impact of such a shift will depend on whether permanent cattle herds are maintained, or whether incentives encourage a focus on using seasonally available range feed resources for sale to fattening operations in the North.

While policy interventions may have had a small measure of success in social terms, these benefits threaten to be short-lived if the environmental consequences of policies are not adequately considered. Income stabilization of small-scale herders will only be temporary if it is achieved through means that result in the degradation of the rangeland upon which the incomes ultimately depend. The long term effects of environmental degradation will ultimately result in the permanent reduction of rangeland productivity and the consequent reduction of herd size and incomes from livestock. In addition, the impacts of increased desertification and soil erosion will find their way into the rest of the economy, affecting agricultural productivity and infrastructure (siltation of reservoirs through increased erosion). The challenge is to introduce less environmentally destructive means to achieve the social objectives.

Table 7-1: Budget Costs of Animal Feed and Fertilizer Subsidies, 1975–91

Year	Animal feed subsidies	Fertilizer subsidies	Total subsidies CGC	Feed and fertilizer subsidies Share of GDP	Feed and fertilizer subsidies Share of government expense
	-------(million current dinars) ------			Share of GDP	Share of government expense
1975	1	5	n.a.	0.4	1.2
1976	3	1	n.a.	0.2	0.7
1977	6	1	n.a.	0.3	1.0
1978	6	3	n.a.	0.4	1.1
1979	10	4	n.a.	0.5	1.4
1980	17	7	n.a.	0.7	2.1
1981	34	10	138.8	1.1	2.8
1982	32	14	161.4	1.0	2.3
1983	9	15	174.2	0.5	1.0
1984	26	16	257.7	0.7	1.5
1985	21	17	262.2	0.6	1.3
1986	11	17	218.0	0.4	0.9
1987	5	14	196.4	0.3	0.6
1988	37	12	274.4	0.6	1.4
1989	49	20	362.2	0.7	1.8
1990	21	14	317.4	0.3	0.8
1991	18	13	289.2	0.3	0.7

Source: World Bank 1993.

Table 7-2: Geographic Distribution of Grazing Lands, 1986

Zone	Grazing area	Percent	Of which improved	Forage bushes	Percent
Humid	89,000	2.4	2,600	n.a.	n.a.
Subhumid	296,500	8.1	1,800	19,500	0.5
Semiarid	303,000	8.2	17,900	15,600	0.4
Arid	1,923,000	52.3	15,400	108,000	2.9
Desert	920,000	25.0	21,000	4,300	0.1
TOTAL	3,531,500	96.0	58,700	147,400	4.0

Source: Chouchen and Alaya 1989.

Table 7-3: Changes in the Composition of Meat Consumption

	1975	1985	1990
Total meat:			
Consumption (kg per capita)	12.9	16.4	18.3
Percent share:			
Bovine	25.6	24.1	17.4
Ovine	52.7	38.7	39.1
Poultry	17.1	33.8	40.4
Other	4.6	3.4	3 1

Source: Chouchen and Alaya 1989.

Figure 7-1: Tunisia's Bioclimatic Zones

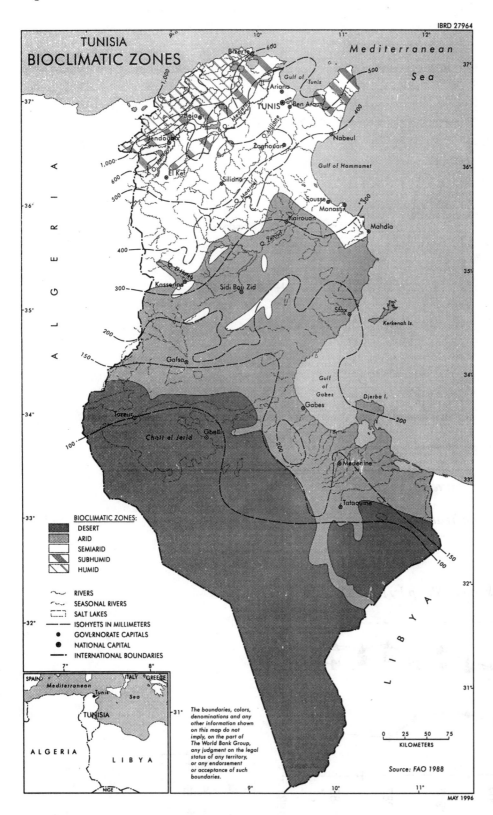

Source: FAO 1988.

Figure 7-2: Rainfall and Herd Size, 1961–91

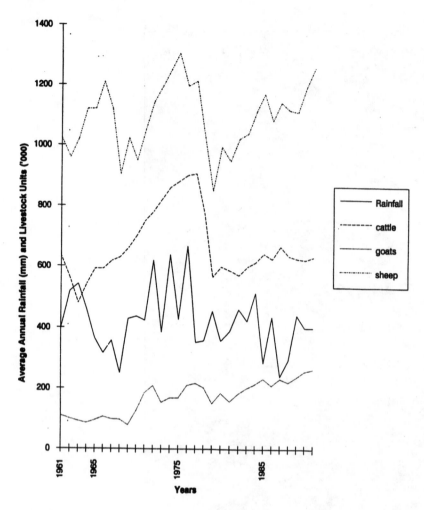

Source: *FAO Production Yearbooks*, various volumes.

Figure 7-3: Distribution of Sheep by Region

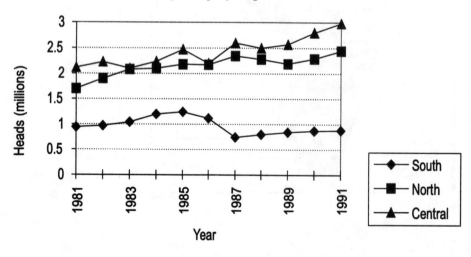

Figure 7-4: Distribution of Goats by Region

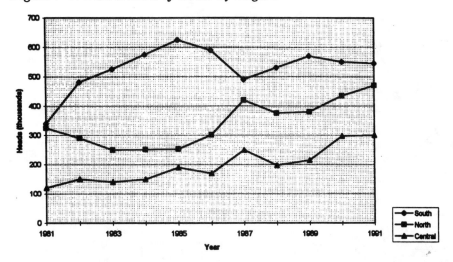

Figure 7-5: Coverage of Feed Requirements by Zone Variation with Rainfall, 1984–86

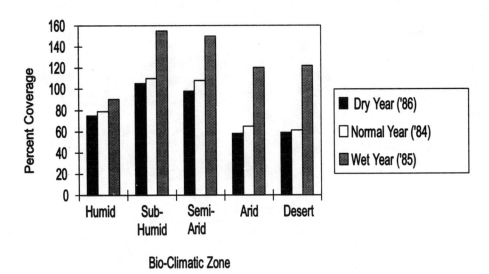

Figure 7-6: Beef and Mutton Prices

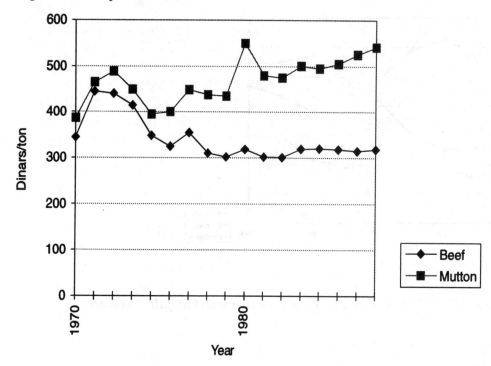

Bibliography

Associates for International Resources and Development (AIRD). 1989. "An Economic Appraisal of the Impact of Government Policies on Rangeland Livestock Systems of North Africa and the Middle East." Unpublished Paper. Somerville, Mass.: AIRD.

Chouchen, A., and K. Alaya. 1989. "L'elevage en Tunisie." In AIRD, *An Economic Appraisal of the Impact of Government Policies on Rangeland Livestock Systems of North Africa and the Middle East.* Somerville, Mass.: AIRD.

Food and Agriculture Organization (FAO). *Production Yearbooks.* Various Volumes. Rome: FAO.

————. 1987. Tunisia Expenditure Review of the Agricultural Sector. The Seventh 5–year Development Plan, the Livestock Subsector, Summary. Rome: FAO.

————. 1988. *Tunisie: Programme de Developpement des Productions Fourrageres et de L'Elevage, Rapport de Synthese, Vol. I and II.* Rome: FAO.

————. 1989. "Rapport du Programme de Soutien a L'Investissement." *Tunisie: Developpement des Productions Fourrageres et de L'elevage, Programme d'Investissement et Projets Prioritaires, Mission d'Identification Generale, Vol I.* Rome: FAO.

Hamza, A., and H. Bennour. 1990. "Essai de cartographie de l'occupation des terres dans les hautes steppes tunisiennes a partir des images landsat thematic mapper." *Revue Tunisienne de Sciences Sociales* 27(102). Tunis: Université de Tunis.

Kennedy, P. 1989. "Monitoring the Vegetation of Tunisian Grazing Lands Using the Normalized Difference Vegetation Index." *Ambio* 18(2).

Khaldi, A., and A. Chaffai. 1987. "Instruments et Institutions d'Intervention dans le Domaine des Prix Agricoles."

Le Houerou, H. N. 1986. "The Desert and Arid Zones of Northern Africa." *Ecosystems of the World: Hot Deserts and Arid Shrublands.* Vol. 12B. New York: Elsevier Scientific Publishing Company.

————. 1990. "Agroforestry and Sylvopastoralism to Combat Land Degradation in the Mediterranean Basin: Old Approaches to New Problems." *Agriculture, Ecosystems and Environment* 33: 99–109.

Ministry of Agriculture (Tunisia). 1989. "Note de Conjoncture No. 3." Tunis.

————. Direction des Sols. 1991. "Etude de l'impact des actions de developpement et de la lutte contre la desertification." Tunis.

Ministry of Agriculture (Tunisia) and Investment Centre, FAO. 1987. "Tunisie: Developpment de la Production Fourragere. Le Controle des Prix et les Subventions dans le Secteur de l'Elevage et des Fourrages." Working Paper. Rome: FAO.

"Tunisia: Review of the Prospects for Agricultural Diversification." Draft.

United States National Committee for Man and the Biosphere. 1981. "Environmental Report on Tunisia." Washington, D.C.: United States National Committee for Man and the Biosphere, Department of State.

World Bank. 1982. *Tunisia Agricultural Sector Survey, Volume 1.* Washington, D.C.: World Bank.

————. 1988a. *Commodity Trade and Price Trends.* 1987–88 edition. Baltimore, Md.: Johns Hopkins University Press.

————. 1988b. *Tunisia: Agriculture Sector Adjustment Loan. The Livestock Subsector.* Washington, D.C.: World Bank.

————. 1989a. *Tunisia Country Environmental Study, Main Report.* Washington, D.C.: World Bank.

————. 1989b. "Tunisie: Rapport sur L'environnement et Plan d'Action National, Rapport d'Experts No. 3. La degradation des ressources foncieres et hydrauliques." Washington, D.C.: World Bank.

———. 1991a. "Tunisia: Agricultural Expenditure Review." Washington, D.C.: World Bank.

———. 1991b. "Tunisia Small Farmers Potential and Prospects. A Technical Study." Washington, D.C.: World Bank.

———. 1991c. "Tunisia Small Farmers Study: Livestock Sub-Sector." Washington, D.C.: World Bank.

———. 1993. "From Universal Food Subsidies to a Self-Targeted Program." Washington, D.C.: World Bank.

8

Economic Policy and Wildlife Management in Zimbabwe

Kay Muir-Leresche and Jan Bojö
with Robert Cunliffe on Environmental Impacts

Wildlife Policy and Utilization in Zimbabwe

The wildlife utilization industry in Zimbabwe's private sector developed rapidly once legislation had been changed to allow landowners to benefit from wildlife conservation through utilization. This development has resulted in significant increases in wildlife in commercial ranching areas and has effectively halted the systematic elimination of wild animals in these areas.

The authors would like to thank Doris Jansen for the cost-benefit analysis; T. Chamboko, F. Murindagomo, and I. Bond for data on CAMPFIRE and communal agriculture; John Dixon and Kent Redford for commenting on a previous draft; and Liisa Hietala for word processing. The authors, of course, retain responsibility for the expressed opinions and possible errors.

Wildlife sector prices had been undermined by macroeconomic distortions and the relatively closed marketing system, particularly in communal areas. More competitive marketing has changed this significantly since the early 1990s. Better access to foreign currency and effective currency devaluation have moved market prices closer to opportunity costs. However, market prices do not reflect the true social value of the wildlife resources because environmental impacts, genetic resources, and existence or bequest values are not incorporated (see Annex 8-A). Where the externalities are significant, attempts could be made to internalize them through a system of taxes and subsidies.

The most lucrative outputs from the wildlife industry in Zimbabwe are photographic tourism and safari hunting. Hunting is important for developing the wildlife option in areas with lower concentrations of wildlife and poor infrastructure. Some specialized wildlife production units are also offering lucrative options—e.g., crocodile and ostrich farming. Meat, hides, and horns are outputs of minor significance, and ivory sales are negligible because of the Convention on the International Trade in Endangered Species of Flora and Fauna (CITES) regulations.

Zimbabwe is well endowed with large mammals, including elephants. The central highveld is intensively farmed with limited wilderness and wildlife, but with some opportunities for recreational tourism. The periphery, particularly along the north, south, and western borders has large concentrations of game. The large-scale ranching areas are not allowed to run buffalo with cattle. Buffalo were totally eradicated in these areas to comply with European Community (EC) veterinary regulations. The lack of buffalo significantly reduces returns to wildlife ranching, but there is a movement to reintroduce buffalo in some ranching areas. Buffalo were not eradicated in those communal areas where the tsetse fly precluded cattle, and the communal areas, which still have buffalo and elephant,

play an important role in the hunting industry.

Zimbabwe follows a policy of sustainable utilization and views all its mammals as a renewable natural resource to be managed. Protection of species and species diversity takes precedence over protection of individuals and groups. The estimated elephant population in 1960 was 32,700 and by 1988 it was up to 52,000, despite the fact that 44,500 elephants were culled during those 28 years (Martin, Craig, and Booth 1989). At the end of 1992 it was estimated that there were some 80,000 elephants in Zimbabwe, and there are increasingly serious conflicts as elephant populations exceed carrying capacity in national parks. Elephants are very important in wildlife enterprises, particularly in the peasant farm sector where they account for some 70 percent of the revenue.

Development of a wildlife industry on privately owned land

From 1960 farmers were given permits to utilize and trade in wildlife. The Department of National Parks and Wildlife Management (DNPWLM) noted the positive response and how quickly wildlife numbers recovered in certain areas. The Parks and Wildlife Act (14/1975) was implemented in 1975. It allocated full custodial rights over wild animals (except for "specially protected" species) to appropriate authorities (landholders) while the animals are on their land. Specially protected animals may only be killed in defense of life, and their remains may not be traded. Restricted species may be utilized upon receipt of special permits. Local committees may also declare a species specially protected within its own area. However, in most instances the animals do not benefit from this protection, since it is loss of habitat rather than hunting that is the major danger.

No person can hunt, capture, or remove any animal or plant from privately or communally-owned land without the appropriate authority's or landholder's permission. The landholder may hunt or market any plant or animal on his land (except those species listed as "specially protected" or "restricted"). However, to market a live animal or a trophy, the landholder must first obtain a specific permit. Under the 1975 Act, appropriate authority was immediately granted to all private landholders, and in the communal areas authority remained with the state.

The introduction of wildlife legislation allowing landholders access to their resource has been successful in the large-scale farming areas of Zimbabwe. Photo-safaris and wildlife-related tourism have grown significantly and rely heavily on the continued viability and attractiveness of the national parks and wildlife estates. From 1972–82 there was effectively only one tour operator, but by 1990 there were more than fifty registered operators. This has resulted in widespread increases in wildlife in all the less arable farming areas and even in the intensive cropping zones where farmers are reintroducing game. In 1960 there were only three game ranches and 350 square kilometers were designated for wildlife outside state land. By 1990, 55,000 square kilometers had been partially or completely allocated to wildlife enterprises in commercial and communal farming areas, with an additional area of about equal size in the parks and wildlife estate and in forest reserves. There is a Wildlife Producers Association (WPA) with a membership of over 10 percent of Zimbabwe's large-scale farmers. Although membership has increased in recent years, it has been the increase from passive to active membership, which has been significant.

Safari hunting is the most important component in large wildlife enterprises, and registered safari operators have increased significantly since 1980. In the predominantly agricultural zones, wildlife tourism is an increasing and generally supplementary enterprise, with some farmers investing in visitor camps, lodges, and recreational facilities. The large wildlife enterprises are found in the arid areas of Zimbabwe where farmers concentrate on

extensive game or mixed game and cattle ranching. The wildlife generally is not used for meat production, and any meat produced is sold locally at prices significantly lower than beef prices. Hunting in ranches is also often sold as a complement to hunting safaris on state hunting concessions and in communal areas. Hunting requires less infrastructural development and lower animal densities than are necessary for general tourism. Once the infrastructure has been developed and areas become less remote—and provided wildlife density is relatively high—the greater volume feasible with photo-safaris may make tourism ventures more profitable than hunting.

Gross income from international safari hunting increased from US$2 million in 1984 to US$9.3 million in 1990. Jansen (1990) estimated that if the entire hunting quota (2 percent of animal populations in state hunting and communal areas) were sold to foreign clients, it would earn US$13 million, which together with an estimated US$7 million by commercial ranchers indicates that hunting revenues could be doubled.

Aside from safaris, other wildlife-based activities contribute to the economy:

- The value of live animals for breeding purposes has increased dramatically. The DNPWLM operates a central allocation system with long waiting lists for animals, and a thriving private trade emerged in the late 1980s. In 1989 there was a waiting list for approximately 5,250 animals to restock private land with wildlife from DNPWLM. Live animal prices in the private sector rose some 400 percent in three years.
- Crocodile ranching has been encouraged since 1960, and producers are required to return a proportion of hatchlings to the wild. Numbers in the wild have increased significantly, and earnings in the crocodile industry have increased from US$300,000 in 1983 to US$2.6 million in 1989.
- Ostrich ranching has been very success-

ful. Where wild eggs are harvested, a proportion of the chicks are returned to the wild. As with crocodiles, those returned are a slightly greater proportion than has been estimated would normally survive to that stage.

- Ivory sales are important only in the state and communal sector where they earned almost $12 million between 1981 and 1988 from approximately 31,000 tusks (Martin, Craig, and Booth 1989). Current elephant ivory stocks held by DNPWLM are valued at over US$10 million with a significant proportion due to be repatriated to peasant communities when sales are made. The CITES ban has meant that very little ivory is sold, with most of the sales being made to Zimbabwean carving companies for sale to the local tourist market.

Development of a wildlife industry on communally owned land

Since 1980 the DNPWLM has managed the wildlife in these areas on behalf of the communities. They have leased hunting rights and collected the fees on behalf of the communities, but were required to surrender revenues to the national treasury. Although in principle the treasury is supposed to reallocate those revenues to the concerned communities on the presentation of proposals for development projects, in practice a large proportion of the revenues was retained. For example, of the Z$ 5.8 million earned by safari hunting in communal areas in 1987/88, only Z$ 3.3 million was paid out to district councils (Zimbabwe Government 1988).

The Parks and Wildlife Act of 1975 enabled the Minister to designate district councils in communal lands as appropriate authorities with full custodial rights to their wildlife, but this only began to be implemented in 1988 under the umbrella of the Communal Area Management Programmes for Indigenous Resources (CAMPFIRE). The limited wildlife revenue generated in communal areas, which

was returned to district councils, was used for development throughout the district, although only a few communities in the district pay the cost and actually live with the wildlife that generated these revenues. Thus, the local communities still have little sense of ownership or control in some districts and subsistence hunting is still illegal. One of the major complaints is that district council authorities receive all the wildlife revenue and then allocate these revenues over a much wider population than that living with wildlife. Both wildlife and tree resources are generally viewed as belonging to all Zimbabweans, but progress is being made in some districts, which have recognized that for people in these marginal areas, "their wildlife is their cattle."

With effect from 1988, legal control over wildlife resources has been granted to districts that apply for it, provided that they meet specified requirements. In 1993 there were twelve communal lands in Zimbabwe with appropriate authority and more than 19,500 square kilometers of communally owned land officially designated to include wildlife in the land use system and managed under the CAMPFIRE program. It was anticipated that communities would form natural resource cooperatives, management trusts, or companies with membership open to all adult males and females in the community. Each community would draw up their own constitution. The allocation of rights would be affected by the population-resource ratio. Defining the boundaries of a communal resource area in the CAMPFIRE[2] program would be a process of negotiation between the national, district and village representatives. Water, forestry and wildlife would be closely controlled with specified community management and access strategies but with arable land being accorded individual responsibility.

---

[2]Communal Areas Management Program for Indigenous Resources. Much has been written on CAMPFIRE; see the original document by Martin (1986) Murphree (1988); Jansen (1990); Child and Peterson (1991); and Murombedzi (1992).

In fact, appropriate authority is only granted to the district council, and local communities have yet to be given the opportunity to form effective resource management units. Most CAMPFIRE projects are still a long way from achieving the objectives of granting control over resources to local communities. CAMPFIRE has, however, succeeded in generating debate over access to resources and may eventually fulfill some of its original goals. Some communities currently see CAMPFIRE as a means of increasing agricultural potential. This development could eventually reduce wildlife and undermine CAMPFIRE, thus creating tension between villagers and implementers.

Wildlife and the economy

It is extremely difficult to ascertain the value of Zimbabwe's wildlife industry. The consumption of bushmeat has been virtually ignored, although the consumption of rabbits, rodents, insects, and wild flora are widespread throughout the country. The consumption of larger mammals is almost exclusively confined to isolated communities with high-wildlife and low-human populations. Assuming that there are some 25,000 households living in such areas, a rough estimate of the value to the nation of large mammal bushmeat is some Z\$ 4 million per annum based on the 60 percent contribution to total income made by wildlife to household income in Angwa, Zambezi Valley (Murindagomo 1988).

The contribution of the wildlife industry to the formal sector is also difficult to ascertain. Published statistics do not separate tourism or wildlife based industries as a proportion of gross domestic product (GDP). Ministerial statements have indicated that in recent years tourism has earned between Z\$ 300 million and Z\$ 1 billion per annum or between 2 and 5 percent of GDP. The most credible revenue estimate appears to have been around Z\$ 500 million in 1990/91. Safari hunting and wildlife management services add another Z\$ 50 million. Crocodiles and ostriches contribute

Z\$ 35 million, and other game products (skins, meat, and ivory) account for Z\$ 1 million. These contribute more than the formal sheep and goats sector. As with agriculture, the multiplier effects of tourism and wildlife are strong, and they are important contributors to foreign exchange earnings. Tourism operations qualifying for the export retention scheme claimed Z\$ 165 million in 1990/91. It has been crudely estimated that during this period, the wildlife sector generated Z\$ 344 million in foreign exchange earnings (Jansen 1992). National data on export earnings are not available for this period, but this is probably in the region of 20 percent of total exports.

The industry has strong backward linkages with the manufacturing sector, as well as some forward linkages with the informal sector, producing curios and clothing. Most tourist industry inputs are locally obtained. In the large hotel sector, 80 percent of fixed costs are local expenditures, but it is close to 100 percent for the safari camps and lodges. For all tourism ventures, 85 percent of variable costs are local—the major linkages being food and beverages. The industry is a high foreign currency converter, but relies heavily on adequate transport and communications facilities, which are foreign currency dependent.

Tourism has grown significantly since 1987, with bed occupancy up to 50 percent in 1990 despite an increase of 86 percent in the number of beds available. Employment grew 20 percent in three years, compared with nonagricultural employment elsewhere in the economy, which grew by 0.5 percent. Nonconsumptive tourism is considerably more labor intensive than sport hunting, and more than 50 percent of those employed in hotels and lodges could be drawn from unskilled local populations (Bond 1992).

The role of wildlife in the economy is significantly increased if adjustments are made to reflect the opportunity cost of the foreign currency earned by the sector (see Table 8-1). For most of the 1980s, various estimates indicated that the average overvalu-ation of the local currency was 50 percent, climbing to over 70 percent by 1990. From mid-1991, the government started a deliberate policy of devaluation to realign the currency.

Tourism in Zimbabwe is wildlife- and wilderness-based and has significant potential for expansion. The great numbers of large mammals, particularly elephants, and the relatively sophisticated infrastructure give Zimbabwe certain advantages over other tourist destinations. The current structural adjustment program will encourage invest-ment in export industries with more realistic exchange rates and easier access to imported inputs. The international recession will have less effect on tourism to Zimbabwe, which relies most on high-income tourism.

Economic Development and Wildlife

The national economy, the resources, and land use systems

Zimbabwe lies within the tropics. However, given altitudes of between 600 and 1,200 meters, most of the country has a subtropical climate, which is perfect for year-round tour-ism. The rainy season coincides with northern winters, but even during this season, the days are mostly sunny, with the rain occurring in sporadic thunderstorms and late afternoon showers. Zimbabwe is broadly categorized into five natural regions, based on rainfall. Region 1 has the most rainfall, but because of topography, production is dominated by exotic timber plantations, tea, coffee, and horticul-ture. Region 2 normally has more than 700 millimeters of rain and is the main crop-grow-ing region in the country. Regions 3, 4, and 5 are increasingly arid and, although cultivated in communal areas, are predominantly only suited to extensive livestock production. The annual variations are large, and the reliability of monthly rainfall is much lower than the seasonal total and decreases in general from north to south. Only 37 percent of the country

receives more than the 700 millimeters' an-nual average considered necessary for semi-intensive farming, and in most parts less than a third of this area is actually arable. In the intensive farming systems followed in Zimba-bwe, the natural growing season is confined to the rainy months.

The indigenous vegetation is *savanna grassland* along the central plateau, with *wooded savanna* throughout most of the rest of the country, and with some *montane forest* in the Eastern Boarder districts. In general, the topography, soils and climate of Zimbabwe are not favorable for intensive agricultural production. More than 75 percent of the coun-try is subject to conditions that make dryland crop production a risky venture. While agri-culture accounts for only some 10–14 percent of GDP, it has a major impact on growth through its backward and forward linkages, and through its contribution to export earnings and to both formal and informal employment.

Since independence, there have been some significant advances in the provision of social services, leading to a decline in infant mortal-ity and increases in education and access to physicians. However, these social services, together with high defense expenditure and large expansion of the public sector, resulted in significant increases in government expen-diture. The economy is highly regulated, and barriers to entry abound. Significant subsidies to the industrial sector, a large proportion of GDP spent on government consumption expenditure, and rapid population growth have resulted in very disappointing economic performance, with GDP per capita declining 7 percent since independence. By 1990 Zimba-bwe had a long-term external debt of some Z$ 12 billion.

Since independence in 1980 there are no longer *de jure* racial divisions, but land-size categories remain effectively unchanged since permission to subdivide is almost impossible to obtain. Ownership of the land in the former Tribal Trust Lands is officially vested in the President, but land is farmed along traditional communal tenure arrangements. This implies good security over homestead and arable land, but the grazing and woodland areas remain effectively open access. Land allocation continues to be a source of conflict within communal areas since local government, political parties, and tribal authorities all have varying degrees of control. The commercial sector is made up predominantly of large-scale farms (the former white farming area) and a few smaller-scale freehold farms (from former African Purchase areas). The communal sector includes resettlement schemes where tenure is not freehold but retained by the state.

The government is involved in an active land resettlement program and has declared its intention to take over 50 percent of the large-scale sector for reallocation to smallholders. Tenure arrangements in the resettled areas are very uncertain. Insecure tenure may have serious implications for environmental integrity. The uncertainty of the resettlement program has also created long-term insecurity for large-scale farmers, which could also affect the environment. For most of the population, however, there are high expectations that old wrongs will be redressed soon by land redistribution. Given the limited capacity for government to implement the program expeditiously, a serious crisis of expectations may result in attempts to settle people on any available land.

This could have serious consequences for communal areas with low human-population densities that are developing wildlife systems. Zimbabwe's population is growing at 2–3 percent per annum and, given the extreme poverty of communities in the marginal lands, population pressure could be translated into demands for access to resources in neighboring parks. The overgrazing and the cultivation of poor land have led to widespread erosion and depletion of the forest and grass cover, so that the neighboring parks appear to have resources desired to support the increasing population.

Political support for wildlife is negligible, and the wildlife sector receives limited alloca-

tions from the central government. This may change with the increased awareness of the potential role of wildlife in generating growth through foreign currency generation and the strong backward linkages which exist in Zimbabwe for the tourist industry. The wildlife sector, despite the advances with CAMP-FIRE, is still seen as white dominated and carries much resentment. Black entrepreneurs need to be given exposure and opportunities to participate in this growth industry.

An economic analysis of wildlife utilization

The large-scale commercial ranching sector

Child (1988) carried out a detailed time-series analysis of cattle and wildlife on Buffalo Range in the southeastern lowveld. The analysis showed that the cattle section gross profits increased during the 1960s, but fell rapidly from a peak in 1975 to losses in 1984. The falling profits were a result of declining herd productivity with calving rates dropping and livemass gains falling off dramatically, even before the major drought. This was primarily a result of veld degradation caused by overstocking.

The wildlife populations on Buffalo Range, however, continued to grow, and the range was less degraded in that sector of the farm. In 1973 Taylor carried out transections on the ranch to compare environmental conditions, but the results between the cattle and wildlife sections were indeterminate (Taylor in Child 1988). These transects were repeated in 1985, and this time environmental conditions in the game section were significantly better than in the cattle section. Child concluded that despite the heavy implicit subsidies for beef which favored the cattle section in most years and the overvalued exchange rates which greatly disadvantaged wildlife, wildlife offered the most lucrative and sustainable option for Buffalo Range (Child 1988).

Jansen, Bond, and Child (1992) carried out a survey of eighty-nine cattle, wildlife, and combined cattle-wildlife ranches in 1989/90 in the more arid Natural Regions 4 and 5 in order to determine the relative profitability of cattle and wildlife. They estimated returns to investment and the comparative advantage of ranching cattle only, wildlife only, and combined cattle and wildlife ranches. The survey year was an average rainfall year, and there were no unusual occurrences which would mean unusually high or low profits for either commodity.

Financial. Cattle-only enterprises had an average 1.8 percent financial (private) return on investment, and the return to cattle on ranches combining cattle and wildlife was 2.6 percent. The weighted average return of cattle enterprises was Z$ 2.78 per hectare. Only four of the seventy-seven ranches producing beef had greater than 10 percent return on investment. The speculative return on holding land was excluded from all analyses. Only three cattle enterprises had returns greater than Z$ 25 per hectare. Thirty-nine percent of the cattle enterprises had a negative adjusted net revenue and to continue in operation most of the ranches were destocking or borrowing. Wildlife-only ranches were the most financially viable with average returns on investment of 10.5 percent. More than half the wildlife enterprises had a greater than 10 percent return on investment, and only four had negative adjusted net revenue. The weighted average return of wildlife enterprises was Z$ 5.8 per hectare.

Economic. An economic (social) analysis of these returns was carried out using estimated opportunity cost prices to incorporate the effects of market prices not reflecting true social values with respect to the price of cattle, the exchange rate, price of land, the interest rate, and the cost of degradation from overstocking. Jansen, Bond, and Child (1992) vary their assumptions in a number of sensitivity runs, but the conclusions essentially all remain the same. The base-run assumptions assumed a particularly conservative estimate of overvaluation of the Zimbabwe dollar to avoid favoring the wildlife option.

The analysis showed both cattle and wildlife to be economically profitable with the average rate of return on investment for wildlife enterprises at 21.5 percent and at 13.1 percent for cattle. The returns to land, however, were higher for cattle than for wildlife after adjusting for government controlled prices and exchange rate distortions, with average economic returns to land for cattle at Z$ 17 per hectare versus Z$ 14 per hectare for wildlife.

The financial results from the study are consistent with the reported shift into more wildlife enterprises, since these lead to a higher net absolute return per hectare than cattle enterprises, even when such are combined with minor wildlife activities. Returns are generally low per area unit, but it should be emphasized that the average farm in the sample is large, some 22,000 hectares, and that returns are net of production costs. Furthermore, many other factors (the possibility to offset losses in these enterprises against capital gains elsewhere, maintaining a certain life style, the prospect of speculative returns to land holdings and attachment to sunk investment, as well as unfamiliarity with wildlife enterprises) all serve to explain the inertia in leaving a financially unprofitable business.

Role of policy. It is clear from a comparison across financial and economic results that profitability is currently greatly depressed by economic policy interventions. Both cattle and wildlife enterprises show much higher profitability under economic prices. With respect to employment, wildlife enterprises are less wage-labor intensive and require more skilled manpower than cattle enterprises, making cattle the preferred option from an employment perspective. This results from the current heavy concentration of the wildlife enterprises on safari hunting. Tourism ventures have much greater employment potential and are becoming an increasingly important component of the wildlife industry.

The communally owned, small-scale farm sector

Between January 1989 and April 1991, twelve districts received "appropriate authority" over their wildlife, although in many of these districts, not all wards have a wildlife resource. All these districts are engaged in obtaining revenue from wildlife utilization (i.e., entering into contracts with safari hunting companies and tour operators), are attempting to manage their wildlife (i.e., protecting it and setting quotas for its exploitation), and are distributing benefits to the participating wards and "producer communities." Administratively, communal areas are divided into district councils which have legal status and are serviced by the Ministry of Local Government and Housing. These district councils are then further subdivided into wards with ward development committees (WADCOs) comprising a number of villages with village development committees (VIDCOs). The WADCOs and VIDCOs are recent political institutions and are more effective in some areas than others.

By 1992 CAMPFIRE had grown to encompass both a large area and a large population among whom the benefits of the wildlife are to be shared. Safari hunting dominates the revenue earned. Most districts now put their hunting quotas out to competitive tender. The safari operators then market the hunting internationally. International safari hunting accounts for more than 85 percent of the revenue in most CAMPFIRE areas. The bulk of the revenue is derived from elephant hunting. Any ban on imports of elephant trophies into the major client regions—Europe and the United States—would have a large negative impact on community wildlife schemes.

Quotas used for culling are normally restricted to those animals that have a limited safari market, e.g., impalas, and no districts have yet established mechanisms to legalize, allocate, and manage subsistence hunting. The communal areas play an important role in the safari hunting industry and complement the plains game hunting sold on most commercial ranches. Fifty-two percent of all elephant and 39 percent of all buffalo trophies came from communal areas in 1990 (Bond 1992).

CAMPFIRE revenue generation and distribution. Although CAMPFIRE programs are administered by district councils there are usually only a few wards which have the wildlife resources to be actively involved in wildlife projects. It would be desirable to devolve authority to ward or even village levels, but this is not possible because the district council is the lowest level of government with legal authority as opposed to advisory powers (Peterson 1992). In addition, the fugitive nature of the resource and the large areas required for safari hunting would make cooperation between neighboring producer units important.

The total gross income from wildlife accruing to the district councils from CAMPFIRE was Z$ 3 million in 1991. Total wealth generated, but accruing more widely (e.g., including safari operators and airlines), is considerably greater. The DNPWLM has issued "Campfire Guidelines" which recommend that no more than 15 percent of revenue be allocated to the district council in the form of a levy, and no more than 35 percent be spent on management costs, so that at least 50 percent of revenue can be passed on to the community in the form of cash or project benefits. These guidelines were not met in four of the nine districts for which data is available. In Nyaminyami and Guruve, community benefits were distributed as ward dividends, but represented only one-third of revenue and in Binga only 40 percent. In Hurungwe none of the wildlife revenue was distributed to the producer communities: the council spent all of it on a truck. In contrast, ward dividends represented considerably more than 50 percent of revenue in four districts.

Not all of the earned revenue is available for the provision of benefits to the communities, since there are costs incurred in managing the wildlife. The larger programs, such as Nyaminyami and Guruve, have wildlife managers who receive salaries and are provided with vehicles and housing. Many districts choose to employ game guards whose main tasks are antipoaching and problem-animal control.

Capital costs, principally for vehicles and electric fencing, have been provided by donors in several districts, and thus far CAMPFIRE revenue has generally not had to be used for capital costs. There is a danger, however, that the recurrent, maintenance, and eventual replacement costs of the donated capital assets may lead to increased management costs, and thus result in a smaller percentage of the revenue being available for community benefits.

The budget of the Nyaminyami Wildlife Management Trust (NWMT), shows a buildup of a "wildlife management bureaucracy." Recurrent costs have increased 360 percent in two years, whereas revenue increased by 79 percent. If the cost of living with wildlife remains higher than the benefits received in the producer communities, then the policing costs will continue to escalate as locals continue to encourage poaching and human immigration. The NWMT has capital assets of nearly Z$ 800,000. In 1991 it withheld 15 percent of its net revenue for a depreciation reserve, further reducing the revenue available for distribution.

In the districts where the CAMPFIRE program has been implemented, more recently the proportion of wildlife revenue distributed to the wards is considerably higher. This may be because the "wildlife management establishment" has not yet had an opportunity to be created. Alternatively, perhaps districts that are only just now beginning to implement CAMPFIRE (and the nongovernmental organization (NGO) collaborative group that assists them), are learning from the mistakes of the "pioneer" districts (Nyaminyami and Guruve) and will try to keep wildlife management costs within or below the 35 percent guideline. Mechanisms could be established that would give full control over utilization

and poaching to the concerned villages. This would give them hunting access to those animals where there is little conflict with the more lucrative safari hunting. However, they should be required to pay royalties to the local village community to avoid overexploitation. The management costs in wildlife protection would be significantly reduced as the villagers would have greater incentives to police themselves and report outside poachers. It is widely accepted that self-policing is very much less expensive and more effective than centralized regulation in theory; the challenge is to develop appropriate institutions for self-regulation.

Cost-benefit analysis of wildlife utilization in communal areas

Jansen (1992b) undertook a cost-benefit analysis in three districts. The analysis projects forward covering a ten-year period, and begins with the first year of the CAMPFIRE program in each district. *Scenario 1 assumes no change* in management, dividend distribution, poaching, and human immigration. This leads to a decline in revenue, and increases in costs and in poaching and immigration in Nyaminyami and Guruve. In Mahenye, by contrast, the status quo is based on continued good management and control of poaching and immigration. Macroeconomic reforms are not implemented, and the Zimbabwe dollar remains overvalued. All values are presented in constant 1991 Zimbabwe dollars.

In Nyaminyami there have been substantial increases in recurrent costs during the first three years. This is in part due to the inexperienced management and to the decision to employ sixteen game guards with conditions of service similar to that provided by DNPWLM. It is important that the community find more cost-effective poaching control mechanisms. Scenario 1 assumes that this situation is not rectified: efforts to date to do so have failed. As a result, it is assumed that recurrent costs increase at a rate of 11 percent in real terms.

Capital costs, which have been substantial and almost totally financed by donor aid (Zimbabwe Trust), are assumed to represent replacement of existing assets plus the additional buildings planned for NWMT. No distinction is made between the source of finance for the capital costs, since they represent use of resources that would presumably be available elsewhere in the economy if they were not used for NWMT. Despite the problems of continuing with the status quo, the net present value (NPV) for the district is positive, Z$ 1.5 million using a discount rate of 10 percent, and Z$ 333,000 using a discount rate of 40 percent.

Scenario 2 is a more optimistic scenario, including 25 percent adjustments for overvaluation of the Zimbabwe dollar. It assumes that the Economic Standard Adjustment Program (ESAP) succeeds, local management improves, and poaching and immigration are controlled. As a result, the net present value to the district, based on a 10 percent discount rate, increases to Z$ 3.6 million. The optimistic scenario assumes that present constraints on performance, particularly in Nyaminyami and Guruve, are eased, and ESAP succeeds. Revenue increases by 10 percent annually as a result of devaluation of the Zimbabwe dollar and good wildlife populations due to declines in poaching activity and immigration. This scenario assumes that recurrent costs do not increase in real terms after 1993 because of improved management, capital costs are restricted to replacement, immigration is controlled, and population increases by 3.5 percent. Ward benefits are distributed only to producer wards.

This type of analysis fails to take into consideration the distribution of the net benefit stream. If the net benefits do not accrue to the producer community, the link between the benefits and costs of wildlife will not be made, and the current trend of encouraging wildlife eradication, immigration, and increased cattle stocking will continue.

Scenario 1 assumes that the ward benefits continue to be spread evenly among all twelve wards. As a result, benefits per household never exceed Z$ 100 per annum and in fact become negative after year 7. Thus, even though this project has a positive NPV for the district, it *should not* be implemented, unless some alternative mechanism of allocating the net benefits is instituted. In other words, a positive NPV is a necessary, but not a sufficient, criterion for going ahead with the project. If the project is to be implemented as an alternative to some other land use option, then its NPV will need to be higher than the competing options, and since wildlife is a less well-recognized option, it will need to be considerably higher before it is chosen in place of conventional options.

Scenario 2 shows that with a more optimistic revenue generation, cost control, lower tax levy, and lower population increase, the benefit per household increases to Z$ 470 per annum (in real terms) in year 10 (Figure 8-1). This assumes that the dividends are paid in the form of household cash dividends, with social service or infrastructure projects paid directly by farmers.

Similar cost-benefit analysis for the CAMPFIRE project in Guruve District shows that like Nyaminyami, the project has received substantial capital investment donated by Zimbabwe Trust, and has a good revenue from hunting and tourism. Also, like Nyaminyami, it has sizeable and increasing recurrent wildlife management costs. If the ward dividends were to be split in the future among all eight wards, as is the case in Nyaminyami, Scenario 1 shows that the benefits per household diminish and in fact become negative by year 10. Under the optimistic scenario 2, with benefits split between only three producer wards, the distribution increases to over Z$ 500 per household and could result in a viable wildlife utilization option. This assumes that the link between the benefits and the wildlife resource is successfully established. This is not yet the case, but the situation is improving steadily as institution building at the ward and village level is taking place. It should be noted that under both scenarios, the NPVs are positive, but the distribution per household is significantly different.

Cost-benefit analyses of the CAMPFIRE project in the Mahenye ward of Gazaland District (Chipinge) indicates that the hunting revenue is considerably smaller there, but so are the recurrent and capital costs. As a result, the NPVs are not much lower than in Nyaminyami and Guruve. Scenario 1 shows the effect of poor macroeconomic policies, but with wildlife revenues distributed solely to the producer community, household dividends peak at Z$ 813 in 1993 and decline thereafter. Under the optimistic scenario 2, the household dividends steadily increase, and are significantly larger than in Nyaminyami and Guruve, exceeding Z$ 1,000 per household from 1993. Although the revenue potential for the district is lower, there are considerably fewer households involved even if Nyaminyami and Guruve focus the benefit distribution more carefully. This indicates the importance of limiting the population benefiting from wildlife if revenues generated are to be meaningful to households and change their decision-making to favor wildlife.

Summary of necessary conditions for success of CAMPFIRE projects

There are a number of principles that can be universally applied. The most important of these is that the *benefits must outweigh the costs for the residents* if they are to encourage wildlife by reducing poaching and habitat destruction. A uniform distribution model of the benefits shared among all the wards in a district, or even all the wards with some wildlife, is unlikely to result in benefits outweighing costs in the important producing areas. Where wildlife revenue is used to fund social services and infrastructure projects in a district, the links between costs and benefits become weak.

With the fugitive nature of wildlife, it is difficult to closely define the producer com-

munities. Even where it is possible to define boundaries, it is difficult to ensure that those paying the highest costs receive the greatest benefits. Even within wards, there are differences in animal densities and in crop and livestock damage due to wildlife. Defining the producer community is difficult and even where the district has decided that the residents "living with wildlife" should be the principal beneficiaries, this is difficult to determine. A number of criteria can be used—according to animal densities, based on the exact location of where the trophies were taken or based on relative crop and livestock damage. This cannot necessarily be done at the ward level, and as in Beitbridge district, it may be one or more village (VIDCO). It is only when wildlife is accepted as "belonging" to those who live with it and pay its costs that the various models that enable the producer communities to receive larger shares will be accepted without creating community strife.

It is important for communities to play an active role in deciding how the wildlife revenue is to be distributed, but even if they are closely involved, there is often a problem with the implementation of community projects. This is largely due to a lack of implementation skills at the district and ward levels. In many wards, the ward dividends remain in the bank, with their purchasing power eroding due to the high inflation rate in Zimbabwe. Also eroding is the link between the wildlife costs and wildlife benefits: the costs are felt immediately in terms of crop damage and threat to human life, while the benefits are delayed. These delays unfortunately parallel the delays these communities experienced in the past in getting wildlife revenue back from Treasury.

It is also essential that the communities receive an adequate proportion of the value of the wildlife sold from their land. Safari hunting involves very high overheads in marketing and operations, but it is only with the introduction of more open and competitive marketing that prices paid by operators increase. *The local communities need to establish openly competitive systems and need to be trained and assisted in marketing their resources to operators.*

Comparative analysis of wildlife and subsistence agriculture in communal areas

In the communal areas in Zimbabwe, animal production regimes largely consist of cattle that are used primarily for draft power, as a store of wealth, and for providing milk and manure. The real and perceived benefits of cattle are high, and the costs are low since for peasant farmers the costs of food and care are negligible: the community bears the costs of depletion of the open access grazing resources and the government bears the cost of most veterinary costs with their animal health and dipping programs.

Small domestic animals are also part of most household economies and in some of the more remote areas, wildlife plays an important role in subsistence income. In a few isolated areas where tsetse flies are still around, wildlife dominates, and even small domestic livestock is limited. Household surveys have shown that in the more arid areas of the country, nonfarm income is very important and that without off-farm income, government sponsored drought relief is necessary even in average rainfall years. Thus, most agricultural officers and farmers prefer irrigation as a strategy for increasing incomes and generating revenues in the marginal areas. However, the irrigation schemes are generally uneconomic, unless the cost of establishing water sources is not included. Even when the water provision costs are excluded, the rates of return are normally around 10–15 percent. The higher return schemes tend generally to be small schemes with limited infrastructural investment.

The analysis of agricultural projects seldom includes any of the subsistence benefits from wildlife, since hunting is illegal. The value of woodland resources are also seldom incorporated as an opportunity cost to clearing land for cultivation (Bradley and McNamara 1993).

This may be partially due to the fact that the irrigation schemes do not necessarily deplete much of the surrounding woodland, even though the increase in population pressure will do so in the long term. These resources play an essential role in coping with drought and in improving the quality of nutrition, and the impacts of reducing access to these resources must be incorporated in all development strategies, particularly in arid areas (Chimedza 1992).

In a recent attempt to compare household returns from agriculture and wildlife, a survey was carried out in four wards in the Sebungwe region of the Zambezi Valley (Murindagomo, forthcoming). The survey showed that in Gokwe over 80 percent of annual household income is from cropping and 8–10 percent from off-farm employment, with 5–15 percent from livestock sales. If wildlife earnings had been paid out in cash, they would have represented 2–4 percent. In the Omay, on the other hand, over 70 percent was from off-farm employment, and only 17 percent was from cropping. Livestock sales were around 3 percent, and the household revenue from wildlife would have been 4 percent if it had been paid out in cash and not retained by the ward for projects. The survey also showed that incomes in noncattle areas were half those in cattle areas. Similar income differentials were observed in Gutsa (mid-Zambezi valley) between houses with and without access to draft power (Barrett 1992) and in most communal household surveys throughout Zimbabwe, access to draft power has been the most important variable in determining income levels.

Even though the CAMPFIRE project is active in three out of the four wards surveyed and considerable wildlife still exists in these areas, wildlife plays a very small role in household revenue generation, particularly where these revenues are retained at the ward level for projects. Wildlife plays a more significant role in household costs (through crop and livestock damage and the time spent protecting resources and people from wildlife), but these have not been estimated.

As a result of tsetse fly eradication, both the Omay and Nenyunka, which have a relatively abundant wildlife population, are faced with land pressure resulting from potential immigrants and their cattle. At this stage of development, where access to land is not the limiting factor, the existing households welcome immigrants because they bring with them the potential of access to cattle for draft power, and increased populations justify more access to government services (roads, schools, clinics, etc.)

It is only under very particular circumstances with very poor agronomic conditions that wildlife can substitute for cattle at the household level, unless a considerably increased proportion of the revenue generated by wildlife can be retained by producers. Draft power is the most valuable output from cattle, and it is possible that where wildlife and cattle cannot be compatible, other forms of draft power may reduce the opportunity costs of wildlife versus cattle for the households. Measures to reduce wildlife predation (e.g., fencing of cropping zones) may also reduce opportunity costs. Localized control systems, which include allowing individual hunting may also result in substantial increases in household welfare at small losses, and possibly substantial gains, to wildlife numbers.

Despite the importance of cropping and maize in revenue generation in the nonwildlife areas, maize gross margins are mostly negative when the cost of own labor and draft power is included in the calculations. The decision to grow maize is rational when the cost of producing the maize is compared to the cost of importing from major urban centers, particularly when the risk of poor access is added to the landed cost. The lack of cash resources to purchase maize also encourages home production. Therefore, it is possible that if markets were more effectively integrated, households would not need to rely on expensive self-sufficiency strategies. Wildlife production systems, which include high-value production of specialty outputs, may become more financially attractive to peasant households and considerably increase both rural and national growth (Muir 1987).

Given the difficulties of comparing cattle and wildlife in peasant farming communities, it may be better to estimate opportunity costs of cattle by comparing the *with* and *without* scenarios. This is carried out in Table 8-2 where the assumption is that cattle and population densities preclude the option of wildlife, but bring with them concomitant increases in average household incomes. The subsistence incomes are higher as a result of direct income generated by livestock, increased cropping incomes, and reduced losses from wildlife. Total area cultivated also increases because there are more households farming. It is assumed that the increased income would be evenly-distributed among households. Income distribution is highly skewed in rural areas, and less than 20 percent of the population normally own adequate cattle for draft.

Under current revenue distribution in communal areas, wildlife is only rarely more profitable to the individual householder than subsistence agriculture. The question therefore is whether wildlife is the more economically viable option in communal areas at the national level. An example is given in Table 8-2 of the opportunity costs of wildlife and subsistence agriculture using Nyaminyami District. The analysis shows that the best option from an international economic perspective is for wildlife with improved agricultural output, but with no increase in population. This is because the increase in human population reduces wildlife revenue and, as the international community benefits by 20 percent more than the nation, it has a larger stake in the wildlife option.

The best option from a national economic perspective is wildlife. This option assumes that population is increasing to 7,500 households because of the additional income generated by more people farming in the area.[3] The crude assumption was that household farm income doubled with improved agriculture by reorganizing the current systems into a best case scenario with wildlife revenue only declining by 12.5 percent. If agricultural incomes cannot be improved while retaining wildlife, the wildlife-only option is preferred from a national social welfare perspective. This option would also be best for the households since they would achieve the increased incomes from better agriculture, as well as from wildlife revenue. If agricultural incomes cannot be improved with wildlife, then the best option for the farmers is to eliminate wildlife and encourage immigrants and cattle.

The calculation assumes that the same per capita agricultural productivity is achieved by reducing revenues by only 12.5 percent, but with only half the new immigrants so that the population is 7,500 households. If agriculture is improved, but there is no immigration, then wildlife revenue remains the same. In reality it would probably improve if the subsistence agricultural system had been reorganized to allow for the interface.

The policy environment and its impact on the future of wildlife

The Zimbabwean economy is characterized by its highly centralized and heavily regulated structure. There are many state-owned enterprises and parastatals. International borrowing subsidized the expansion of the civil service and expenditures for social services. In the 1980s real gross national product (GNP) per capita stagnated, and debt service problems arose. This was the context in which Zimbabwe embarked on an economic structural adjustment program (ESAP) in the 1990s.

The impact of macroeconomic policies on the wildlife sector

Foreign exchange

For most of the 1980s, overvaluation was greater than 50 percent, but with ESAP this had fallen to 15–20 percent by the end of 1993. The overvalued exchange rate has had a significant negative effect on the wildlife industry. The limited access to foreign exchange had severely constrained access to imported inputs, particularly vehicles, spare parts, and the luxury commodities high-value tourism and hunting demands. The regulations pertaining to access to foreign exchange significantly increased transaction costs and favored established industries and firms, constraining wildlife sector growth and effectively reducing returns to CAMPFIRE. For example, in a survey of safari operators, the most significant constraint to growth cited was the shortage of foreign exchange.

Recent changes under ESAP have considerably improved the wildlife sector's access to foreign exchange. For example, the introduction of the export retention scheme (ERS) in July 1990 allowed exporters the right to utilize 35 percent of export earnings to import inputs (except for those in a "negative list"[4]). Although it favors existing operators, ERS quotas are now tradeable at a premium of between 20 percent and 50 percent, and that has helped new entrants. There are still considerable transaction costs in accessing these rights and delays in clearing imported inputs, but the situation has improved. The increased retention scheme also has reduced incentives to engage in illegal foreign currency deals and underinvoicing.

---

[3]These estimates all assume that the immigrants are moving from overcrowded areas and that all the slack created by their exodus is taken up by the remaining population. This is not likely to be true in the short-term.

[4]However, some of the items on the "negative list" (imported luxuries and vehicles above a certain value) are necessary for the wildlife industry, and there may need to be some exceptions for wildlife enterprises.

Fiscal policy

The Zimbabwe government has greatly expanded its bureaucracy since independence, and expenditure on salaries is extremely large. By contrast, the Ministry of Environment and Tourism (which includes DNPWLM) received 0.68 percent of total government expenditure in 1990/91. DNPWLM received only half the expenditure on Veterinary Services and only 60 percent of that allocated to the Ministry of Political Affairs. This is an indication of the low priority accorded wildlife despite its potential for growth.

The budget deficit and high government expenditure have directly contributed to the need for tight monetary controls. This has affected the wildlife sector at a time when it appeared ready for major expansion. Continued fiscal imprudence with expenditure directed toward party rather than national priorities is a serious threat to the entire Zimbabwe economy, including the wildlife sector.

Monetary policy

One area in which the government does appear to be committed to structural adjustment is in monetary policy, since interest rates have been forced up by requiring the banks to remain very liquid. This has been part of the policy to contain inflation, but unfortunately this tight monetary policy has not been matched by austere fiscal policy. The position has been made significantly worse by the drought, which has forced government to incur large deficits in the importation of essential food and raw materials.

Given the lack of government progress on containing nondrought-related expenditure, the prognosis for the future must include the burden of very high national debt. Monetary policy alone can only control inflation at the expense of growth, through severely high interest rates. These high interest rates also affect the wildlife industry. This situation excludes new entrants with limited collateral and will therefore exacerbate the trend of a

white-dominated industry, unless an affirmative action program with special credit facilities and training is put in place.

Employment

The government is very concerned about increasing employment and reducing under-employment. The industrial sector cannot grow fast enough to absorb the rapidly increasing population, and the agricultural resettlement program is supposed to help. However, limited employment generation means that the current trend of informal settlement will continue, and this population pressure threatens communal lands, including many of the CAMPFIRE areas. Most wildlife options in communal areas at the moment are land intensive and absorb very few people, relative to subsistence agriculture. It is important to develop institutions and technologies which enable wildlife systems to employ or at least accommodate more people, without reducing wildlife densities.

Investment policy

The Zimbabwe Investment Centre (ZIC) has been established to facilitate private sector investment. Government policy places a premium on investment in the mining and manufacturing sectors as compared to the wildlife sector.

The impact of sectoral policies on the wildlife sector

Sectoral allocation

The viability of the wildlife industry in Zimbabwe rests very heavily upon an effective national parks structure. Capital expenditure for the Department of National Parks and Wildlife Management in 1991 had declined 27 percent since independence. Recurrent expenditure for DNPWLM has fallen 6 percent in real terms since 1988. This is despite the significant increase in the demand for DNPWLM services.

The result of inadequate financing has been a decline in the capacity of this department to service the rapidly expanding wildlife industry and to sustain the national parks estate. In addition to the very low budget, DNPWLM has had to service an expanding mandate and has had to face significant increases in poaching. Time, skills, financial, and other resources have been directed away from traditional concentration on park management and research to service all these new demands. The decline in funding has resulted in deterioration of roads, boreholes, buildings, plant, vehicles, and equipment. It has also affected research, extension and interpretive services, park management, and law enforcement, thus threatening wildlife conservation, habitat protection, and the economic productivity of the wildlife sector as a whole.

Land

The current land policy aims to reallocate half the land in the large-scale freehold sector to the small-scale sector, but it will retain the same basic dualistic structure. There is considerable concern that farms with wildlife enterprises will be targeted for resettlement. These fears arise from the belief that wildlife is considered a luxury and not a productive land use system by some bureaucrats and politicians. *There is, therefore, an urgent need to disseminate information on the productivity of wildlife.*

The country is to introduce a land tax that will encourage large-scale farmers to utilize those areas of their properties currently underutilized. On areas that cannot be used for agriculture, there may be increasing investments in wildlife and recreational tourism, and this would increase the growth of the wildlife sector. Regulations that discourage subdivision will reinforce this trend, since the farmers will not be able to sell the land they are not using for agriculture. There is some uncertainty as to the nature of the land tax, with some inference that it may be used to affect production systems. If this is the case, the

subsequent distortions will have severe impacts on the economic efficiency of agriculture and may lead to disincentives for wildlife-based activities.

The negative attitudes of most of the agricultural bureaucracy to wildlife derives from uncertainty over its actual economic value, as well as lack of technical and business expertise in wildlife enterprises. This has more serious consequences in the communal areas and resettlement schemes, since land use planners hesitate to allocate land to wildlife. Similarly, those responsible for resettlement find wildlife to be land intensive, and very restrictive to their mandate to resettle the maximum number of people from overcrowded communal farming areas.

Marketing and price policies

In the large-scale sector, cattle are the major competitor with wildlife for land. Beef production has been heavily supported by the government since the 1930s. This included large marketing and processing investment in beef by the state. Producers or consumers (and at times both) have been directly and indirectly subsidized by government marketing and pricing policies for beef over the decades. The distortions created by the implicit and explicit support for beef have particularly affected the development of the goat industry and have probably had similar effects on game meat. Since independence the Cold Storage Commission (CSC) has received subsidies of Z\$ 40 million per annum. Prior to 1985 both producers and consumers were subsidized, but subsequently producer prices were reduced, and only consumers have been subsidized by the state, and indirectly by farmers.

Veterinary and health controls

The erection of fences and the eradication of buffalo from large-scale ranches have had negative effects on both the economy and the viability of wildlife enterprises on ranches. It is unlikely that the value of the buffalo eradicated in order to allow for beef exports to Europe can ever be recouped, despite the very high prices obtained from privileged access to their controlled markets. No analysis has been carried out on the economics of the fences nor on their impact on wild animal migrations. The continued effect of keeping buffalo out of cattle areas affects wildlife profitability, since buffalo add significantly to the value of hunting on ranches (Child 1988). Movement controls implemented to satisfy EC requirements considerably increase the cost of live animal sales by requiring long quarantine periods. There are also a number of municipal and national regulations that restrict the free movement of game meat sales and require various inspections.

External trade controls

Exports of wildlife products and of live animals are subject to various permits, licenses, and restrictions. These restrictions are normally either to fulfill the requirements of international conventions (e.g., CITES) or are an attempt to build up the local industry. The restrictions on the sale of live animals are controversial and tend to result in industry concentration. The export of game meat and other wildlife products are severely restricted by the importing countries.

Sale and utilization controls

Although landholders or appropriate authorities may utilize wild animals found on their land, the method and sale of various services and products are controlled (Booth 1992). In the communal areas, residents are still prohibited from hunting any wild animals, even in districts that have been granted appropriate authority. The Zimbabwean economy is very highly regulated, and these national, municipal, and industry restrictions often act as barriers to entry and have restricted the growth of wildlife and tourism ventures.

Conclusions

Wildlife in the commercial ranch sector is often more financially profitable than cattle, particularly in the more arid parts of Zimbabwe. An improved macroeconomic environment and a less regulated economy will contribute to its viability and continued growth. This will also benefit cattle enterprises greatly and may even tilt the balance in its favor vis-à-vis wildlife. *In the remote, semiarid communal sector, the CAMPFIRE program appears to be the most economic option from a social welfare perspective, but it is seldom the rational choice for households living in these areas.* Thus, more effective mechanisms and institutions need to be developed so that the gainers compensate the losers.

Finally, the direct benefits to the world community from retaining wildlife can be considerable. These would include greater species diversity, greater tree coverage, and the bequest and existence values of the animals. If these can be appropriately valued, then in certain areas the international community clearly benefits from land allocated to wildlife. Such global benefits need to be considered through institutions such as the Global Environment Facility (GEF).

Table 8-1: Adjusted Contribution of Wildlife to the Economy, 1990/91

Sector	Total Earnings (Z$ million)	Forex Earnings (Z$ million)
1. Tourism	731.0	531.0
2. Hunting	81.5	81.1
3. Wildlife management services and live animals sales	6.2	negl.
4. Game products (meat, hides/skins, horns)	1.0	negl.
5. Crocodile production	26.6	26.6
6. Ostrich production	35.4	35.4
TOTAL	881.7	674.1

Note: Based on Equilibrium Exchange Rate. All the figures must be considered very rough estimates due to severe data limitations.
Source: Jansen (1992a).

Table 8-2: Comparative Analysis of Wildlife and Subsistence Agriculture: Total Revenue Estimates Using Nyaminyami District, Zimbabwe

Part 1: Wildlife Revenue Estimates and Allocation (U.S. dollars per annum 1992)

	International	National	District	Households (HHs)	All HHs	Wildlife HHs
Direct Revenues						
Hunting	1,034,066	827,252	212,000			
Tourism	781,250	625,000	7,200	70667	14	35
Total	1,815,316	1,452,252	219,200			
Airfares	450,000					
Outfitting	200,000	51,703				
Taxidermy	51,703	10,000		6,000		
Curios	10,000	20,000	--	10,000	17	43
Meat	20,000	--	219,200	--		
Ivory	--	1,533,956		86,667		
Total	2,547,019					
Environ. protection	Not quanti-	Not quanti-	Not quanti-			
Genetic resources	fied, but signifi-	fied, but	fied, but			
Bequest	cantly	signifi-	signifi-			
Existence	positive	cantly	cantly			
TOTAL wildlife		positive	positive			

(continued)

Part 2: Alternative Land Use Scenarios for Nyaminyami

		International	National	District	Households (HHs)	All HHs	Wildlife HHs
Subsistence agriculture with wildlife							
5,000 HHs agric income	US$	262,000	262,000		262,000	52	52
TOTAL incl. wildlife income	US$	2,809,019	1,795,956	219,200	348,667	70	96
Subsistence agriculture with no wildlife							
10,000 HHs	US$	1,048,000	1,048,000		1,048,000	105	105
5,000 HHs	US$	524,000	524,000		524,000	105	105
Retain wildlife with reorganized and improved agriculture							
7,500 HHs	US$	3,014,641	2,128,211	219,200	872,667	122	148
5,000 HHs	US$	3,071,019	2,057,956	219,200	610,667	122	148

International refers to revenue generated for the world population.
National refers to the revenue generated which remains within Zimbabwe.
District refers to the proportion paid to district council.
Households refers to proportion of income accruing to producers.
All households refers to per household distribution based on 5,000 households, in the two lines and as indicated for the remainder.
Wildlife households is based on 2,000 households living with wildlife.
Refer to the notes that follow for detailed assumptions used in Table 8-2.

Notes to Tables 8-1 and 8-2

1. **Hunting revenue.** The estimated total value from the hunting sold based on projected international hunting prices for 1993 with 5 percent deducted for international inflation. International safari prices have not in fact risen, and it is possible that the 1992 value should be the same as that for 1993, but a conservative estimate was preferred. Precise 1992 data were not easily available.

2. **Hunting revenue retained in Zimbabwe.** A deduction of 20 percent to cover external marketing costs, convention, wholesaler and agents commissions and fees. The remainder is what is paid into Zimbabwe.

3. **Hunting revenue retained by the district council.** The trophy and concession fees paid to the district council (Z$ 1,060,000 converted to US$ at 5:1).

4. **Tourist revenue generated by Nyaminyami wildlife.** An estimate of the revenue earned by Bumi Hills Safari Lodge and Tiger Bay because of the wildlife in Omay. If there was no wildlife it is estimated that Bumi would loose 50 percent of its custom and Tiger Bay 25 percent (it is closer to the national park and caters more heavily to fishermen). Both were estimated at 5000 bed nights, Bumi at US$250 per night and Tiger Bay at US$125 per night, full board and tours.

5. **Tourist revenue retained in Zimbabwe** A deduction of 20 percent for external marketing agents fees etc - this is probably too high as much of the marketing costs and fees may be retained locally.

6. **Tourism revenue paid to district council.** Tourism numbers for 1992 were calculated as lower than 1991 (particularly for Bumi) because of the effect of drought on international visitors. Assuming that the per visitor fee to be paid to the district council in 1992 is higher, the revenue to the DC, is assumed to be the same as in 1991 (Z$ 36,000).

7. **Hunting and tourism revenue allocated for wards.** Assumes that the DC pays 33 percent of its total earnings as ward dividends

(as for 1991)

8. **Ward allocation to individual households.** Assumes 5000 households in Nyaminyami. Assumes that the ward dividends are distributed evenly between the 5000 households (whether as cash or projects)

9. **Ward allocation if only to wildlife households.** Assumes that the revenue is shared only by those living in areas with substantial wildlife resources (Omay). The number of households is estimated to be 2000.

10. **Value of airfares of incoming hunters.** It is guesstimated that there are 145 hunters and companions based on the number of hunts. No airfare value is given for those coming in for tourism on the assumption that they would fly to Zimbabwe, even if there was no Nyaminyami wildlife.

11. **Value of guns, etc.** Assumes that each safari party spends $1,400 in their home country on equipment, ammunition and outfitting (safari outfits etc).

12. **Value of taxidermy.** Each client spends 5 percent on mounting trophies.

13. **Value of curio sales.** An estimate based on Binga sales of Z$ 80,000 - estimated that the handicraft center at Bumi will earn Z$ 50,000.

14. **Value of curio sales to households.** The producers retain 60 percent. Although averaged over all Omay residents in fact it is likely to be much more concentrated income and cannot be easily represented in the individual household dividends.

15. **Value of meat.** Includes meat, hides, etc, from cropping and problem animal control - assumes less available but at higher price so remains same as 1991. National social price is doubled as meat was sold at subsidized price. Opportunity cost value not adjusted at household level because for those individuals the opportunity cost is hunting time and illegality risk which may even be less than the money saved by access to cheap meat.

16. **Current value of subsistence agriculture**

in Nyaminyami. Based on Z$ 262 per household per annum currently generated by crop, livestock and beer sales and grain retentions (average crop returns for Negande Ward in Murindagomo 1992). Most household income is from off-farm work and drought relief. Z$ 262 by 5,000 households converted to U.S. dollars.

17. **Value of subsistence agriculture with cattle and no wildlife.** Using survey results of vidcos with and without cattle (Zhomba and Ntamo, Nenyunka Ward, Gokwe in Murindagomo 1992) average farm income doubles. This would be as a result of increased access to draft power, immigrants with greater access to cash or credit for input purchases and reduced wildlife depredation. It is assumed that there are no agronomic differences between the vidcos which may have caused the differential. It is further assumed that with the elimination of tsetsefly and increased demand for land, immigrants move in and the population is doubled resulting in increased habitat destruction and poaching which reduce wildlife to insignificance. The calculation is double Z$ 262 multiplied by 10,000 households converted to U.S. dollars.

18. **Household value of subsistence agriculture with cattle and no wildlife.** This assumes that the increased incomes are evenly distributed when in fact they are usually highly concentrated with those who own cattle. The current residents will benefit from increased access to cattle, more people in the area to lobby for services and to sell beer to; but it is unlikely that they will in fact double their current incomes.

19. **Value of wildlife and subsistence with project to reorganize agriculture.** Some wildlife experts maintain that it is not currently desirable to incorporate cattle into subsistence agriculture systems in wildlife areas and furthermore that any increases in population would not be sustainable. However, it seems that reorganization including possibly greater separation of people and wildlife, access to alternative draft or livestock holding pens etc could be used to try to enable increased agricultural production alongside continued wildlife enterprises - this has been achieved in the commercial ranch sector. It is more difficult in the communal sector but may be possible.

Figure 8-1: Comparison of Projected Household Income

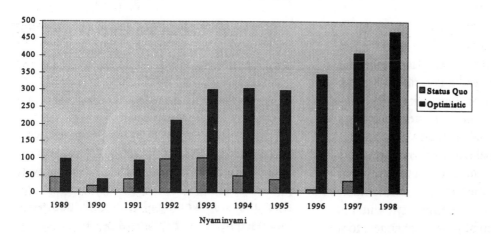

Nyaminyami

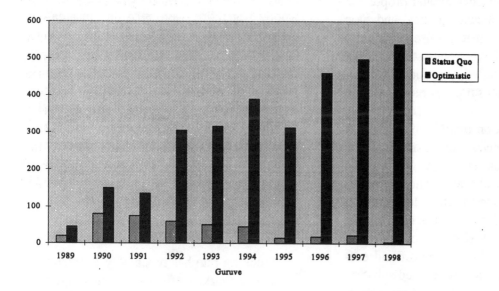

Guruve

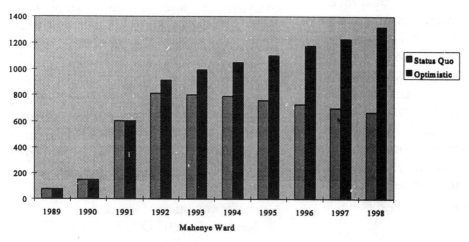

Mahenye Ward

Annex 8-A: Relative Environmental Impacts of Wildlife[5]

Introduction

Concerns about overgrazing and rangeland degradation have played a central role in the shaping of the national livestock policy, giving rise to schemes of limiting stock numbers and in some cases of actually destocking. Attention has also been drawn to the impacts especially of elephants in the destruction of woodlands. Degradation is seen as manifesting itself where a plant community, which is dominated by perennial grasses changes, to a community that includes a greater proportion of woody species, annual grasses, and bare ground. Thus, rainfall that was used efficiently in the production of a relatively stable supply of fodder is now wasted, less fodder is produced, and the fodder supply is more variable from year to year.

Initially utilization results in changes in the herbaceous species composition of the veld, especially from perennial grasses to a combination of annual grasses and less palatable perennial grasses with reduced vigor. Ground cover and litter cover decrease, thus leading to increased soil compaction and crusting, and thus enhanced runoff and erosion. Rainfall infiltration is reduced substantially and, because the density of grass roots near the soil surface is lower, a greater proportion of the water that does enter the soil becomes available to deeper-rooted woody species. This gives them a competitive advantage, which they are able to maintain at the expense of grasses, so that the supply of fodder is permanently reduced. As bush encroachment and the above induced drought conditions continue to develop, sheet and gully erosion become more widespread, and previously permanent streams become more intermittent.

The Evidence on Herbivore Impacts on Zimbabwean Rangelands

National surveys

For Zimbabwe as a whole, over the ten-year period from 1963 to 1973, closed woodland and open woodland declined in area by 4 percent and 16 percent, respectively, while the area of sparse woodland and cultivated land increased by 12 percent and 8 percent, respectively (Whitlow 1980). The main decreases in woody vegetation were recorded in areas of high to moderate population densities, particularly within the communal lands. This was ascribed primarily to the expansion of cultivated lands, and to a lesser extent to the collection of firewood and building materials. Attention was also drawn to the rapid rate of destruction of woodlands on some of the state land in the west and northwest of Zimbabwe, which was ascribed mainly to the buildup of high elephant densities within these areas.

Commercial livestock production systems

Stocking rate has repeatedly been shown to have a marked effect on both rangeland composition and animal productivity (Clatworthy 1989). There is a consistent trend for perennial grass cover to decline with an increasing stocking rate. For animal performance, both wet season gains and dry season losses are affected by stocking rate, with the former decreasing and the latter increasing as the stocking rate is increased. However, for a given stocking rate, the wide range of grazing procedures examined have had almost no differential effects on botanical composition nor on the condition of the veld.

Kennan (1969), O'Connor (1985), and Clatworthy (1989) all emphasize that the

---

[5]This annex is based exclusively on the background paper prepared by Robert Cunliffe.

impact of livestock on veld condition is dependent on both rainfall and soil conditions. A number of studies have demonstrated that long-term rainfall variability has an overriding effect on herbaceous compositional trends, independent of grazing regimes, particularly in the drier rangelands where rainfall is more variable and primary production is strongly limited by soil moisture availability. In moister savannas, annual variability in rainfall is lower, and the relationship between vegetation production and rainfall is less marked. The influence of grazing varies, with the most pronounced effects being observed in low rainfall regions.

Wild herbivore systems

Despite the diversity of large herbivores, which is a characteristic of African savanna communities, only a limited number of species have been reported as having dramatic effects on the environment. Analysis shows that communities tend to be dominated by a few large species, such as elephant, hippopotamus, buffalo, zebra, and wildebeest (Cumming 1982). It is these species, particularly the elephant, which have been reported as having a dramatic effect on the environment.

Craig (1992) and Martin (1992) have calculated that elephant densities need to be held below about 0.5 animals per square kilometer, in order to maintain the existing woodland canopy cover intact. This is far lower than the densities currently occurring in many of the national parks and safari areas, which in 1991 were estimated to range from 0.25 to 2.12 animals per square kilometer.

Communal land agro-pastoral systems

Since early in the colonial period, overstocking and degradation of communal rangelands have caused concern. For much of this century, and continuing to the present, government officials have sought ways in which to control or even reduce livestock numbers in the communal lands. Stocking rates in the communal lands, frequently of the order of 2–3 hectares per livestock unit, are typically higher than those found on other types of land. Livestock, particularly cattle, form an integral part of the agro-pastoral farming system, particularly through the provision of draft power and manure, which is widely used to maintain or improve soil fertility. Recent studies, such as those by Swift et al. (1989) on nitrogen cycling in communal land farming systems and Barrett (1992) on the economic role of cattle in communal land farming systems, indicate that the majority of households do not own sufficient livestock to satisfy their needs for draft power and manure.

Despite the widespread concern about the deterioration of communal land rangelands, remarkably little research has been directed at this problem. This has been highlighted by a number of recent studies that question the official view of the extent and significance of degradation in these areas (Abel and Blaikie 1989; Barrett, Brinn, and Timberlake 1991; Sandford 1982; Scoones 1990; Warren and Agnew 1988).

Scoones (1990) examined livestock production records over several decades for seven heavily stocked communal lands in southern Zimbabwe. Government officials, in 1944, considered the stocking rates of six of the seven communal lands studied by Scoones to be in excess of the recommended carrying capacities for these areas. Yet for each communal land, the 1986 cattle population density was considerably in excess of its 1944 stocking rate. Despite large fluctuations in response to rainfall, cattle populations appeared to have been successfully maintained over the last twenty-five years for all communal lands. There were obvious signs of soil erosion on the rangelands, and yet there was no evidence that cattle populations were declining, and neither was their potential productivity being detrimentally impacted. Scoones (1990) suggested that the impact of erosion on secondary production is sufficiently low as not to be felt on a relatively short time scale, or else that the sites where erosion is occurring might not contribute significantly to the overall livestock production, or both.

The Save study (Campbell, Du Toit, and Attwell 1989), however, perceived the environment as being degraded through deforestation, overgrazing, loss of soil, loss of soil fertility, siltation of rivers and increased runoff. It concluded that there was a severe imbalance between the human population and the resource base, such that the environment was less able to satisfy the needs of current and future human populations.

Comparative studies

Kelly and Walker (1976) undertook a comparative study of four sites under different land tenure, which were apparently similar in every respect, except for the type and intensity of grazing and browsing by large herbivores. Fifteen years later De Jager (1988) repeated measurements of vegetation and range condition. Kelly and Walker's study concluded that the intensively utilized communal land site was in fact degraded in comparison to the other three sites, in that the perennial grasses had largely been replaced by annual grasses; herbaceous production was more variable between years.

De Jager's follow-up study failed to reveal any firm evidence of directional trends that could be related to differences in the intensity of utilization by herbivores. The herbaceous vegetation of the communal land site was still dominated by annual grasses, as opposed to perennials on the other three sites. Basal cover of grasses was also lowest for the communal land site, as was the litter cover and the rate of infiltration. There were indications that the communal land soils were now of lower fertility than those of the other three sites, but none of these differences were significant. Woody vegetation had changed considerably in density and the heterogeneity among plots within sites tended to mask differences between sites.

A comparison of separate game and cattle enterprises, which have been run since 1960 on adjoining, ecologically very similar areas, under the same overall management was undertaken on Buffalo Range (Child 1988). Rangeland condition has been assessed in detail in 1973, in 1986 (Child 1988), and in 1990, although the results of this latest survey have not yet been made available.

In 1973 the cattle section was ecologically in better condition than the game section at this time. Thirteen years later there were definite indications that range condition on the game section had improved, whereas it had deteriorated on the cattle section. The area under cattle now exhibited twice as much erosion as that under game, and although there was an increase in soil capping on both the cattle and game sections, the increase on the former was threefold that of the latter. These changes in range condition can be related directly to trends in secondary production. The levels of meat harvested fluctuated, but over a twenty-six-year period show the two systems yielded very similar amounts of meat. Cattle productivity, however, was reduced by declining calving rates.

Child (1988) relates declining cattle productivity to the overstocking. The stocking rate of wildlife fluctuated considerably, increasing rapidly during the high rainfall years of the 1970s but declining massively during the drought years from 1982–84. After 1984 populations increased through natural growth at a slower rate than on the cattle section, which was restocked with cattle from elsewhere. At no point in time has the stocking rate of wild herbivore grazers on the game section ever exceeded that of cattle on the cattle section. At the time of the 1986 measurements, the cattle stocking rate was some 1.5 times that of game.

This study suggests that the meat production potential of the cattle and game enterprises is similar and that rangeland impact is largely a function of the stocking rate of herbivores. Child (1988) makes the important point that the generation of revenue from the cattle enterprise is directly related to the secondary production of beef, whereas for the wildlife enterprise, the major form of revenue generation is through safari hunting operations, thus enabling more conservative stocking rates to be maintained.

The Major Factors Influencing Environmental Impacts

There is no single biological optimal carrying capacity that can be defined independently of the different management objectives associated with different forms of animal exploitation. Thus, for semiarid rangelands, which are subjected to erratic rainfall and characterized by large fluctuations in plant species composition, cover, and biomass, the problem becomes one of distinguishing between drought-induced fluctuations and permanent changes in vegetation states. It is doubtful that our current knowledge of savanna systems allows these distinctions to be made at present with any degree of confidence.

Comparisons of herbivore community structure between wildlife and domestic livestock systems, in terms of the biomass contributions of the different classes of feeders, lead to the important conclusion that the impact of wild, as opposed to domestic, herbivores on the environment, is more likely to be a question of degree rather than of fundamentally

different kind, associated with the unique effects of different herbivore species (Cumming 1982). The comparison of Child (1988) between wildlife and a commercial cattle system suggests that the environmental impacts of wildlife and cattle are determined largely by the stocking rate, rather than by the different types of herbivores, and this is supported by the literature reviewed by Clatworthy (1989). The research reviewed above further suggests that, particularly in semiarid environments, vegetation changes are unreliable indicators of rangeland degradation. Rates of soil loss and changes in soil chemistry, and physical properties may be more reliable indicators.

Given that the *environmental impacts of different herbivore communities are determined essentially by the stocking rate rather than the types of herbivores involved*, some consideration of the stocking rates required to meet the specific objectives of different animal production systems, becomes important. Data from Buffalo Range illustrate that *wildlife can be profitably stocked at a significantly lower rate than that required for cattle*, due to the high values associated with hunting safaris. Studies of communal land farming systems show that the current high livestock numbers consistently fall far short of the populations required to satisfy the multiple needs of farmers. Thus, the communal lands are likely to continue to be heavily stocked.

Bibliography

Abel, N. O. J., and P. M. Blaikie. 1989. "Land Degradation, Stocking Rates, and Conservation Policies in the Communal Rangelands of Botswana and Zimbabwe." *Land Degradation and Rehabilitation* 1:1–23.

Agritex. 1990. "Feasibility and Design Report of Nabusenga Small-scale Irrigation Scheme." Irrigation Division, MLARR, Zimbabwe Government, June.

Anderson, G. D., and B. H. Walker. 1974. "Vegetation Composition and Elephant Damage in the Sengwa Wildlife Research Area, Rhodesia." *Journal of the Southern African Wildlife Management Association*, 4:1–14.

Barrett. J. C. 1992. "The Economic Role of Cattle in Communal Farming Systems in Zimbabwe." *Pastoral Development Network Paper* 32b. London: ODI.

Barrett, J. C., P. Brinn, and J. Timberlake. 1991. *Tsetse Control, Agropastoralism and Land Degradation: A Case Study in Chiswiti Communal Land. Final Report.* Unpublished report of the Tsetse and Trypanosomiasis Control Branch, Department of Veterinary Services, Harare.

Behnke, R. H., and I. Scoones. 1992. "Rethinking Range Ecology: Implications for Rangeland Management in Africa." Dryland Networks Programme Paper No. 33, Overseas Development Institute, London.

Behr, J., and J. A. Groenewald. 1990. "Commercial Game Utilization on South African Farms." *Agrekon* 29(1):55–58.

Benson, D. E. 1986. "Game Farming Survey." *Farmer's Weekly*, April–May.

Berry, M. P. S. 1986. "A Comparison of Different Wildlife Production Enterprises in the Northern Cape Province, South Africa." *S. Afr. Tudskr. Natuurnay* 16(4): 124–28.

Bond, Ivan. 1992. "Tourism, Hunting and Management Services." In Price Waterhouse and Environmental Resources Ltd. *Wildlife Management and Environmental Conservation Project* Task 2 The Role of Wildlife in the Economy. Reports prepared for Dept. National Parks and Wildlife Management, Zimbabwe.

Booth, V. 1992. "Wildlife Utilization, Management and Planning Outside the Parks and Wildlife Estate." In Price Waterhouse and Env. Resources, *Wildlife Management and Environmental Conservation Project* Background Papers prepared for DNPWLM funded by Japanese Grant Aid, coordinated by World Bank, AF6IN.

Bradley, P., and K. McNamara (eds.). 1993. "Living with Trees, Policies for Forestry Management in Zimbabwe." WB Technical Paper Number 210.

Campbell, B. M., R. F. Du Toit, and C. A. M. Attwell. 1989. "The Save Study: Relationships Between the Environment and Basic Needs Satisfaction in the Save Catchment, Zimbabwe." *Supplement to Zambezia*, University of Zimbabwe, pp 1–119.

Child, Brian. 1988. "The Role of Wildlife Utilization in the Sustainable Economic Development of Semi-arid Rangelands in Zimbabwe." Unpublished D.Phil dissertation, School of Forestry, Oxford University.

Child, B., and J. Peterson, Jr. 1991. *CAMPFIRE in Rural Development: The Beitbridge Experience.* DNPWLM and CASS Joint Working Paper 1/91.

Child, Graham. Forthcoming. Wildlife in Zimbabwe, draft book in preparation.

Childes, S. L. 1984. The Population Dynamics of Some Woody Species in the Kalahari Sand Vegetation of Hwange National Park. M.Sc. thesis, University of Witwatersrand.

Chimedza, R. 1992. "Women, Household Food Security and Wildlife Resources." Draft working paper, Dept. Agric. Econ.& Ext., University of Zimbabwe.

Clatworthy, J. N. 1989. A review of rangeland utilization trials in Zimbabwe, 1970 to 1985. In A. R. Maclaurin and B.V.

Maasdorp (eds), *Rangeland Potential in the SADCC Region, Proceedings of a Regional Workshop, Bulawayo, 1–5 June, 1987*, Ministry of Lands, Agriculture and Rural Resettlement, Harare.

Collinson, R. F. H. 1979. "Production Economic of Impala." In M. A. Abbot (ed.), *Proceedings of a Symposium on Been and Game Management*, pp 90–103. Pietermartizburg: Cedara Press.

Colvin, I. S. 1984. *An Enquiry into Game Farming in the Cape Province*. M.Sc. Thesis, University of Cape Town.

Conroy, A. M., and I. Gaigher. 1982. "Venison, Aquaculture and Ostrich Meat Production." *South Africa of Animal Science* 12:219–22.

Conybaere, A. M. 1991. Elephant Occupancy and Vegetation Change in Relation to Artificial Water Points in a Kalahari Sand Area of Hwange National Park. Ph.D. thesis, University of Zimbabwe.

Coulson, I. C. 1992. Elephants and Vegetation in the Sengwa Wildlife Research Area. In R. B. Martin, G. C. Craig, V. R. Booth, and A. M. G. Conybeare (eds), *Elephant Management in Zimbabwe*, Second Edition, pp. 55–62, Department of National Parks and Wildlife Management, Harare.

Craig, G. C. 1992. A Simple Model of Tree/Elephant Equilibrium. In R. B. Martin, G.C. Craig, V. R. Booth, and A. M. G. Conybeare (eds), *Elephant Management in Zimbabwe*, Second Edition, Department of National Parks and Wildlife Management, Harare, pp. 81–86.

Cumming, D. H. M. 1982. The Influence of Large Herbivores on Savanna Structure in Africa. In B. J. Huntley and B. W. Walker (eds.), *Ecological Studies, Vol 42: Ecology of Tropical Savannas*. Berlin: Springer-Verlag.

Cumming, D. H. M., and I. Bond. 1991. *Animal Production in Southern Africa: Present Practice and Opportunities for Peasant Families in Arid Lands*. A report prepared for the International Development Research Center, Nairobi.

Dassmann, Raymond F., and Archie S. Mossman. 1961. "Commercial Use of Game Animals on a Rhodesian Ranch." *Wildlife* 3, September/December.

De Jager, P. 1988. *Environmental Degradation in Communal Land*. M.Sc. thesis, University of Zimbabwe.

Dublin, H. T., A. R. E. Sinclair, and J. McGlade. 1990. Elephants and Fire as Causes of Multiple Stable States in the Serengeti-Mara Woodlands. *Journal of Animal Ecology* 59:1147–64.

Dunham, K. M. 1990. Biomass Dynamics of Herbaceous Vegetation in Zambezi Riverine Woodlands. *African Journal of Ecology* 28:200–212.

Ellis, J. E., and D. M. Swift. 1988. "Stability of African Pastoral Ecosystems: Alternate Paradigms and Implications for Development." *Journal of Range Management* 41: 450–59.

Elwell, H. A., and M. A. Stocking. 1974. Rainfall Parameters and a Cover Model to Predict Runoff and Soil Loss from Grazing Trials in the Rhodesian Sandveld. *Proceedings of the Grassland Society of Southern Africa* 9:157–64.

——. 1982. "Developing a Simple yet Practical Method of Soil-Loss Estimation. *Tropical Agriculture (Trinidad)* 59:43–48.

Epstein, H. 1971. *The Origins of the Domestic Animals of Africa*, Volumes I and II. New York: Africana Publishing Corporation, 573 pp. and 719 pp.

Gambiza, J. 1987. Some Effects of Different Stocking Intensities on the Physical and Chemical Properties of the Soil in a Marginal Rainfall Area of Southern Zimbabwe. M.Sc. thesis in Tropical Resource Ecology, University of Zimbabwe.

Guy, P. R. 1981. "Changes in the Biomass and Productivity of Woodlands in the Sengwa Wildlife Research Area, Zimbabwe." *Journal of Applied Ecology* 18: 507–19.

Hawkes, R. K. 1991. *Crop and Livestock Losses to Wild Animals in the Bulilima Mangwe Natural Resources Management Project Area.* CASS/MAT Working Paper Series 1/91.

Hitchcock, P., and F. Nangati. 1992. "Interim Assessment of Zimbabwe Natural Resources Management Project." Draft report, Price Waterhouse, Zimbabwe.

Ivy, P. 1969. "Veld Condition Assessments." In Proceedings of the Veld Management Conference, Bulawayo, May 1969, 105–112, Department of Conservation and Extension, Salisbury.

Jansen, D. 1990. "Sustainable Wildlife Utilization in the Zambezi Valley of Zimbabwe: Economic, Ecological and Political Tradeoffs." WWF Multispecies Animal Production Systems Project, Paper No. 10.

———. 1992a. "The Role of Wildlife in the Economy." In Price Waterhouse and Environmental Resources.

———. 1992b. "The Economics of Campfire: Lessons to Date" Background report prepared for AFTEN, World Bank, November.

Jansen, D., I. Bond, and B. Child. 1992. *Cattle, Wildlife, Both or Neither: Results of a Financial and Economic Survey of Commercial Ranches in Southern Zimbabwe* WWF, Multispecies Animal Systems Project Paper No. 27, Harare.

Jansen, D., and K. Muir. 1991. "Trade and Exchange Rate Policy and Agriculture." Paper presented at Conference on Zimbabwe's Agricultural Production Revolution, Victoria Falls, Zimbabwe.

Jansen, D., and A. Rukovo. 1992. *Agriculture and the Policy Environment in Zambia and Zimbabwe: Political Dreams and Policy Nightmares.* OECD Technical Paper No. 74.

Johnstone, P. A. 1973. "Evaluation of a Rhodesia Game Ranch." *Journal of Southern African Wildlife Management Association* 5(1):43–51.

Kaufman, I. 1992. "Development of Wildlife Tourism in Zimbabwe." In Price Waterhouse and Environmental Resources.

Kelly, R. D., and B. W. Walker. 1976. "The Effects of Different Forms of Land Use on the Ecology of a Semiarid Region in Southeastern Rhodesia." *Journal of Ecology* 64:553–76.

Kennan, T. C. D. 1969. "A Review of Research into the Cattle/Grass Relationship in Rhodesia." *Proceedings of the Veld Management Conference, Bulawayo, 27–31 May,* pp 5–26, Government Printer, Salisbury, Rhodesia.

Kerr, M. A. 1972. Annual Report: Rhodesia. Department of National Parks and Wildlife Management.

LaGrange, M. 1988. "Innovative Approaches in the Control of Quelea in Zimbabwe." In R. Marsh (ed.), *Proc. 13th Vert. Pest Conf.* Univ. of California, Davis.

Marks, S. A. 1973. "Prey Selection and Annual Harvest of Game in a Rural Zambian Community." *East African Wildlife Journal* 11:113–28.

Martin, R. B. 1986. "Communal Areas Management Programme for Indigenous Resources (CAMPFIRE)." Working doc. 1/86, Dept National Parks and Wildlife Management, Harare.

———. 1989. "The Status of Projects Involving Wildlife in Zimbabwe." DNPWM, Harare.

Martin, R. B. 1992. Relationship between Elephant and Canopy Tree Cover. In R. B. Martin, G. C. Craig, V. R., Booth, and A. M. G. Conybeare, (eds), *Elephant Management in Zimbabwe,* Second Edition, pages 77–80, Department of National Parks and Wildlife Management, Harare.

Martin, R., G. Craig, and V. Booth. 1989. *Elephant Management in Zimbabwe,* DNPWM, Harare.

McDowell, R. E., D. G. Sisler, E. C. Schermerhorn, J. D. Reed, and R. P. Bauer. 1983. *Game or Cattle for Meat*

Production on Kenya Rangelands? Cornell University, 77 pp.

Monke, E. A., and Scott Pearson. 1989. *The Policy Analysis Matrix for Agricultural Development.* Ithaca: Cornell University Press.

Mossman, S. L., and A. S. Mossman. 1976. "Wildlife Utilization and Game Ranching." IUCN Occasional Paper No. 17.

Muir, Kay (ed.). 1983. "Agricultural Marketing In Zimbabwe." Working Paper 1/83, Dept. Land Management, University of Zimbabwe.

———. 1987. "Marketing Wildlife Products and Services." In IGF, Paris, Proceedings of *International Symposium on Wildlife Management in Sub-Saharan Africa* October, Harare.

———. 1989. "The Potential Role of Indigenous Resources in the Economic Development of Arid Environments in Sub-Saharan Africa: The Case of Wildlife Utilization in Zimbabwe." *Society and Natural Resources* 2.4:307–18.

Murindagomo, F. 1988. "Preliminary Investigations into Wildlife Utilization and Land Use in Angwa, Mid-Zambezi Valley." Unpub. M.Phil thesis, Dept. Agric. Econ. & Ext., Univ. of Zimbabwe.

———. 1992. "Wildlife Management in Zimbabwe: The CAMPFIRE Programme." *UNASYLVA (International)* 43(168):20–26.

———. Forthcoming. "A Comparative Analysis of Wildlife and Agriculture in Communal Subsistence Communities in Gokwe and Nyaminyami." Doctoral dissertation in preparation.

Murombedzi, James. 1992. *Decentralization or Recentralization: Implementing Campfire in the Omay Communal Lands of the Nyaminyami District Council of Zimbabwe's Wildlife Management Programme.* CASS Working Paper 2/1992, Center for Applied Social Sciences, Univ. of Zimbabwe.

Murphree, M. 1988. "Decentralizing the Proprietorship of Wildlife Resources in Zimbabwe's Communal Lands." Paper presented to African Studies Association, Cambridge.

———. 1991. *Communities as Institutions for Resource Management.* Center for Applied Social Sciences, Univ. of Zimbabwe.

O'Connor, T. G. 1985. "A Synthesis of Field Experiments Concerning the Grass Layer in the Savanna Regions of Southern Africa. South African National Scientific Programs." Report No 114, Foundation for Research and Development, Council for Scientific and Industrial Research, Pretoria.

Pangeti, G. 1989. "Administration and Interagency Co-ordination of Wildlife Management and the Effects of Legislation in Implementation." *Wildlife Resource Management* workshop, Hwange.

Peterson, J. 1992. *A Proto-Campfire Initiative in Mahenye Ward, Chipinge District* CASS Occasional Paper 3/1992, Center for Applied Social Sciences, Univ. of Zimbabwe.

Richardson, F. D. 1983. Short and Long-term Influences of Under-nutrition on Range Cattle Production. *Zimbabwe Agricultural Journal* 80:175–82.

Sandford, S. 1982. "Livestock in the Communal Areas of Zimbabwe." Report prepared for the Ministry of Lands, Resettlement and Rural Development, Harare.

Scoones, I. C. 1990. Livestock Populations and the Household Economy: a Case Study from Southern Zimbabwe. Ph.D. thesis, University of London.

Smithers, R. H. N. 1988. *The Mammals of the Southern African Subregion* Univ. of Pretoria, Pretoria.

Stanning, J. 1987. "Household Grain Storage and Marketing in Surplus and Deficit Communal Farming Areas." In Rukuni and Eicher (eds.) *Food Security for Southern Africa* Dept. Agric. Econ., University of Zimbabwe, pp. 145–84.

Stocking, M. 1986. The Costs of Soil Erosion in Zimbabwe in Terms of the Loss of Three Major Nutrients. Consultants' Working Paper No. 3, Soil Conservation Programme, Land and Water Division, AGLS, FAO, Rome, pp. 164.

———. 1992. "Land Degradation and Rehabilitation Research in Africa 1980–1990: Retrospect and Prospect." Dryland Networks Paper No. 34, International Institute for Environment and Development, London.

Swanepoel, C. M. 1989. Patterns of Habitat Use by African Buffalo in Mana Pools National Park, Zimbabwe. D.Phil. thesis, University of Zimbabwe.

Swift, M. J., P. G. H. Frost, B. M. Campbell, J. C. Hatton, and K. B. Wilson. 1989. "Nitrogen Cycling in Farming Systems Derived from Savanna: Perspectives and Challenges. In M. Clarholm and L. Bergstrom (eds.), *Ecology of Arable Land*, Kluwer Academic Publishers, pp. 63–76.

Thompson, P. J. 1975. "The Role of Elephants, Fire and Other Agents in the Decline of *Brachystegia boehmii* Woodland." *Journal of the Southern African Wildlife Management Association* 5:11–18.

Walker, B. H., D. A. Matthews, and P. J. Dye. 1986. "Management of Grazing Systems—Existing versus an Event-Orientated Approach." *South African Journal of Science* 82:172.

Warren, A., and C. Agnew. 1988. An Assessment of Desertification and Land Degradation in Arid and Semi-arid Areas. *Drylands Programme Research Paper*, No. 2, International Institute for Environment and Development, London.

Watt, M. 1913. "The Dangers and Prevention of Soil Erosion. *Rhodesian Agriculture Journal* 10:5.

Western, D. 1979. "Size, Life History and Ecology in Mammals." *African Journal of Ecology* 17:185–204.

Whitlow, J. R. 1980. "Deforestation in Zimbabwe." *Supplement to Zambezia*, 1980, University of Zimbabwe, pp. 1–35.

———. 1988. "Land Degradation in Zimbabwe: A Geographical Study." Natural Resources Board, Harare.

Whitlow, J. R., and B. Campbell. 1989. "Factors Influencing Erosion in Zimbabwe: A Statistical Analysis." *Journal of Environmental Management* 29:17–29.

Zimbabwe Government. 1988. "Value of Wildlife" Parliamentary Debates, House of Assembly, Hansard series, Sept. pp. 1628–44.

Zimbabwe Government, DNPWLM. 1992. "Wild Life Policy." Dept. of National Parks and Wildlife Management, Harare.

ABBREVIATIONS AND ACRONYMS

AFC	average financial cost
AIC	average incremental cost
AIM	Action Impact Matrix
BAT	best available technology
CAC	command-and-control (measures)
CEB	Ceylon Electricity Board
CEE	Central and Eastern Europe
CES	constant elasticity of substitution
CET	constant elasticity of transformation
CFC	chlorofluorocarbon
CFL	compact fluorescent lighting
CGC	*Caisse de Compensation General*
CGE	computable general equilibrium (model)
CIDIE	Committee of International Development Institutions on the Environment
c.i.f.	cost, insurance, and freight
CITES	Convention on the International Trade in Endangered Species of Flora and Fauna
CMEA	Council of Mutual Economic Assistance
CSC	Cold Storage Commission (Zimbabwe)
DC	district council (Zimbabwe)
DHE	district heating enterprises
DNPWLM	Department of National Parks and Wildlife Management (Zimbabwe)
DSM	demand-side management
EA	environmental assessment
EAP	environmental action plan
EC	European Community
ECLAC	U.N. Economic Commission for Latin America and the Caribbean
EER	energy-efficient refrigerator
EPRI	Electric Power Research Institute
ERS	export retention scheme
ESAP	Economic Standard Adjustment Program
ETP	Economic Transformation Program
FGD	flue gas desulfurization
f.o.b.	free on board
FY	fiscal year
GATT	General Agreement on Tariffs and Trade
GDP	gross domestic product
GEF	Global Environment Facility
GHG	greenhouse gas
GJ	gigajoule
GNP	gross national product
GTZ	German Technical Assistance Agency (*Gesellschaft für Technische Zusammenarbeit*)
IAST	Institute of Agrarian Studies

IPCC   Intergovernmental Panel on Climate Change
LP   linear programming
LRMC   long-run marginal cost
LSS   Living Standards Survey
MADIA   Managing Agricultural Development in Africa
MEC   marginal external cost
MIT   Polish Ministry of Industry and Trade
MOC   marginal opportunity cost
MPC   marginal private cost
MUC   marginal user cost
NAFTA   North American Free Trade Agreement
NEAP   national environmental action plan
NEPP   National Environmental Policy of Poland
NGO   nongovernmental organization
NPR   nominal protection rate
NPV   net present value
NWMT   Nyaminyami Wildlife Management Trust (Zimbabwe)
OECD   Organisation for Economic Co-operation and Development
OED   Operations Evaluation Department of the World Bank
OLS   ordinary least squares
OS   oil steam-electric
p.a.   per annum
PFBC   pressurized fluidized bed combustion
PM   particulate matter
PPGC   Polish Power Grid Company
PPP   Purchasing Power Parity
SAM   social accounting matrix
SNA   System of National Accounts
SOCB   state-owned commercial bank
SOE   state-owned enterprise
SRMC   short-run marginal cost
T&D   transmission and distribution
TJ   terajoule
UN   United Nations
UNSO   United Nations Statistical Office
VIDCO   village development committee
VIM   vehicle inspection and maintenance (program)
WADCO   ward development committee
WCED   World Commission on Environment and Development
WHO   World Health Organization
WPA   Wildlife Producers Association
ZIC   Zimbabwe Investment Centre